AUTOCRACY

Autocracy

by
GORDON TULLOCK
(George Mason University)

1987 **KLUWER ACADEMIC PUBLISHERS**
DORDRECHT / BOSTON / LANCASTER

Distributors

for the United States and Canada: Kluwer Academic Publishers, P.O. Box 358, Accord Station, Hingham, MA 02018-0358, USA
for the UK and Ireland: Kluwer Academic Publishers, MTP Press Limited, Falcon House, Queen Square, Lancaster LA1 1RN, UK
for all other countries: Kluwer Academic Publishers Group, Distribution Center, P.O. Box 322, 3300 AH Dordrecht, The Netherlands

Library of Congress Cataloging in Publication Data

Tullock, Gordon.
Autocracy.

Bibliography: p.
1. Dictators. I. Title.
JC495.T85 1987 321.9 86-18114
ISBN 90-247-3398-7

ISBN 90-247-3398-7

PRINTED IN THE NETHERLANDS

Table of contents

AUTO'CRASY. n.s.
Independent power; supremacy.

DICTATOR. n. [Latin]
One invested with absolute authority.
Unanimous they all commit the care,
And management of this main enterprize,
To him their great dictator.
Milton's Paradise Regain'd

KING. n.s.
Monarch; supreme governour.
The great king of kings,
Hath in the table of his law commanded,
That thou shalt do no murder. Shakes. R.III
A substitute shines brightly as a king,
Until a king be by; and then his state
Empties itself, as doth an inland brook
Into the main of waters. Shak. Merch. of Venice
True hope is swift, and flies with swallows wings;
Kings it makes gods, and meaner creatures kings. Shakesp.
The king becoming graces,
As justice, verity, temp'rance, mercy, stableness,
Bounty, persevrance, mercy, lowliness,
Devotion, patience, courage, fortitude,
I have no relish of them. Shakespeare's Macbeth
Thus states were form'd; the name of king unknown,
'Till common int'rest plac'd the sway in one;
'Twas virtue only, or in arts or arms,
Diffusing blessings, or averting harms,
The same which was in a sire the sons obey'd,
A prince the father of a people made. Pope

- A Dictionary of the English Language
-by Samuel Johnson

AU-TO-CRAT
A monarch ruling with unlimited authority; a governor with absolute power. in.0

DIC-TA-TOR

One ruling absolutely, typically with brutality, oppression, and ruthless supression of opposition [political dictators who attempt to accomplish by calculated brutality and aggression what they lack in intelligence and magnanimity to consummate.

Lewis Mumford

KING

A male monarch who rules over a major territorial unit : the ruler of a kingdom [kings were makers of the laws - James I]; [distinguish between the king and the crown - C.H. McIlwain].

- Webster's Third New International Dictionary

Preface

My first serious thought about a scientific approach to politics was in Communist China. When the Communists seized China, the American Department of State, which was planning to recognize them, left its entire diplomatic establishment in place. At the time, I was a Vice Consul in Tientsin, so I found myself living under the Communists. While the Department of State was planning on recognizing the Communists, the Communist plans were obscure. In any event, they weren't going to recognize us in the Consulate-General until formal relations were established between the two governments, so I had a great deal of leisure.

As a man who then intended to spend his life as a political officer in the Department of State, I decided to fill in this time by reading political science. I rapidly realized, not only that the work was rather unsatisfactory from a scientific standpoint, but also that it didn't seem to have very much relevance to the Communist government under which I was then living.[1]

I was unable to solve the problem at the time, and after a number of vicissitudes which included service in Hong Kong and South Korea, neither of which was really a model of democracy, I resigned and switched over to an academic career primarily concerned with that mixture of economics and political science which we call Public Choice.

Most of my work in Public Choice has dealt with democratic governments. This is not because I thought that democratic governments were the dominant form of government, either currently or historically. That more people are ruled by autocracies than democracies today, and that the same can be said of earlier periods, is obvious. I did think that democratic governments were better than the 'various alternatives which have been tried from time to time', but the basic reason that most things that I have published have dealt with democracies is simply that I've found dictatorships a very, very difficult problem.

I have, however, thought a great deal about the problem, and this book is the result of that thought. I am sorry that I cannot say that it is a complete logical theory of dictatorships. Indeed, it is far from complete. There is a consistent approach, and I think that approach is far more realistic than that of most writers who have written on dictatorship.[2]

This book, then, is in essence a summary of what I have learned. I regret to say that it is not as perfect as I would like. I am, however, getting on in years and it seemed best to get what I know down in print now, rather than taking the risk that it would perish with me. It is my hope, not that this book will be a last word on the study of autocracy, but that it will be the first. I hope it will inspire or irritate other scholars into further studies which will lead them to solve those remaining problems which I have been unable to handle.

In general, the book differs from what little material already exists on this topic, in that it is concerned with the internal functioning of dictatorial governments, not the policies they adopt. An absolute ruler, once he is an absolute ruler, has as his most important problem retaining control. It is likely that his policies will always be subordinated to that overriding priority. Absolute rulers are, of course, like the rest of us, not 100 percent selfish. They are willing to make some, although probably not very large, sacrifices for the public good, to help the poor, to advance the arts, etc., even as you and I. Just as most of us do not voluntarily transfer more than 5 percent or so of our income to those goals, and keep most of our income to spend on ourselves, so the dictator is likely to devote only a certain amount of his political capital to doing things that he thinks are good, and the bulk of it to doing things that will strengthen his power. In addition, it should be said, that most people who get into this kind of position have relatively weak policy ideas. They are specialists in political manipulation, not in scientific choice of substantively desirable policies.

There is little empirical research in this book. This is not because I am against empirical research,[3] but because there is relatively little such research. Further, a good part of what does exist has resulted from my stimulating various graduate students to work in the field. The basic problem here is the absence of data. By this I do not mean that history does not tell us a great deal about a very large number of autocracies, but that mining of this immense historical record to produce internally coherent statistical series has not been carried out.

Compiling such statistics would be an extremely difficult task. It requires work in many different languages. Take a few minor questions: How much do absolute rulers spend on their personal living expenses? How much do they spend on their personal guards? Indeed, do they have a single unified guard or several different agencies which are balanced against each other, and if the latter, how much do they spend on each one? Absolute rulers are fairly free in their denunciations of plots against them. How many of these plots are genuine, and how many are invented by the ruler for political reasons, or as a third possible explanation, how many are invented by other courtiers of the ruler who wish to get rid of the 'plotters' in order to improve their own position with the ruler? As far as I know, there is no available data on any of these subjects, although a large research staff of trained historians with knowledge among them of 50 or 60 languages could produce a definitive collection of such statistics.

But these are merely a few samples. Until this type of research has been done, the scholar is compelled to turn to essentially anecdotal evidence, as I have done. In a way, however, when I give an example of something happening in ancient Greece, I am not offering that as evidence that it can happen often – it is, of course, evidence that it happened once – but explaining a theoretical point. In order to actually prove empirically that the theory was correct, we would need very many observations, not one or two.

What is really offered in this book, then, is a coherent approach to autocratic government with great emphasis on its internal functioning. This general picture is clearly in close accord with what we see in real-world autocratic governments. What we need, however, is detailed empirical research on each aspect of the picture. I hope that the book will inspire such work, but I do not think that we will have definitive statistical tests based on large bodies of data in the immediate future. The data collection is just too hard.

But that is the basic theme of this preface and, indeed, of the book. I hope that the book is a significant step forward in the study of autocracy; I do not doubt, however, that we have much farther to go.

NOTES

1. This was particularly true of the Marxist literature.

2. Machiavelli is, of course, the most important of my predecessors in this regard, interestingly, he too apparently found autocracy a difficult problem. *The Prince* is a fairly short book written by a man whose total volume of writing on political matters was immense. Almost all of the rest dealt with systems which made decisions by voting.

3. Although I do tend to feel that my comparative advantage is not in that field.

CHAPTER I

Introduction

Most governments in the world today are dictatorships of one sort or another.[1] In spite of this fact there has been almost no scientific analysis of this form of government since Macciavelli. Scholars such as Karl Loewenstein and Carl Friedrich have written learned and perceptive[2] studies, but they are essentially contributions to political philosophy, not Public Choice. This book is intended to take the first steps towards filling the gap.

I have chosen to call it 'autocracy' instead of 'dictatorship' because I also want to discuss Kingdoms and Empires. The difference between a dictatorship and a kingdom is, as far as I can see, simply that the kingdoms tend to be hereditary. I should like to emphasize the word 'tend', because disputed successions are by no means uncommon. We English speakers, in essence, descend from what was probably the most unstable monarchy in Europe, with undisputed succession for three generations almost unknown.[3] Most other monarchies in Europe were somewhat stabler, but still there was the Fronde in France,[4] and the wars of Austrian and Spanish succesion.[5]

In the actual government, however, there is not all that much difference between a hereditary ruler and a dictator.[6] There are differences, and they will be discussed below, but they clearly belong in the same family of governments. The word 'autocracy' encompasses both.

This form of government, as I said, is the dominant one in the world today. Further, more of the world is now ruled by such autocratic governments than, let us say, twenty-five or thirty years ago. It is dangerous to base predictions on historic trends, but since 1914 on the whole democracy has become a less significant form of government and dictatorships more important.[7] The situation is highly unstable, however. At the time I prepared the final draft of this book there were only 6 dictatorships in Latin America, possibly an historic low. In the few months between then and the final proofing, the number went up to 7. I hesitate to guess how many there will be when you read it.[8]

But having said that autocracy is the commonest form of government, I should like to briefly discuss two other forms of government, mainly because that is the easiest way of limiting what I mean by autocracy. Governments that depend on voting of some sort or are feudal are not autocracies. I am not at all sure there may not be other forms of government than these three, but these make up the overwhelming majority of all historic governments. Indeed, autocracy by itself is the dominant form of government, and most governments that are not autocratic are either feudal or electoral. As we shall see, however, there are intermediate stages between these three forms of government.

It is common for most people to think that their own experience is universal, and it is common of most countries and areas to think that their history is universal history. It happens that the Western European area was essentially feudal for at least five hundred years. From this a great many people, including Marx, have come to the conclusion that feudalism is a necessary stage in development.[9] As a matter of fact, feudalism is quite rare in the world, the only other clear cut case that I know of being Japan. Perhaps the Rajputs were a third and Mycenean Greece a fourth.[10]

It is particularly astonishing that the myth that feudalism is universal could arise since one of the great periods of feudal history was the Crusades, in which the feudal lords attacked centralized non-feudal Mohammedan kingdoms[11] either in alliance with, or sometimes opposed to the centralized Byzantine empire.[12] In fact, centralized Mohammedan, Byzantine, Persian, Chinese, and Indian kingdoms paralleled the feudal epoch. Much more of the human race lived under these systems than lived in feudal Europe or feudal Japan. The Rajput case, which I mentioned as possible feudalism, is somewhat later than the European feudal period.[13] Most of India, however, was not part of this Rajput feudal confederacy, but a set of independent despotic states which were, for a short period of time, united under the rule of the Great Mogul, also not feudal.[14]

The feudal system was a complex blend of different powers. In theory the king was surrounded by a group of nobles who each held territory from him, who were loyal to him, and who subinfeudated this territory to lower nobles, etc. In practice, anyone who reads the history will realize the degree of loyalty to the king was distinctly limited. Further, the system in Europe was complicated by the existence of another very great power, the Church, and the further existence of a large number of free cities.[15]

Lord Acton, no mean judge, thought that the 13th century was the highest point in human freedom.[16] The immediate thought one has when hearing this is that he was crazy, but actually he had a not bad argument. He pointed out that the existence of quite a number of powers meant that any individual had a great deal of bargaining power in dealing with someone who nominally was his superior. A peasant, legally, was bound to the land. As a matter of fact, if he became annoyed with his lord, he could decamp quietly at night feeling fairly confident that about twenty miles down the road there would be another lord who would welcome him because he needed additional peasants to operate his land.[17] There was, of course, also the Church and the free cities, both of which would offer him protection.

This is, of course, not the standard historical picture of this era, but new economic historians have pretty much demonstrated that the average peasant could, if he wanted, change lords.[18] An overlord, meeting with Parliament in London and passing vigorous laws to prohibit peasants from leaving their land and prevent lords from accepting strange peasants, might at the same time, be writing to his steward, encouraging him to accept any peasant who came along.

In Japan, the peasants were not as free as they were in Europe, but it was nevertheless true that the small scale of the land held by any given feudal lord meant that movement was possible. Further, the control of the feudal lord was by their superiors, and the Ashikaga who preceded the Tokagawa were able to exercize little or no control. The Tokagawa, in fact, were an intermediate station between autocracy and feudalism, but a rather different intermediate station than that found in Europe as the feudal system gradually changed, during the Renaissance, into despotsism.[19]

This definition of feudalism is not quite the ordinary one, although very close. A great many people think that feudalism is just an earlier state of society, and by that definition, of course, almost everything that is not modern and western is feudal.[20] Marxists have, of course, contributed a great deal to this definition, with serious debates as to whether the Ching Dynasty in China was or was not feudal.[21] Traditional histories of China did refer to the Chou Dynasty as feudal, and it may have been in its earliest days. By the time that it becomes actually part of history, however, it is clear that the Chou emperor was a shadowy figure with no real power. The individual 'feudatories' were actually independent monarchs whose governments within their own territory were despotic and not feudal.[22] It was not, for example, like the government of the medieval Holy Roman Emperor in which the great feudatories who held from the emperor had their own feudal retainers and did not have direct control over the bulk of the land which was within their kingdom or dukedom.

The earlier, possibly feudal, government in ancient Greece in which Menalaus, the King of Men, led an army to the siege of Troy is relatively little known. It was destroyed by the Dorian invasion.[23] When the night of the Greek dark age receded, there were a series of independent city-states.[24]

Western feudalism, of course, died with the development of the Modern Age. It was ended in France and Spain by the king establishing complete power over the lords, and in Germany and Italy, with the lords becoming independent rulers with the nominal emperor simply a ceremonial figure.[25] England had a unique solution to this problem, a sort of compromise. This compromise was, of course, of immense importance for the development of democracy in the western world. Unfortunately, I know almost nothing about the Rajputs. As far as I can see, they retained their feudal organization right down to the end of Mogul Dynasty and could even be said to have continued under the British Raj, albeit the individual Rajas were immensely restricted in their power at that time.[26] This book is not about feudalism and we will only discuss feudalism occasionally when we are discussing possible transitions between it and despotism.

Democracy is also not the subject of this book, but I am compelled to deal at some length with a more general category of governments, of which Democracy is a member. Specifically, if the government proceeds through votes by a considerable number of people I shall call it an 'Electoral System'. Dahl has coined another word 'polyarchy'[27] which I would prefer to my 'electoral system' if he had not given it a meaning which is different from mine, but close enough to cause confusion if I used it.

Democracy, is, of course an example of an electoral system, but there are others. A greek city state, for example, emerges from the greek dark age governed by a council of about 30 heads of noble families. They make decisions by voting, but we would hardly call this a democacy. Such 'electoral systems' will be referred to from time to time, because they are historically important. Normally the electoral systems which are discussed in this book will not be democracies because the franchise is limited. The word 'democracy' will be reserved for governments in which the entire sane and non-criminal adult population can vote. I am simply trying to separate off despotic forms of government.

Thus, with this definition, Athens had an electoral system in spite of the fact that there was widespread slavery and that there were a number of people, foreigners in residence, who were not permitted to vote.[28] But also, those Greek states which were referred to as oligarchies would be electoral because they also depended on the votes of a considerable number of people, even if not a large part of the population.[29] Similarly, Venice, Bearn and most of the city-states, used the electoral system. Modern Israel and South Africa are are also electoral, although in both cases a considerable number of the residents of the geographic area are not permitted to vote.[30]

Note that my definition of 'democracy' is stricter than the normal one. For most writers, 'democracy' is defined by the number of voters being large. Exactly what 'large'means in this definition is not very clear. Anthony Downs[31] feels that universal adult suffrage is necessary for the usage of the word 'democracy'.[32] Both the Downs definition and mine rule out almost all historical examples. England was never a democracy until the end of World War I. Indeed, there were practically no democracies before World War I and certainly none before 1850. Washington, Jefferson, etc., were not democratic statesmen, nor was Pericles. Caesar did not overthrow Roman democracy, etc. Most people do not put such extreme limitations on the use of the word 'democracy', but the exact size of the neccessary number of voters is blurred. Fortunately this book is not about democracy, so I don't have to solve the problem.

I must here make a few more rather rough distinctions within the autocracy category. Firstly, there is currently in the literature a good deal of talk of totalitarian as opposed to authoritarian governments. These terms aren't necessarily clear, but it is clear to anyone who looks at the data that it's easy to tell a certain class of governments, most of which in the present day world are communist, from the others. I shall use the word totalitarian for those governments where the government actually makes a strong effort to control all aspects of the lives of its subjects. Present day Russia and China are obvious examples.

It is an open question whether the type of ancient hydraulic civilization described in Karl Wittfogel's *Oriental Despotism*[33] was or was not, as Wittfogel thought it was, the logical predecessor of modern communist states. Certainly these governments exerted a great deal of power over their subjects, but it's also notable in most of them that the local villages were self-governing and used essentially democratic methods to govern themselves. Wittfogel explains this in terms of the declining marginal return on administration, ie., that the government knew that if it tried to control everything, its control would disintegrate in the outer reaches of the government apparatus.[34] The problem is of great historic interest, but no great importance for our purposes. We can distinguish quite readily between modern totalitarian governments and other dictatorships.

Consider, for example, Spain during the heyday of Franco. This was clearly a rather inefficient, badly run dictatorship. It was not, however, totalitarian in the sense that Russia was. Franco made little effort to interfere with the private life of his citizens. He did not, during most of the time that he was dictator, even have a death penalty. Further, throughout the time that he was dictator, foreign newspapers and magazines were reasonably available in Madrid.[35] After the first few years of Franco's reign there were not even very many political prisoners in Spain although, of course, there always were some.[36] This is radically different from the government of Stalin or even the government of Gorbachov.

In this respect, Franco is relatively typical of the average African, South American, or Asiatic dictator of the present day. We will discuss this kind of situation in great detail throughout the book, so there is no point in elaborating here. The dominant form of autocracy has been the non-totalitarian type presented by Franco, Lee of Singapore, or Mobuto of Zaire. I've chosen those names, incidentally, with animus forethought. Zaire is surely one of the worst governed countries in the world, and Singapore one of the best. They both fall, however, within our category of standard dictatorships.

There are, of course some intermediate stages between autocracy and various other forms of government. We all know the history of the development of English democracy, which essentially came out of feudalism rather than out of autocracy. Looking around the world today, however, we find a number of governments which I am going to call 'limited autocracies'. They are places like the Philippines under Marcos, South Korea, and Mexico, where you have a pretty clear cut dictator, but[37] there is also an elected legislature. This legislature, like the legislature of George II in England[38] usually is elected by methods which would not meet with the approval of the ACLU, but nevertheless is not completely dependent on the ruler. It's relationship to the ruler is also rather unclear. It is clear that the ruler is not controlled by the legislature in the same way that Margaret Thatcher is controlled by the House of Commons in England, but it's also clear that the legislature does put some checks on the power of the ruler. This intermediate form of government will be discussed at some length later.

The intermediate stage between feudalism and autocracy will not be discussed very much in this book mainly because I don't know very much about it. Historians of the gradual switch of both France and Spain from feudal monarchs to 'enlightened' despotism may be able to shed some light here.

The intermediate stages between feudalism and the electoral system may, or then again may not, be important. We know almost nothing about what happened during the Greek dark age after the previous probably feudal society had been destroyed by the Dorians.[39] The conversion of Japanese feudalism and Rajput feudalism into democracy came essentially through outside influences. This leaves us with England.

It is not at all clear exactly what happened there. The Wars of the Roses killed a good many feudal lords and they were succeeded by the strong Tudor monarchs, who clearly proposed to wipe out what was left of the power of the lords.[40] One of their tools, a rather minor one, was the House of Commons.[41] Elizabeth, the last Tudor, died without issue.[42] The throne went to the King of Scotland.[43] The House of Stuart became involved with some of the nobility and the House of Commons in what is called the English

Civil War.[44] It should be pointed out that it was, in this case, the king who revolted rather than the House of Commons. The king went to Oxford to raise his standard and the only permanent professional military force, the navy, remained loyal to the House of Commons in London.[45] Essentially, however, the war seems to have been fought on religious grounds.[46] The immediate outcome was the establishment of a much stronger monarchy under Cromwell, but he died leaving matters in the hands of weakling son and a constitutional monarchy was established.[47] What we can make of this for our present purposes isn't obvious. It is clear, however, that the period from, let us say, the return of Charles II through George III's insanity[48] was a period of what we have been calling limited autocracy, ie., a very strong ruler who nevertheless has to put up to some extent with the votes of an elected body which he does not completely control.

The reader will no doubt by now have gotten the general idea of what this book is about, but also a feeling that the boundaries are rather vague. Vagueness seems to be inherent in the subject matter. It's easy enough to produce very sharp definitions and divisions, but if you do, you'll find that the world doesn't seem to divide up that way. It seems to be easier and more efficient to accept the vagueness of our historic evidence and work forward from there.

Another problem is the nature of the historical evidence I will use. It will, unfortunately be mainly anecdotal. This is not because I would not like more sophisticated methods, but because the neccessary data for their use is not available. Further, granted the diversity of autocracies, collecting such evidence would require knowledge of quite a number of languages. I have been unable to undertake the task, but I hope this book will lead other scholars to begin the work. As some help in empirical testing of my theories, I have put in an appendix at the end which lists hypotheses which could, in theory, be tested. I hope other scholars will take up the challenge.

Now a few words about the remainder of the book. I have said dictatorship or some type of autocracy is clearly the dominant form of government both in the world today and throughout history. Western history, it is true, had occasional upsurges of electoral governments but in earlier centuries these were followed by restoration of autocracy. Although that does not prove it will happen this time it still must be accepted as a statement about history up to now. It is therefore important to understand this, the commonest form of government.

The organization of the book may impress the reader as a little bizarre. I will begin by discussing how an existing dictator remains in power. He faces essentially three potential sources of danger. The first of these is the high officials of his own regime. Most dictators are overthrown by higher officials of their own regime, simply because the higher officials want to promote themselves with at least one of them becoming the new dictator. If the reader has doubts about this I suggest he consult the New York Times Index for the previous six months or so and check the number of cases in which dictators have been overthrown. In most cases the persons overthrowing it will be either officials or former officials in the government which was overthrown. The consequence is simply the establishment of a new dictatorship.

Normally the new dictatorship will announce that it's going to have different policies but the policy changes are usually modest. In fact the whole policy change between dictatorial regimes is rather similar to the policy change when the party in power changes in a democracy. In both cases there is a lot of talk about what changes will be made, but mainly the changes turn out to be modest. Occasionally in both, quite radical changes will be made. As a democratic example, we may take Franklin Roosevelt in 1933.

The second most frequent cause of the overthrow of a dictator in recent years has been foreign intervention. Over the long sweep of history, however, foreign conquest has been the most common source of the termination of dictatorial power. It has not been very important in the last forty years, but this I believe represents a peculiarity of that historical period. This was a time when the United States dominated the world. The United States has a rather irrational objection to 'aggression'. It is true that Israel and India were permitted to annex pieces of their neighbors.[49] But during most of this period any other country attempting to grab neighboring real estate would have had trouble with the United States. Apparently one of the results of the Vietnamese War is that this is no longer true. Qaddafi has been permitted to seize a substantial (and apparently worthless) piece of the Sahara.[50] The Vietnamese government conquered Laos and Cambodia, Indonesia took Timor, and Russia has invaded Afghanistan, all without anything except expressions of pain and surprise from the United

States. The current rather bloody war between Iran and Iraq started with an Iraqi effort to invade Iran, and when that failed, it has now developed into an Iranian effort to conquer Iraq.[51] Once again, the American reaction has been pretty largely simply expressions of pain and surprise. Naturally, the U.N. has done nothing about any of these things. The basic difference is that the U.N. doesn't even show pain and surprise. It seems likely that we can expect a good deal more of this kind of thing in the near future.

The last, and in many ways least likely , way in which a dictator may be overthrown is by a genuine popular uprising. This is rare, not only in my own opinion but that of most people who have seriously looked into the matter. 'Armed insurrection in some form or other is the classic method of making a revolution, and... it is bound to imply a clash with professionally trained troops equipped with all the gear of scientific warfare. History shows that, in the last resort, success or failure hinges on the attitude which those armed forces of the status quo government will take toward an insurrection... Whatever government or party has the full allegiance of a country's armed forces is to all intents and purposes politically impregnable'.[52] This is quoted with full endorsement and approval by Johnson.[53] If it is rare in the study of actual overthrows of dictatorship, it is very common in the romantic literature. The Bastille was actually taken by a regiment of regular infantry, but it is still the legend that it was a Paris mob.[54] It is true that the King of France, like the Shah of Iran, felt that his troops should not fight and hence, left himself rather defenseless.[55] The Napoleonic Dynasty took a different position. Napoleon I became ruler of France to a very considerable extent because he was the only general in the French army who was willing to order cannon to fire grapeshot into the Paris mob.[56] Napoleon III converted himself from prince-president of France to emperor in part because he personally led a cavalry charge into the grandchildren of the victims of his Uncle's grapeshot.[57] Although popular uprisings are rare, they are not totally unknown. It can, however, be said that they occur only when for one reason or another the military machine is immobilized. The matter will be discussed in greater detail later.

There will then be a discussion of the apparently irrelevant subject of ethics. This concerns the fairly obvious fact that some dictators, even some of the worst of them, seem to have convinced their subjects the there is an ethical duty to support them. The subject is related, of course, to the traditional political science discussions of 'legitimacy'. How and why ethical importance can be attached to an existing regime, or for that matter to someone who wants to overthrow it, is an important subject and will be given a chapter by itself.

Having discussed the problems a dictator faces in holding his job we will discuss how he selects policies and administers them. We will then turn to what an ambitious man who wants to overthrow the dictator should do. It is, in a way, looking at the problem of maintaining power from the other direction. In the final section of the book we will turn to some technical problems such as: how a dictator can arrange a reasonably peaceful succession to himself without providing an opportunity for someone to kill him; the intermediate stages between dictatorship and democracy, which are quite common in the present day world; and to why very small voting bodies normally develop into dictatorships.

As one final introductory note, I think that I should explain my view of dictators. At a recent conference two scholars both of whom are emotionally much more antagonistic to dictatorships than I am, denounced me for having an unduly low opinion of dictators. Basically, they thought of dictators as people who had acquired dictatorial power for the purpose of implementing certain policies. The policies were ones that they disliked, hence their strong emotional aversion to the dictator. What they objected to about my attitude was that I thought that dictators were people who acquired power essentially because for personal reasons they prefer being a dictator to being a lower ranking official. Policies in my view were then adopted largely, not entirely, but largely, in terms of their effect on the dictators career rather than in terms of their intrinsic desirability.

It can be seen that in this case I am simply carrying over what I might call the public choice view of politics. Anthony Downs is frequently quoted as having said, 'Political parties do not seek power in order to select policies: they select policies in order to seek power.' This has been the general view of most people in the public choice movement. It is, in a way, one of the more radical differences between public choice and traditional political science. We think politicians are like the rest of us in that most of the time, not always, but most of the time, they seek their own advantage. We can buy reasonably good cars not because the car manufacturers have our interest at heart, although to some extent they do, but basically because they want to make money. Similarly, if we have a choice of policies offered by different political groups, this is because those political groups are seeking political power and hope to use the policies as incentives to collect our vote if it is a democracy.

The basic advantage of a democracy is that those people who seek power must seek power by attempting to please a majority of the population. A dictatorship is ruled by people who seek power and must please other people, but the people who must be pleased are a much smaller group.

This is indeed, different from the normal attitude towards politics, both democratic politics and dictatorial politics. Nevertheless, I think it is also realistic. If a dictator comes from a society where most of the people who could effect his future are firmly convinced of the truth of some political proposition, he is likely to accept it because that is the way to power. His convictions are however, rarely deeply held and can be changed very rapidly if there is a political gain to be obtained from it. Lyndon Johnson and George Wallace were not of course dictators, but both were at different times in their career in favor of keeping the blacks firmly down and of civil liberties for blacks. In both cases they made considerable political gain from the switch. Similar startling changes of position will be found in the career of most dictators.

It may be that in taking this point of view, I am indeed, being unjust to the dictators, but I think not. Dictators may follow extremely bad policies when looked at from our value system. The normal reason however, is not that they are devoted to those policies on ideological grounds, but that they think that those are the policies that are most likely to permit them to obtain and maintain power.

I should not close this chapter, however, without making one point clear. This is a book about dictatorship. It is not a book advocating dictatorship as a form of government. The average person in our society knows of dictatorships, or autocratic governments, only that they are bad things. I don't deny that they are bad, but they are very, very common. We should try to understand them. This book is dedicated to that end.

NOTES

1. Dahl estimates about 80% of present day governments. Dahl, p. 202, see also his Table 5.3, p. 67.

2. Not always perceptive. In 1946 Loewenstein expected the early overthrow of Franco. (Loewenstein, p. 152) Presumably my book will also show clouds in my crystal ball if it is read 40 years from now.

3. Between 1400 and 1900 there was only one case of undisputed succession involving three or more monarchs in England – the Hanoverian line, from George I to Victoria. There were major risings against the Hanoverians in 1715 and 1745 and George III lost both 1/3rd of his kingdom and the real power of the dynasty. See Ward, Prothero, and Leathes 1911, Tables 1-4.

4. Fronde is a word used to refer, collectively, to two open revolts in France in the Seventeenth Century. The first revolt, which was led by the parliment of Paris and joined by many of the old nobility, occurred in June 1648. It was inspired by what was perceived to be the financial excesses of the Italian-borne Finance Minister Jules Magarin. This revolt quickly collapsed. The second revolt occurred in 1650 and was again led by the old nobility and their private armies. Plagued with infighting and shifting allegances this revolt ceased in 1653. See Blum 1966, pp. 224-25, and also see Blum, Cameron and Barnes, 1970, pp. 235-237, 269.

5. The War of the Austrian Succession (1740-1748) occured after Maria Theresa's claim to the Hapsburg throne was disputed by Philip V of Spain, who considered himself a more suitable heir. Eventually Spain, France, Saxony, Bavaria, Prussia and Great Britain were involved (with Austria, of course). See Dupuy and Dupuy 1977, pp. 630-637. The War of the Spanish Succession (1701-1714) resulted from England and Holland, objecting to the inheritance of the Spanish throne by a grandson of Louis XIV of France (ibid., pp. 617-627).

6. The word 'king' has two meanings in modern parlance. Firstly, a pleasant, powerless man like the present King of Sweden. Secondly, somebody like William the Conqueror (r. 1066-1087; see Cantor 1969, p. 62), or Louis XIV (r. 1661-1715; see Goubert 1970) who actually rules as well as reigns. Sweden is as democratic a state as the United States. The fact that the Swedes rather enjoy spending some of their resources maintaining certain ceremonies in downtown Stockholm is of no more importance in determining the form of their government than the elaborate ceremonies that the Marine Corps performs at Iwo Jima Monument every Tuesday during the summer are in determining the American form of government.

7. Predictions are particularly hard here. In 1959 Tad Szulc wrote a book entitled *Twilight of the Tyrants* which dealt with South America. As we now know *Tyrany Resurgent* would have been a better title for that date.

8. Albert O. Hirschman began a survey of the problem: 'The point of departure of any serious thought about the chances of democracy in Latin America nust surely be pessimism.' On Democracy in Latin America,' *New York Review of Books*, Apr. 10, 1986, p. 41.

9. See the discussion of Ingram 1925, p. 705

10. On the form of feudalism in ancient Greece which developed between 1200 and 800 B.C., see Forrest 1979, pp. 45-46.

11. Or Turkish tribes, in some cases. The first Crusade (1096-1099) attacked the

Seljuk. See Dupuy and Dupuy 1977, p. 311.

12. In fact, one Crusade (the fourth, 1195-1200) had as its object, the conquest of Constantinople and is generally considered to have constituted for all practical purposes the death knell of the Byzantine Empire. See Dupuy and Dupuy 1977, pp. 380-382.

13. Japanese feudalism lasted much longer than European feudalism and, in fact, started later also.

14. The Rajput princes retained their feudal system under the Moguls. In fact they provided most of the Mogul Cavalry.

15. See North 1981, pp. 126-129.

16. See Himmelfarb 1968, pp. 82-84.

17. North and Thomas state 'would-be founders of new manors had to seek out peasants aggressively, even to the point of limiting their own powers by offering grants and privileges to entice potential emigrants...Peasants who succumbed to the lure of the frontier could either purchase their freedom from their lord, have it purchased for them by the lord, organizing a new manor, or steal away in the night. It is clear that large numbers of them followed one or another of these paths to the frontier.' North and Thomas (1973).

18. See North and Thomas, 1973, p.25-37

19. See Blum, 1966, pp. 64-72 and Thorndike, 1917, pp. 576-612.

20. See the account of this debate in Smith 1983, pp. v-xi.

21. See Hofheinz, 1977, pp. 3-9.

22. See Coulborn, 1965, pp. 54-8 and 65-71.

23. See Forrest 1979, p. 10., A. R. Burn, pp. 56-60

24. See Forrest 1979, p. 45., A. R. Burn, pp. 56-83 is a compact account of the dark age.

25. As a matter of fact, during most of this time the nominal emperor was also the ruler of Austria-Hungary and, hence, the most powerful single lord'. But his control over what actually went on in, say, Brandenburg was probably no stronger than that of the Russian emperor, Brandenburg regarding, in practice, both of them as foreign sovereigns.

26. The Rajput nobility were forced to sign a treaty with the British Governor-General which substantially restricted their powers. (See Edwards 1961) In regards to the Rajput status maintaining their organization under the British rule, A.C. Lyall, British Chief Commissioner in the 1870's wrote in 1875 that the Rajputs are 'still very much in the position which they took up on first entry upon the lands' (See Asiater Studies)

27. Dahl

28. See Forrest 1979, p. 48ff.

29. Ibid., pp. 98-101.

30. The number is, of course, very much larger in South Africa than in Israel. Israel has a Jewish population of about 3.5 million, and an Arab population of about 1,650,000. Of the later, about 1.15 million live in the area conquered by Israel in 1966 and cannot vote. There are about 5.4 million whites with full franchise, and about 18 million blacks and Asians with either restricted or no franchise in South Africa. See Dunnigan and Bay 1985, pp. 48-49; and pp. 170-171.

31. See Downs, 1957, p. 23-24.

32. He has a footnote in which he says that possibly not letting women vote would not deprive the nation of the right to be called democratic. P. 23.

33. See Wittfogel 1981.

34. See Tullock 1965, pp.137-165,for a formal elucidation of the point.

35. By foreign here I mean things not written in Spanish. Franco apparently felt that people who could read foreign languages either could be trusted or, perhaps, were not controllable. See Johnson 1983, p. 607 on the restricted tyrrany of Franco's dictatorship.

36. Ibid., p. 608.

37. In Mexico he rules for only six years and then has to appoint his successor and retire.

38. See Namier, 1957.

39. See Forrest 1979, p. 45.

40. See Aubyn 1983, pp. 11-15.

41. Ibid., p. 16. There is a myth that the Commons had been a significant part of the government in the middle ages. For an accurate account of its very minor role, see Sayles.

42. See Cantor 1970, p. 807.

43. Ibid., pp. 809-810.

44. See Ashley 1966, pp. 93ff.

45. See Dupuy an Dupuy 1977, p. 511.

46. See Ashley 1966, pp. 43ff.

47. Ibid., pp. 350-358.

48. On Charles II's return in 1660, see Dupuy and Dupuy 1977, p. 556. On George III's insanity see Canter 1970, p. 892.

49. See Johnson 1983, pp. 305; 481. India seized Portugese Goa in 1961, an event largely ignored in the West (outside of Portugal).

50. See Dunnigan and Bay 1985, p. 132.

51. See Dunnigan and Bay 1985, pp. 72-75.

52. See Chorley 1943, pp. 11, 16. Also see, Marx & Frederick Engels, 'The Class Struggles in France 1848 to 1850', *Selected Works*, Vol. 1, p. 136. 'Let us have no no illusions about it: a real victory of an insurrection over the military in street fighting, a victory as between two armies, is one of the rarest exceptions.'

53. See Johnson, 1966. p. 102

54. See Montague 1928, p. 164.

55. The Shah also, in the last eighteen months of his reign, stopped torturing people.

56. See Macdonald 1928, p. 396.

57. See Bourgeois 1982, p. 113.

CHAPTER II

COUPS AND THEIR PREVENTION

It may seem odd to begin our discussion of absolutist government not with the way one becomes a dictator, but with the way one keeps the dictatorship once one has it. This is dealing with the second stage, not the first stage of the career of most dictators. Nevertheless, for most dictators the period which they are in power is much longer than the period in which they achieve power. There is also a structural reason. In order to understand the problems faced by a man attempting to seize power, it is necessary to have a good idea of the barriers which were placed in his way by the existing dictator. The internal history of any dictatorship is largely a jockeying for power. The dictator lives continuously under the Sword of Damocles and equally continuously worries about the thickness of the thread. His high ranking courtiers, on the other hand, are well advised to shake their head in order to make certain it is still firmly attached every time tney leave his presence. Of course, politics in most modern dictatorships is not as bloody as that in the ancient autocracies which led to these two legends, but great personal insecurity is still part of them.

In any event we're going to talk about how you keep power if you are a dictator or king. There are, of course, differences between the hereditary monarchy and the ordinary dictatorship. Indeed, as a rough rule of thumb, historically, dictatorships are transitory, with the eventual switch to heredity control being likely. The Duvalier 'Presidency' of Haiti lasted two generations.[1] and the apparent establishment of the Kim dynasty in North Korea[2] are, I believe merely the precursors of what will with time, become the normal procedure. The situation in Singapore is less clear, but apparently the throne will be hereditary.[3] Enver Hoxha, dictator of Albania 1945-1985, actively promoted his son as his successor[4] but the son failed to take control when his father died.

The Somoza family governed Nicaragua through three generations and Trujillo would probably been able to pass the throne on to his son if the American navy had not intervened. Looking over the long reach of history, the usual situation is a hereditary succession interrupted from time to time by dynastic overthrows.

But there are differences between the hereditary King system and the dictatorship. firstly, the change of dictator is apt to be a fairly disturbing event; occasionally large numbers of people are killed. There are some technical ways of avoiding that which I will discuss later, but normally transmission from one dictator to another is a rough period. The succession in the royal dynasty usually is not, although quarrels within the ruling family, or between it and other families can cause a good deal of bloodshed.

The second major difference here, is that the Kings through the accidents of gene selection can be fairly stupid and inept people. Louis XVI, of course, is a good example.[5] Dictators on the other hand, although they may not be nice people, are pretty invariably talented. They tend to be intelligent, tough, and aggressive. They also tend to be much less secure than a hereditary monarch. Napoleon is sometimes quoted as having said that a hereditary monarch could go out ever summer for ten years and lose a battle and then return to his capital and live quite happily. But that he (i.e., Napoleon) would be finished if he lost one battle. This is a slight exaggeration, but it does point in the generally correct direction.

In this chapter I'm going to talk mainly about dictators rather than hereditary monarchs, mainly because they are much commoner in the present day world. Having said that I'm going to talk about how dictators stay in power, I must now once again confess that I do not have a general theory of dictatorship or a general theory of how dictators stay in power. I've been concerned about the problem of dictatorship for almost as long as I've been interested in Public Choice. Indeed, my first work on what now is thought of as Public Choice, was undertaken while I was in Communist China and I was thinking more of the government there than I was of democracies. The reasons that my writings have mainly been concerned with democracies is simply that dictatorship turns out to be a very difficult subject.

Theoretically the problem of maintaining power in a dictatorship is really very similar to that of maintaining a majority for redistributional purposes in a voting body. It is easily demonstrated, of course, that it is always possible to build a majority against any particular program of redistribution by offering something to the 'out's' on the original program and fairly high payment to a few of the 'in's'.

The situation in a dictatorship is similar. It is always possible at least in theory to collect together a group of people which is more powerful than the group supporting the status quo. This group will be composed of important officials of the regime who could benefit from its overthrow and their concomitant promotion. The reason that this is so, is that the rewards now being received by the supporters of the status quo, and it should be kept in mind that the dictator himself usually is very well paid, are available for redistribution to their successors.

As an example, which doesn't really fit most dictatorships, but nevertheless, may be familiar, suppose that Reagan is a dictator in the United States and his cabinet is in complete control. The ambitious Secretary of State, shall we say, offers to Undersecretary of Defense a promotion to Secretary of Defense, and makes similar offers to other officials. Since the Dictator himself and his prominent supporters are to be removed, there is clearly plenty of room for promotion of other people. This is like the circulating majority problem in a democratic voting body.

It should be said here that it's something of a mystery why the voting bodies do not behave in the highly unstable way that the Arrow Theorem would imply they should. Indeed, I have been conducting a long debate on this subject under the title 'Why So Much Stability' in my journal.[6] The purpose here, however, is not to contribute to that debate, but to discuss the dictatorial counterpart.

How then, does the dictator avoid this problem. The first thing to be said is that most of them don't avoid it permanently. There have been many dictators who have died peacefully in office and over time the tendency for rulers to pass the throne on to their son has been strong. Although there have been many such dictators, the number who have been overthrown is much larger. Thus the problem I have stated although successfully solved by some dictators has not yet been solved by all. Even those who are overthrown however, have usually a number of years of success before the overthrow occurs.

Traditional discussions of dictatorships, rarely bring this matter up. The problem however, surely dominates the activities of the dictator. To quote an American euphamism, 'In order to be a great Senator, one must first of all be a Senator.' Similarily, if you are to do anything as a dictator, you must first of all be a dictator.

I am not here discussing the overthrow of the dictator by popular forces. If the Police and Army are even reasonably efficient and willing to shoot to kill, that won't happen. Indeed, I'm not positive there is any clear cut case of a popular overthrow of the government. Generally speaking, it is a fight within the government itself, although the government may have democratic aspects. In the United States for example, the local legislatures and sheriffs of the thirteen colonies were already elected.[7] These elected legislatures threw out the Royal governors. This was clearly a fight within the government rather than a rising against the government. I believe that most other cases of what is claimed to be democratic overthrow of dictatorial regime will be shown to have the same pattern although I cannot claim to have made a careful study of all of them.

Characteristically, however, the overthrow of the dictator simply means that there will be another dictator. This second dictator will normally announce that he has popular support and for that matter he may have it at the beginning. Basically however, it is one dictator replacing another and the policies they follow will probably not be radically different. If we look at the world, we quickly realize that these policies will not be radically different from those that would be followed by a democracy either.

Here we must point out once again that the modern totalitarian dictators, Hitler, Stalin, Mao Tse-Tung, Pol Pot, are exceptional and unusual people and I'm not talking about them here. I suggest that the reader think of Francisco Franco, a more normal dictator even though he originally maintained that he was a follower of Mussolini and Hitler. It's hard to find any policy other than keeping power which he followed throughout his reign. Although he, of course, prevented centers of opposition from developing, his government was not violently oppressive.

As mentioned before, during most of his reign, Spain had no death penalty. The reinstitution of the death penalty in his last year came after extremely severe provocation in which his political opponents had ‘executed’ something like one hundred of Franco’s supporters. Even here when they murdered his prime minister instead of striking back hard, he chose to make concessions and select as new prime minister, a man who was thought to be more acceptable to his opponents. All of this is not intended to argue for Franco’s regime, in fact, I think it was a very poor government. Nevertheless, it was not a violently repressive regime. Franco in no way compares with Pol Pot.[8]

But this has been a digression. Let us return to our main topic of how the dictator holds his power, inspite of the fact that he will inevitably be in a position where a coalition of let us say, the Commander of his Army and the Chief of the Secret Police could jointly remove him while benefiting themselves.[9] Hume pointed out that although a ruler could rule the people by the power of his police and army, he could not rule the police and army by that power. As he put it, rule depended on opinion.[10]

It seems to me that this insight of Hume, like most of Hume’s other insights was an extremely good one. Hume did not, however, properly describe the opinion. I should like to repair this deficit and say the the opinion which a dictator must maintain among the people around him is not so much that he is a good, just, or God ordained dictator, but simply that if it comes to an effort to overthrow him he will win.

A more modern Social Scientist than Hume, Schelling, has pointed out the situation in which people can agree without discussing the matter in advance. If there are a number of people all of whom will gain a great deal if they make the same choice and all of whom will lose if they do not make the same choice, there may be certain characteristics of the environment which act as cues and lead them to, in fact, make the same choice. On the other hand, of course, there may not.[11]

For a political example, let us consider the Brams and Riker view of what happened in American nominating conventions back in the days when the convention was not a mere puppet of pre-existing primaries. All of the people attending the convention were professional politicians who hoped very strongly to be rewarded because they had provided support for whomever was nominated as president. On the other hand, usually they didn’t know when they arrived who was going to be nominated. There was then a cautious feeling out of the situation with individuals moving to the support of whomever they thought was in fact, going to win. The early movement tended to give more information to others and very quickly everyone was rushing to get on the band wagon of the winner. Those who waited too long, of course, were not rewarded because their vote had not been necessary. Further, those who failed to get on or who pushed to hard for one of the losers would not be rewarded. The result here is a combination of Hume and Schelling. The opinion which counted here was opinion as to who was likely to win. The decision had to be made while it was still uncertain who was going to win, because if you waited too long, you would get no reward and the result was at first caution, and then a cascade of people rushing to join who ever they thought would win.

Efforts to overthrow a dictator have somewhat the same structure. The basic difference is that everything is much more concealed than it was at a convention, and secondly, if the dictator himself will win as he usually, but not always, does, the thing may proceed so rapidly that we don't even see the early stage at all.

The basic problem can be seen in figure 2.1. The top panel has on the vertical axis the probability that a dictator will be overthrown and on the horizontal axis the strength of opposition against him. Note that the individuals would have different lengths along the axis with a private in a provincial garrison taking up very little space and the Chief of Staff a great deal.

The extreme example of this disproportion was the events in France in 1958. Before De Gaulle decided to overthrow the government of France, there was substantially no chance of it being overthrown, as soon as he has made up his mind, the government collapsed.[12] In essence, he himself, occupied a space on the horizontal axis which perhaps extended from point A to point B.

The vertical line which extends from the top panel through all the other panels cuts the curve on panel a at a point where the probability is 50/50. In other words, anything to the right of that line has a better than even chance of overthrowing the dictator, anything to the left has a worse chance.

On panel b, we continue the same horizontal axis, but the vertical axis is the reward from successful participation, with the reward from the overthrow of the dictator above the line, and the penalty for failure to overthrow the dictator below the line. Note that I have drawn these lines not on the basis of empirical evidence, but more or less the way I think they should be. The reader is invited to experiment with other lines if he doesn't like these.

The lower line, which is actually on the second quandrant of the Cartesian axis of panel b shows the punishment which the individual is likely to receive if he joins the revolutionary effort and it fails. The bottom panel simply shows the net present discounted value of joining the revolutionary conspiracy for some individual contemplating such an action. It is computed from the first three lines. The problem of the dictator is making certain that everyone thinks that they are in the negative payoff portion of this diagram. The problem of the person attempting to organize conspiracy, is to convince people that the present discounted rewards of joining the revolution are positive.

This rather simple set of diagrams is, of course, intended for heuristic purposes and is not intended as an empirically accurate measure of probabilities, etc. Nevertheless, it does I think, represent quite accurately the type of calculation that must be undertaken under these circumstances.

Suppose then, that the commanding General of the 3rd Army Corps suddenly announces that the government is corrupt, wicked, etc., and that he will save the country from these depraved rulers. He tries to make this announcement as convincing as possible and what he is trying to convince people of, in general, is not that he is good, just, etc., but that he is strong and will win. Of course, there is no reason not to claim virtue and he no doubt will, but this is less important. He will try to obtain control of communications (Under present circumstances, this means the TV or radio stations.), because he wants his message, which is 'I am strong and will win!' concealed under 'I am virtuous', to be transmitted and the current dictators message not.

At this point various other people in the country, particularly the higher officials, are presented with a difficult problem. Is it better for them to jump on the revolutionary band wagon or join with the dictator in supressing the revolution. Further, it's very dangerous to show hesitation. This is particularly so if you think that the dictator himself might win because he is likely to regard hesitation or neutrality in these cases as treason. Strength comes from an appearance of strength but strength also gives an appearance of strength.

This discussion of how dictators are overthrown is extremely brief. I have not, for example, even dealt with the not particularly uncommon situation in which the attempted overthrow is strong enough so that it seizes part of the country physically and there is then a protracted civil war. Here again, the real point of the civil war is to convince people that one side or the other is going to win.

But how does a dictator prevent this kind of overthrow? He must always have as one of his primary objectives, the presentation to the world of a picture of strength. Note here that the world is not the average citizen although the dictator should try to convince them too. The world is actually his higher officials. An impressive looking, but actually hollow armed force, may frighten the citizenry, but it's not likely to frighten the higher officials who know how hollow it is. On the other hand, the hollowness of this force may mean that the officials feel they cannot rely on it in an effort to overthrow the dictator.

The dictator must prevent subversive coalitions from forming. His basic rule in preventing them from forming is convincing people they will be unsuccessful. Since there is always the possibility both in theory and in practice of a successful coalition against him, a coalition of people who will gain from overthrowing him and who have power enough to do so, he cannot rely on the low possibility of such a coalition at any point in time. What he must try to do is make it appear to anyone contemplating either starting a conspiracy or joining a conspiracy not that any conspiracy against the dictator is impossible, because that is absurd, but that that particular conspiracy will fail. In essence, he has to interrupt communication among potential conspirators by making communications dangerous.

In order to attract potential conspirators into a given conspiracy, it is necessary to offer them rewards in the form of promotion, etc. inside the hierarchy. It is hard to do this while keeping matters a secret. Once the revolutionary coup is announced, of course, such promises can be made with no difficulty.

How does a dictator deal with this? A precaution that he normally will take is stringent enforcement of the law against treason. Any conspiracy even discussion of overthrowing a dictator is apt to be severely punished if the dictator finds out about it, and he'll make every effort to do so. His reasons are, of course, simple. Things which indicate his strength are plainly visible. He has

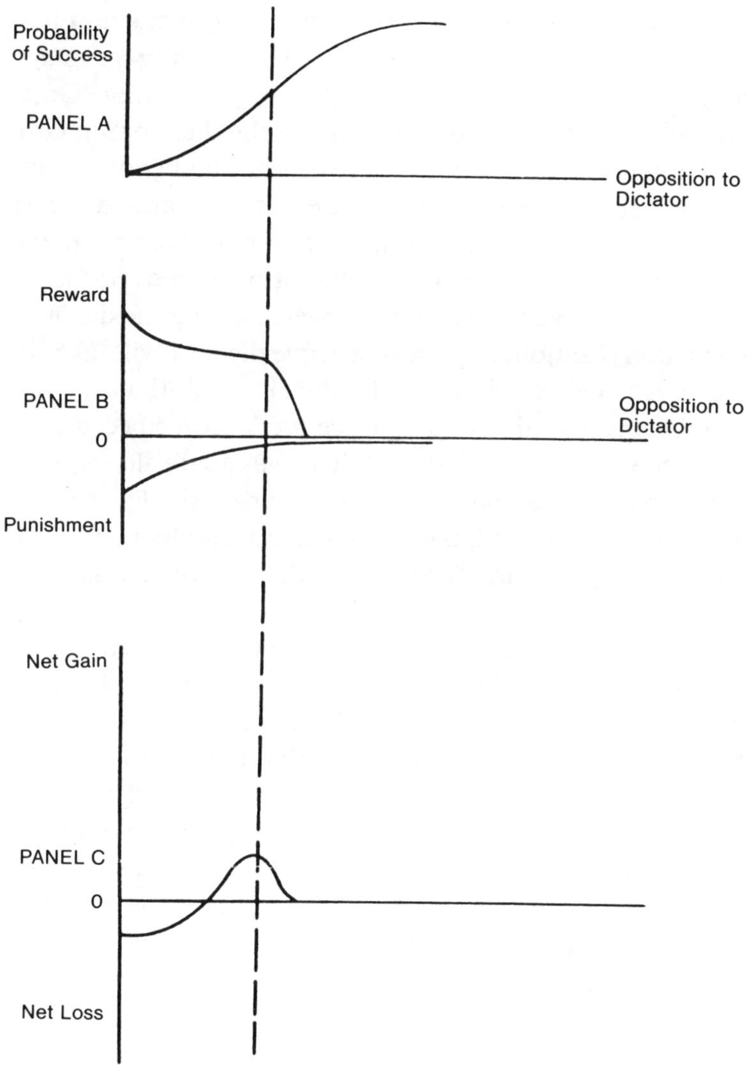

Figure 2.1

guards, police, and the military, to say nothing of possible public demonstrations. People involved in these various activities are apt to feel that the other people involved in the same activity are loyal to the dictator unless they have some positive information to the contrary. By making it illegal to even discuss overthrowing a dictator, the dictator makes it difficult for such positive information to develop. thus the dissatisfied lieutenant in the dictator's personal guard is apt to feel that his dissatisfaction is a limited phenomenon and not realize that there are a great many other people who'd be delighted to overthrow the dictator. On a more cold blooded level, if the lieutenant in the dictator's guard realized that it must be true that there are a large number of people who could benefit by overthrowing the dictator and moving upward themselves, he is unable to safely communicate with them and hence insure his own future in the revolutionary movement.

This prevention of even discussion of overthrowing the dictator is an important precaution which any sensible dictator will take. It has, however, a serious defect. Macciavelli said that it was astonishing that any overthrow of a prince ever occured because of necessity, the conspiracy was risky and there was a safe alternative, which was to betray the conspiracy to the prince.[13] The prince would then, naturally reward highly the person who had betrayed the conspiracy and take care of those members of the conspiracy that had not informed.

In general, Macciavelli correctly identified the phenomenon. He overlooked, however, another problem here. One of the ways of rising in the entourage of any dictator, Macciavelli's 'reward', is to denounce a conspiracy. It's not necessary that there actually be a conspiracy there to be denounced. The dictator is apt to be surrounded by skilled and subtle courtiers all of whom are trying to convince him that all of the others are disloyal to him. Their reason is simply a desire to rise in his favor. Thus the dictator has very strong motives to suppress conspiracies against himself, and to reward highly people who inform him, but the reward system in and of itself, tends to generate false alarms.

All of this makes life difficult for the dictator and indeed is by no means the only thing that makes it difficult.[14] He can neither trust his officials not to conspire against him nor can he necessarily trust reports of these conspiracies. It should be said that in recent years the development of very small recording devices has made it somewhat easier for the person who wants to betray a genuine plot to do so. Unfortunately, most of the people who are in a position to plot (i.e., the higher officials) are rather subtle individuals who are accustomed to communicating by allusion and indirect methods and hence recording their conversation is not all that helpful. A general conspiracy may not sound like it and casual conversation may possibly be interpretable as a conspiracy.

But if the ruler cannot prevent subtle conspiracies among the people of high rank around him, he pretty surely can prevent any wide spread conspiracy from developing. Thus higher officials may feel that there are enough of them antagonistic to the current dictator so that a conspiracy would work, but there is no way that they can assure themselves that their subordinates will follow their orders. It was of course, this problem that stopped coup and attempted coup by the German Military against Hitler.[15]

Firm enforcement of the law against treason is certainly highly desirable for the dictator, but he will find it very difficult to do and it is certainly not a solid final reliance. In practice, dictators tend to respond to reports that one particular official is conspiring against them, not by killing him, but by appointing him Ambassador to some far off place. He can then be brought back later. Stalin, of course, followed the policy of simply killing and it must be admitted that he was extremely successful.

Let us now return to the positive methods that the dictator has for demonstrating strength; for convincing all the people around him that in the event of any effort to overthrow him he will be successful in supressing it. The first of these, of course, is simply seeing to it that any group of people that he particularly suspects are kept physically from doing anything about it.

The current King of Morocco has suffered several efforts by military men to replace him. In consequence at the moment, the army is almost entirely kept out of Morocco proper and engaged in a war against the Polisaro. When they are in Morocco, they are not permitted to leave their base without police permission and are escorted by the police whenever they do leave the base. This offers a good deal of protection against the army, although the possibility that it might decide to march into Morocco cannot be totally ruled out. It doesn't offer any protection against the police.[16] The current dictator of Syria has chosen to balance matters. Not long ago his brother commanded a special very well equipped military force which in essence guarded the dictator. He has since been exiled to Switzerland and then brought back. The dictator does not permit any force to get large enough so that it could independently overthrow him. The Special Defense Companies, formently commanded by his brother were matched (and watched) by the Special Forces of the same size. Neither could safely take on the current dictator and the army.[17] Such balancing is more common than the kind of thing the King of Morocco is doing.

The problem here is that in a real sense a dictator lives in a state of nature. He is not the owner of important assets in a well run state. There is no overwhelmingly powerful state which can protect him. What he needs to be protected from is parts of the state. All of this makes his life dangerous and in some ways unpleasant, but presumably the dictators regard the advantages greater than the disadvantages.

The situation is analogous, to a very typical Public Choice problem; the self enforcing constitution. It's fairly easy to design a constitution for a state which would lead to an at least reasonably good government. The problem is designing this constitution in such a way that it enforces itself. How do you, to give but one example, prevent a supreme court from deciding that it should be supremer than the designers of the constitution intended? At the moment we don't have very much of a solution to this problem in democratic politics and the dictator must face it every day.

The gang of four in China lost their position of power because the commander of their guard force chose to arrest them rather than guard them.[18] Arevalo, a dictator of Guatamala, was assassinated by one of his own guard while he was walking towards the dining room of his house with his wife.[19] President Park of Korea was shot by the head of his secret police.[20] But this problem can to some extent be mitigated in a dictatorship by attempting to enforce the law against treason and by a variety of other techniques to which we will now turn.

The first of these is simply preventing others from getting positions of firm power. The dictator should practice what Mussolini called 'Changing of the Guard', i.e., he should move his high officials around so that they never develop a firm personal following in what ever job they hold. This is particularly important in the case of the army and police force, and it is of course, in those areas where most modern states rotate higher officers with regularity. This shifting around firstly, demonstrates the power of the dictator. Any individual knows that at any time he can be removed. Secondly, it provides a way of quietly rewarding services.

The dictator if he's well advised will not only rotate people from one military command to another but will at least occasionally remove individuals from command totally and then a few years later bring them back. It should be said here that in Mexico the 'Party of Revolutionary Institutions' originally was simply a coalition of military men. The conversion of a rather disorderly state to one which is rather orderly as dictatorships go, largely involved imposing on the higher military officials, all of whom were in fact bandit chiefs with their own little armies, rotation with their troops not going with them.[21]

There are many cases of this. When Mao Tse-Tung seized control of China, he actually was the head of an organization in which there were in essence 5 armies all of which had been built up by one leader from practically nothing and which were to a considerable extent loyal to that leader. Mao might have been able to deal with this by ordinary methods, but the Korean war gave him a wonderful opportunity. He in essence drafted from each of these armies specific units to send to the Korean war. These units were then rotated back to China on a regular basis, but were not returned to their original army. As a result at the end of the Korean war the 5 major armies had been melded into one. Mao Tse-Tung was then able to remove the four most important generals from their positions of personal power.[22]

One thing that most dictators should at least give careful thought to is personal command of the army. At the least, the dictator must devote a lot of attention to who commands it and if possible should fix it up so there is no true commander, but a number of officials with titles like Minister of War, Chief of Staff, etc. He can, however, take direct command himself and this frequently is very helpful in retaining power.

Another technique is collegial control (i.e., putting a board or commission at the head of almost everything.) the Lords of the Admiralty are an example of this from the present day.[23] Cabinets and Councils are others. A group of this sort cannot effectively conspire because somebody will talk, nor is any individual likely to be able to use it to build up a personal following.

Another technique, a very traditional one, is 'cutting off the head of the tallest flowers', disposing of people who are rising in power and influence.[24] When the Great Captain returned to Spain after having won most of Italy for the King of Spain, he was almost instantly exiled to his estates and prevented from having any influence in the government of Spain.[25] Khrushchev disposing of Zhukov right after Zhukov had made Khrushchev a success in the

'Anti-Party Plot' affair certainly is another example.[26]

As a minor, but nevertheless possibly important aspect of keeping power, a lot of pompous ceremony surrounding the dictator is a good idea. It should be said here that I suspect that the dictator also enjoys it. It is particularly helpful if the dictator can arrange to have himself surrounded by a great deal of pomp and ceremony while putting on an appearance of being a very simple man himself. Lord Montgomery during World War II insisted that all of his staff officers be absolutely perfectly dressed with shoes shined, etc., while himself, wearing less than perfectly tailored uniforms. His public relations officer made quite a bit out of this contrast.[27] This kind of thing frequently pays off to a dictator.

There is another important aspect which is that the dictator should always get his way. In order to always get your way without making a lot of mistakes, the dictator has to be careful. Macciavelli said, 'a dictator should continuously solicit advice, but never take unsolicited advice.' (Macciavelli, p. 117). This is still a good bit of advice for any for dictators if they're willing to accept an unsolicited suggestion from me. Secondly, the dictator should normally make up his own mind late in the discussion of any particular problem. And lastly, if he runs into a particularly difficult problem, he should push the whole thing off on an inferior. He can blame the inferior if things work out badly. Once he has taken a position however, in general, it is dangerous for him to change. A dictator can get away with this sometimes, but not frequently.

The basic problem here is one which has been discussed in connection with nuclear war called 'escalation dominance'. The dictator should be surrounded by people all of whom feel that opposition to the dictator has less chance as it proceeds to a higher level. In other words, the individual courtiers should believe there is no point in starting a serious argument with the dictator because the dictator will win; that if he tries to arrange a coup the dictator will win; and that if he actually starts a civil war the dictator will win. As long as every courtier thinks all of these things are true the dictator is safe.

These problems are clearly very difficult for the dictator and it is also clear that the solutions that I have suggested are incomplete. This is, of course, characteristic of the real world. Dictators do not, on the whole, keep their power permanently. Further, the lack of true intellectual precision of my discussion here, I believe, also reflects the real world. The dictator is faced by a set of very difficult problems and his solutions to them are, generally speaking, not the neat mathematical solutions that we would like to find.

When I discuss matters of this sort, I normally find that I get two reactions. The first of them is that this is obviously absurd, and the second, sometimes from the same person a little bit later in the conversation, that everybody has always known these matters. I believe the second is, in fact, correct, at least when we are talking about dictators themselves. Although I think most dictators have been on the whole aware of the kind of problems I have been discussing, and for that matter the kind that I will be discussing in the next two chapters, they have rarely spoken about them. This is probably because they regard any open discussion on these matters as likely to weaken their power.

Political scientists, when talking about dictators, have tended to pay little attention to these problems. The existing literature on dictatorship is sparse and in my opinion, very poor. It is very heavily dominated by moral considerations and in fact, to a considerable extent, consists of simple attacks on the whole idea.[28] These attacks can be rather restricted. It's an intriguing characteristic of communism that it does not have any political science at all for its own governments (which are, of course, always dictatorships), but that it does have an elaborate attack on other governments. All of them are accused of being dictatorships and this accusation is apparently intended to hurt. But even there they have no theoretical structure.

If we turn to the few things that I can find in western sources, Macciavelli is perhaps the most informative. A mixture of moralistic attacks on dictators, moralistic advice to dictators (i.e., they're told to be good) and occasional discussions in terms of the class structure of the dictatorship are almost all we find. In my opinion, all of these things are beside the point. Dictatorship may indeed be immoral and wicked, but we should try to understand it. Further, offering moral lectures to dictators is not likely to be much help.

NOTES

1. Francois Duvalier was dictator of Haiti from 1957-71, and was succeeded by his son, Jean-Claude. Both proclaimed themselves 'President for life'. Although the son was eventually overthrown, he was ruler for a longer period than his father.

2. The North Korean dictator Kim Il Sung has publicly designated his eldest son Kim Jong Il his successor, and has taken the precaution of ordering the state-controlled press to print numerous stories concerning the son's infallibility ('So This is Paradise: North Korea Will Be More Perfect When the Great Leader Meets His Maker', *Washington Post* Oct. 31, 1982; p.c 1).

3. Prime Minister Lee Kuan Tew, the dictator of Singapore, appears as of this writing to be grooming his son Lee Hsien Loong as his successor, *Wall Street Journal*, Oct 8, 1984; p.31.

4. (Dunnigan and Bay 1984, p. 78).

5. Louis XVI spent most of his time playing with mechanical toys and hunting, and frequently fell asleep during Council meetings when matters of grave importance were under discussion. According to one of his more admiring biographers, he 'was unequal to prolonged toil or daring resolution, and so self-distrustful as to be readily swayed this way or that by those whom he liked or who had frequent access to his company... His lack of will was phenomenal' (Montague 1928, p. 79).

6. *Public Choice* It has now lasted three years and shows no sign of ending.

7. Knollenberg (1961), pp. 49-57.

8. Trythall (1970).

9. It's very hard to tell who will remove you. Batista was a mere sergeant when he staged his first successful revolution. He and his fellow non-coms removed most of the regular officers of the Army and appointed themselves in their place. (Johnson, 1983, p.619; Thomas 1970, p.639). The current dictators of Surinam and Liberia did somewhat the same thing (on Surinam, see *New York Times*, Feb. 26, 1980, p.5; on Liberia, see *New York Times*, Apr. 13, 1980, p. l).

10. Hume p.23

11. Schelling's first example involved two people who would be highly rewarded if they met in New York without prior consultation. He (at the time a professor at Yale) reasoned each would independently go to the information booth in Grand Central Station.

12. The French army was a critical factor in the overthrow, and support from the army coalesced around De Gaulle following his decision (Crozier, 1973, pp. 453-478).

13. Macciavelli - p. 96.

14. Xenophon is largely a discussion of these difficulties. He exaggerates some, but not a great deal.

15. In this case the army major commanding troops sent to arrest Goebbels allowed the latter to talk him out of it (Fitzgibbon, 1968, p.210).

16. *Washington Post*, January 27, 1984; p. 19. The army further has no Minister of Defense, or Chief of Staff, and has only one active general for 170,000 men (*Time*, September 24, 1984; p. 44).

17. Hafez al-Assad's brother Rifaat is the colonel in command of the elite

Special Defense Companies. His rival, General Ali Haidar, commands the Special Forces (of similar size); the two organizations spend a lot of time watching each other (Dunnigan and Bay 1985, p. 57). At the time which this page was actually written, Damascus was an armed camp with different military factions pointing their guns at each other and occasionally engaging in light gun fire (*Washington Post*, February 9, 1984; p. 7). This is a more overt expression of the normal situation in the Syrian Dictatorship or indeed in any dictatorship. Normally it is better concealed.

18. Onate, 1978, p.562.

19. *New York Times* , July 28, 1957; p.1.

20. Park was shot to death during a dispute between KCIA director Kim Jae Kyu and his chief bodyguard (*New York Times*, October 27, 1979; p. 1).

21. On the history of the Insitutional Revolutionary Party, (PRI), see Smith, 1979,pp. 11-20.

22. On the five Field Armies, see Karnau 1972, pp. 68-69. For the rotation policy and postwar reorganization see Gittings 1967, pp. 294-99. It should be said that I believe that I am the actual source of this idea. So far as I know, a secret despatch written by me to the Department of State from the Korean Embassy was the first mention of it.

23. Originally established under Henry VIII, the Admiralty (composed of five lords commissioners) was in charge of Royal Navy operations until 1964. After this date, the Admiralty became the Navy Department, within which the Admiralty lords still exist although their functions are undefined.

24. Thrasyboulos was.. said to have given advice on how to be a tyrant to the young Periandros of Corinth, taking his messenger for a walk by a cornfield and thoughtfully lopping of with his walking stick the head of any stalk that looked superior to the average.' S. R. Burn, p. 126.

25. El Gran Capitan was Gonzalo de Cordoba, who Dupuy and Dupuy (1977, p. 488) describe as an 'organizational and tactical genius'. He was recalled to Spain following his spectacular successes and never given another opportunity to command 'due to the jealousy of [King] Ferdinand' (ibid., p. 470).

26. Four months after Zhukov (the famous victor of Moscow, Leningrad, Stalingrad, and Berlin), then Chief of Staff, saved Khruschev from being ousted as Premier, Khruschev removed him from office – ostensibly for statements Zhukov had made in a speech *supporting Khruschev* implying that the army was an independent political force. (Worth 1961, p.16).

27. See Barnett 1960, pp 269,280. Interestingly, it was only after taking command of the Eighth Army in August 1942, that Montgomery began dressing eccentrically (most notably wearing outlandish headgear); until then his dress had been quite orthodox (ibid.). In Montgomery's *Memoirs* (1957, p.111) he admitted that this reflected a conscious policy.

28. See those by John J. Johnson, and Hugh M. Hamill, Jr. for examples.

CHAPTER III

WAR

Napoleon, Hitler, and Mussolini all lost their power as a result of unsuccessful wars. Alexander, Ghengis Khan, and Stalin on the other hand, all greatly increased their power as a result of war. To an absolute autocrat, then, war offers both an opportunity for increasing his power and a risk that he will lose it. In this chapter we will be primarily concerned with the essentially defensive problem of preventing an autocrat's overthrow by an outside army rather than his ability to increase his power or to overthrow other autocrats. We'll also ignore the apparently real entertainment value of war when contemplated from the position of the chief player. The statement frequently made in the 17th and 18th centuries that war was the sport of kings does seem to have had a good deal of truth in it.

It's not at all clear whether over the sweep of history as a whole the foreign invasion or a domestic coup is the greatest danger to an autocratic ruler. In recent years, domestic coups have clearly greatly outnumbered foreign invasions, but I believe that this situation may be in a state of change. Recently, there have been some rulers removed by invasion. Afghanistan is particularly interesting in this case because the Russians first put in a puppet and then sent the army in to kill him.[1] This is by no means the only case. Qaddafi periodically intervenes in Chad and the intervention is sometimes countered by the French.[2] Indeed, the French have throughout almost the whole of their former empire taken active interest in local politics through defending the existing dictator, or withdrawing the defense under circumstances in which it's fairly certain he'll be removed.[3] England did some of this kind of thing in the days right after her granting freedom to the bulk of her empire. Nyere, for example, is dictator of Tanzania to a large extent because a British Naval Task Force put down a military rebellion against him. Britain, however, apparently has given up this particular activity.[4]

Nyere, of course, sent his army in to throw out Idi Amin and, in fact, at the time of this writing, his army of occupation is still holding Uganda.[5] The Vietnamese government conquered Laos, installed a puppet government, and has also installed a puppet government by force in Cambodia. In these cases the previous dictator, of course, lost his job.[6]

The current bloody war between Iraq and Iran started when the dictator of Iraq decided that he would take the oil fields away from Iran. He was not, apparently, interested in overthrowing the government of Iran, but of course, depriving it of its principal source of revenue might have done just that. The army acted with almost incredible ineptitude with the result that it is now on the defensive inside Iraq against Iranian forces. The Iranian forces make no secret of their desire to get rid of the current dictator of Iraq and, in fact, apparently propose to change the governments throughout the Persian Gulf if they are able to destroy the Iraqi army.[7]

But all of this is fairly minor compared to the number of dictators who have been overthrown by coups in recent years. I've said several times I believe this is a transitory phenomena. In essence the period of American domination and an enforced peace is dying out, and the world will, I think, return to its traditional state of disorder. If so, dictators will find foreign invasion as much of a risk as domestic coups. It is likely, of course, and partial compensation, that at least some dictators will regard this as an opportunity and not a danger. We may see some genuine empires in Africa. The Fulani crusade may be restarted and/or Mali may become as great an empire as its namesake was.[8]

The basic problem that this gives to a ruling dictator is rather well represented by Iraq. Iraq has had a series of vigorous military uprisings with the government overthrown, and the current dictator is the product of one of these overthrows. He, for various reasons decided to spend his very great oil revenues on buying arms and ammunition from the Russians, but at the same time, he clearly worried about the armed forces overthrowing him. He thus promoted to high rank a group of people whose primary characteristic was that they were not likely to try to overthrow him.

Even so, they were watched carefully by a secret police and kept divided among themselves. This gave him a great deal of security domestically, but when he decided to take over the oil wells of Iran he discovered these people might indeed be no danger to him, but they were not much of a danger to the Iranians either.[9]

At the start of the war, it should have been an Iraqi walkover. The almost incredible military incompetence of the Iraqi higher command[10] meant that they did not do very much damage to Iran and, of course, irritated it. Iran's natural military capacities are immensely greater than those of Iraq, particularly granted the fact that Hassan did not take their oil wells, and hence that they were able to continue drawing in large amounts of arms from abroad. Hassan had, apparently, not thought about the war very much, and therefore had started it in circumstances in which they could cut off the bulk of his oil exports. The result is that after a considerable period of time in which his heavily armed, highly inept army failed to do very much, the Iranians began pushing him back.[11]

He may lose his throne because his army, although very unlikely to overthrow him directly, will lose the war. But once again, these things are complicated. His higher officers are now in a better position to overthrow him than they ever have been before. Further, some of them, with time, seem to have developed a certain amount of military ability.[12] Some of these more confident officers may have acquired loyalty among the troops and may be wondering whether they would not like to be dictator of Iraq themselves.

This is the sort of dual problem that the possibility of foreign war presents to an absolute ruler. He may be overthrown by his neighbor's armies, or by the armies that he organizes to defend him against his neighbors. There is also the possiblity of increasing his own strength by conquering his neighbor, but once again, the army that he organizes for this purpose may overthrow him. This problem is added on to the problems that we have been discussing in the last chapter.

It is a consideration of problems like this, probably, that have led the African dictators to enter into a sort of cartel under which they agree not to invade each other. It permits them all to keep relatively small military units, and what is more important, military units that are weak because the senior officers have little loyalty from the troops under their command.[13] The problem with this cartel, like the problem of all cartels, is that it is prone to break down. I have mentioned Nyere's successful invasion of Uganda and Qaddafi's invasions, some successful and some unsuccessful, of the Chad. There are a few other examples of the same kind of thing. Algeria has been backing the Polisaro in its effort to take a bit of the Sahara Desert from Morocco.[14] Intermittant war between Somalia and Ethiopia is, of course, another area where this has been broken,[15] and various dictators have given quiet support to efforts to overthrow the government of their neighbor by refugees from that neighbor in their country.

The basic response of the African countries to this breech in the cartel is to try and pretend that it isn't happening. Nevertheless, this is getting harder and harder, and it is now becoming quite difficult to get the Organization of African Union to even meet because of various wars that are, in fact, going on at low level among its members.[16]

In general, military invasion of one country by another is to be distinguished from simply offering support to citizens of a neighbor who want to overthrow that government. Both are the kind of activity that the receipient government probably resents, but they do involve quite different levels of risk for the country which is engaging in the offensive activity. Algeria, for example, can provide the Polisaro with arms and refuge without building up the personal prestige of any officer in the Algerian army. The dictator doesn't have to worry particularly about his own military success being followed by a revolt against him by his own army.

But, let us take the matter up in an orderly manner. We will begin by discussing a dictator's protection of himself against foreign invasion, and then denote a tiny amount but not very much attention to his advantages from engaging in invasion himself. We will then discuss his problem playing off military strength and efficiency against the danger that an effective military force poses for him. It should, of course, be kept in mind, that an effective military force does indeed pose a danger. But not markedly more of a danger than a highly efficient secret police or, indeed, any subordinate whose natural capacities are such that he develops a good deal of support in the state. After all, President Park of Korea was, as we have mentioned above, killed by the chief of his secret police. Further, that most suspicious of all rulers, Stalin, quite regularly killed the leaders of his secret police because he thought they were conspiring agianst him. The final chief of Stalin's secret police, Beria, was killed almost immediately after Stalin's death either because he was plotting against the others of Stalin's successor, (which is what they said), or simply because they thought he was too powerful.[17] The Pretorian Guard, which although it was a fighting unit, was basically the central guard and police of the emperor of Rome, was always at least as much danger to the emperor as anyone else in the empire.[18]

Let us think about the military problem. The first thing to be said is that the military problem, to a considerable extent, is also a diplomatic problem. A weaker army may be compensated for by changing the international environment in a way in which you are in less danger. Note that I say here a weaker army, not a smaller army. The matter will be discussed below, but the Roman army, which gave continuous trouble to the emperors, was a fairly small army granted the size of the empire.[19] Stalin maintained a vastly larger army which, in fact, ignoring some accusations made in the 1930's, never caused him any real concern.[20] And France maintained a monster army which was no danger to the king.[21]

The English military forces, of course, were comprised dominantly of colonial forces scattered around the empire. But they were, nevertheless, an immense power and of course they were backed by a navy that was even more powerful. Their structure, with its rather unusual internal organization, will be dealt with below. It should be pointed out, however, that although it gave security against a military rising, it gave rather weak security against other parts of society rising. The army available in England was usually quite small, a fact which led various people to think they could overthrow the king.[22] The American colonists, of course, were successful, as was William while James II, James III, and Charles III were all unsuccessful.[23] The same could be said of the various Irish rebels.[24] Nevertheless, there was far more fighting by Englishmen attempting to overthrow the king of England than by Frenchmen attempting to overthrow the king of France.[25] Once again, all of this will be discussed in greater detail later.

Basically, a dictator, like a republic, depends on its own forces and on allies for its defense against possible foreign enemies. Let us begin with allies. The first thing to be said is that the history of alliances is not one of friendship and loyal cooperation. Indeed, at most times throughout history the normal attitude among allies was one extreme irritation. Each ally always wanted to use the power of the others for its own ends. There were almost always severe difficulties in planning particular military operations and in the general thrust of the war. All of the allies in traditional times were aware of the fact that their ally of today might be their enemy of tomorrow.[26]

Nevertheless, in spite of this lack of confidence among allies, the potential existence of allies was a strong safeguard on the part of any country or any dictator who was under attack. The reason is simple: the balance of power. If A attacks B and it appears to C that A is going to win decisively, then C, if it is sensible, will enter on the side of B. This is not because it likes B, but because it does not want A to be in the position where it can combine the power of A and B and then turn against C.

This simple bit of foresight on the part of each country, that it is not to their interest in general to permit any one country to become overwhelmingly powerful, means that any country which is weak can expect at least some allies to try to protect it. They do so not because they like it but because they do not want it added on to another country.[27]

Occasionally, it is true, arrangements have been made among three or four countries to barbecue another. The partition of Poland is probably the most famous single example of this.[28] Normally, however, this is does not happen. Normally, a country that is being beaten can expect that it will find allies suddenly springing to its defense. This leads to rapid changes of position. When the Conference of Vienna met after Napoleon was deported to Elba, the first order of business transacted there was treaty of alliance between Austria, England and France against Russia. The ostensible reason for the conference was to establish the conditions of the peace between the allies, England, Austria and Russia on the one hand, and France on the other.[29] Thus, this involved a very, very sharp change in position.

However, there is more to this story. When Napoleon returned from Elba and seized France, the then king of France, Louis XVIII, a rather inept man, left his copy of the alliance in his desk. Napoleon promptly sent it to the Czar of Russia. The Czar, however, who fully understood the nature of the balance of power, was completely unimpressed.[30] No doubt he expected something of this sort, even though it had been successfully kept a secret from him until Napoleon sent him the treaty. All of this is in no way uncommon. Rapid changes of this sort are normal in history. Charles V spent a long military career fighting various people, but over that period of time the German princes that were on his side changed radically from time to time. His allies in one victory would decide that he was becoming too powerful and become his enemies while his former enemies whom he had weakened by his previous victories would first form an alliance with his former allies, and then when that alliance seemed to be getting a little overpowerful, possibly become allies with Charles.[31]

But all of this, although an important principle for history and important for any ruler who wishes to keep his throne, in essence involved protection of the country, not the ruler. Shortly after Louis XVI was beheaded his close relatives, the other branch of the Bourbon family which ruled Spain, formed an alliance with republican France. This alliance stuck until Napoleon much later decided to make his brother king of Spain, thus terminating it.[32]

But nevertheless, although what we see in our example was primarily preventing B from being absorbed into A, normally C will not have any particular devotion to the present government remaining in B, but will regard a revolution or uprising there as, on the whole, destabilizing. Mainly however, they defend B against A, not against enemies of the dictator of B inside B.

Although a country is, to a considerable extent, defended by a balance of power, it would be unwise to depend entirely on that balance of power. A partition can sometimes be arranged under which C is compensated by getting part of B when A takes the rest. If B were totally disarmed, this would tend to be a more attractive alternative, firstly because the partition would be cheaper, and secondly, because C would know that in any event B would not come to their aid if they later had trouble with A or some other country. The military force maintained by a country under the balance of power, and that is of course the normal status of the world, offers protection for that country partly by being able to directly protect it, but partly by being able to participate in the balance of power, ie., preventing neighbors from becoming too powerful.

All of this has assumed the balance of power is a normal phenomenon of international life. On the other hand, I have not described the balance of power as something which does any particular good. What it actually does is make it very, very difficult for one country to conquer all the others either in the world, a continent, or in some local area, by giving them a continuing motive to combine against the conqueror.

Why the balance of power has had such a bad press in the United States I don't know, particularly since we owe our independence to it. During the Seven Years War, England, aided only by Frederick the Great of Prussia, took on substantially the whole of Europe and won.[33] At the end of the war England formally became the leading power in Europe, a fact which was solemnized by the British ambassadors being everywhere given precedence over the French ambassadors.[34]

This upset almost everybody, certainly the French, but also interestingly enough, the Prussians, who had been England's only ally in the previous war. France thought that the easiest way of weakening England would be to reduce its population by one third, specifically supporting a revolution in the thirteen colonies. It was not, of course, solely French influence that led to the revolution, but it certainly was primarily the French and Spanish military forces that led to the success of the revolution. England found herself at war with France and Spain, and with her power sharply restricted by what was called the League of Armed Neutrality, which involved practically every other country in Europe.[35] Faced with this immense aggregation of power, on the whole, England did quite well. But she did have to deliver a number of colonies in various parts of the world to France and Spain, and grant the thirteen colonies their independence.[36]

The balance of power weakened England and gave us our independence.[37] Thus, military forces have three different roles in defending the dictator against potential foreign enemies. Firstly, they can directly fight against potential invaders [and, of course, directly fight against potential victims if the dictator is trying to strengthen his power]. Secondly, he can go to the aid of another country which is under attack when the conquest of that other country by a third country would be contrary to the long run survival prospects of the dictator. Thirdly, the fact that they would be available and in condition for the second cause means that foreign countries are particularly willing to come to the aid of our dictator in the event that he is attacked by a stronger foe.

A strong military force is an important protection for the dictator in dealing with foreign enemies. It is also, of course, an important protection for the dictator in dealing with those domestic enemies that are not in the military force itself. The problem that the dictator faces here is, of course, that he may be overthrown by members of his own armed forces. This is, indeed, the common fate of South American and African dictators. What he needs is a strong military force to deal with foreign enemies and, at a lesser level, to deal with domestic enemies who are not in the military, and at the same time a military force which is weak enough so that it cannot overthrow him. If it were not for the potential for foreign enemies, this would be a reasonably easy problem to solve. He could arrange four or five not terribly strong military forces, and arrange to keep them quarreling with each other. This is not an absolute insurance, but it is pretty good. Unfortunately, this kind of military force is apt to be inefficient when dealing with a major force.

Another protective measure is to put people who are not strong, tough, aggressive types at the top of the military force. A fairly weak general will probably not try to overthrow you, and if he does, you can probably arrange to dispose of him. The problem is that he probably will not be very effective in dealing with your enemies abroad, either. The present dictator of Iraq is learning that lesson the hard way.

The other approach to this problem, which is to have tough, efficient generals, has its risk, too. President Rhee of Korea was not, strictly speaking, a dictator in spite of what is frequently said in the American press.[38] He did, however, face a severe problem in the existence of a powerful military force in North Korea dedicated to the destruction of South Korea. He built an army, the higher commanders of which were fairly tough, competent people. Street riots developed against President Rhee, and the army participated in a coup against him which led to an interim elected government dominated by his civilian enemies, and then after a few months, complete military control.[39]

It could be said here that, looked at from the standpoint of the average Korean citizen, this seems to have been a major improvement. Korea's rate of growth under President Rhee had been quite moderate, but under President Park, the military dictator, it achieved rates of growth that were as high as any in the world.[40] It is not possible to say whether General Park's successor will be able to sustain these rates of growth. He had the misfortune to take over in the middle of a world depression and has not yet been in office long enough so that we can make reliable judgements of his economic success.

Having mentioned President Park's great economic success, I should perhaps pause here to say that it is not at all obvious that this indicates that he was a brilliant economic manager. Indeed, he seems to have known almost nothing about economics. I have not kept up with Korea in recent years, but it would appear that General Park's success in economics was an accidental byproduct of political moves. When he became dictator he may have been ignorant about economics, but he did know that the bulk of the civil part of the government opposed him. He responded by firing a very large portion of that government, and thus moved Korea from an inept and corrupt controlled economy to a very open economy. It is likely that this was the major reason for the rapid growth under his control. With time, of course, he began finding higher officials who were his friends and expanded their control over various parts of the economy with the result that the rate of growth was slowing down. The long run prognosis was not very good even if the short run performance was excellent. Neither President Rhee nor President Park basically believed in a free enterprise economy, but President Park created one as a byproduct of a massive political purge.

To return to the main theme, the problem is maintaining an army which is both efficient and so weak domestically so it won't overthrow the dictator. Obviously this is a very difficult problem, and I have no final solution. In general, hereditary monarchs have found it less of a problem, although the number of hereditary monarchs who have been removed by the commander of their army is not even remotely close to zero. Let me discuss two examples which rather delimit the problem. Firstly, Rome. Rome never succeeded in achieving a situation in which their danger of military overthrow was not high. Indeed, there were more Roman emperors established by military means than cases of peaceful succession.[41] This is particularly remarkable, because we generally tend to think of the Romans as being exceptionally able governors. They were, in most respects, but not in maintaining domestic peace.

The basic problem that appears to have caused difficulty for Rome was the combination of a very large empire, which meant that many military units would by necessity be vastly distant from the capital.[42]

The Turks faced a somewhat similar problem because although their empire was only about half the size of the Roman, nevertheless it was hard to move troops about in it. The solution was to keep the major army in the capital during the winter, and then march towards whichever frontier the Padashah had chosen for war that year each summer. This both left most of their frontiers unguarded much of the time, and put an intrinsic limit on the size of their empire.

This wide dispersion of the forces meant there was a prospect for developing local loyalties. The Romans never seem to have understood the idea of rotating either their higher officers or the units as a whole. Individual legions might spend generations in the same camp. An officer might be sent to the Rhine frontier and gradually be promoted to the rank of commander of the Rhine frontier without ever holding a command elsewhere.[43] It's not at all obvious that this system had any strictly military advantages and it certainly had very severe political disadvantages. Rome was kept in turmoil.

Now contrast this with England let us say from 1700 to 1900. During this time, as I have said before, England was always a major military power if one counted all of its military forces including, of course, those of the honorable East India Company. If one looked only at the forces that were actually in England at any given point in time, they tended to be quite small.[44] In time of war they expanded their army quite considerably, but these units were characteristically committed to continental combat almost immediately after being trained. Further, the individual units followed a system (earlier as a result of the purchase of commissions, and later as a matter of policy probably based on the tradition of the purchasing commission) of having all of the officers in the individual regiments in essence permanently assigned to a particular regiment. The officers above regimental level got their original training in one particular regiment but were then promoted to higher rank thus leaving their regiment.[45] No permanent military structure existed above the level of the regiment, with the regiments being put into brigades or sometimes divisions for specific wars.[46] So there were no really large permanent military formations. The bulk of the officer corps serving its entire career in one regiment had little contact with officers from other regiments. Conspiracy, etc., would have depended on the generals, and they did not have very much in the way of permanent contact with individual military units.

The navy was, of course, more important for British military matters than the army, but larger parts were laid up in peacetime,[47] and the bulk of the officers spent the peacetime parts of their career as officers in ordinary merchant ships.[58] It may not be of zero importance here that the Thames is shallow enough so that heavy ships could never reach London.

This system kept what was in many ways a rather unstable and weak central government firmly in power. There were no military coups of the sort there had been in Rome. It's obvious that the system depended very heavily on the island nature of England,and the fact that it could during this period send out armies to fight elsewhere and did not need to worry terribly much about invasion of England. Indeed, the uprisings of 15 and 45 both came reasonably close to success against the rather weak forces that were kept in England under this system.[49] It made little or no difference in the 19th century, by which time the Hanoverian succession and the parliamentary supremacy had become well enough established so that they had deep popular support. In the 18th century, however, with a foreign and not very popular dynasty in charge, military weakness was of considerable importance. Bonnie Prince Charley might have won.

It is unlikely any modern dictator could follow this kind of a system. In the first place, it takes a long time to get started. A permanent regimental officer corps cannot be created overnight. Further, it did not, as I have pointed out, provide all that much domestic security when the government was unpopular. Thus, it's unlikely that a dictator will turn to this method.

It is, however, probably sensible to regularly rotate senior officers so that they do not develop close connections with their troops, and to have committees, like the Joint Chiefs of Staff, make basic decisions. Again, you have a group of people who are likely to betray each other if any one of them contemplates overthrowing the government and who will, in any event, have little direct affiliation with the troops under their command and, hence, cannot feel that the troops would follow them. Once again, this was the problem that scuppered the Germany army's various efforts to dispose of Hitler.[50]

The problem with this is that it's really not a very good way of running an army. A general, who through long association, is trusted by his troops and who trusts them, is almost certainly a better commander than the man who has been brought in a year ago as part of a regular rotation who is, more or less, unknown to his troops and does not for that matter have a very good knowledge of them. A dictator, and for that matter a republic, must make up its mind whether it prefers to have a domestic or a foreign menace when dealing with this problem. A military machine designed to be of optimal military efficiency is dangerous and, on the other hand, a military machine designed to be perfectly safe from the standpoint of domestic coup is unlikely to win wars (except against similar armies).

There is here, it should be said, another possibility which was important for Hitler and has been important for many hereditary dynastics; that is, the development of a loyalty to the ultimate sovereign on the part of the individual soldiers. If such a loyalty can be developed, then the higher officers are not in a position to overthrow him. This will be discussed later.

In the last chapter, we talked about the problem of preventing coups. Coups are, of course, not by any means entirely military. If we look over the long and unfortunate history of most South American 'republics', civilian dictators have been reasonably common. Perhaps the worst of them all, Dr. Francia of Paraguay, was a civilian.[51] Nevertheless, the military is always a standing organization which can pull off coups. Diem, just before President Kennedy arranged his death, was so concerned about the prospect of the military rising against him[52] that he was prohibiting the movement of any unit of battalion size or larger without his direct knowledge. Although Vietnam, at that time, was more peaceful and the Communists weaker than at any time after Diem's death, it was clear that this was not a good system of command. Diem could only have followed this policy because he had in the previous years been really quite successful getting the Communists under control. The country was not completely pacified, but fairly close. I believe at the time he was probably more concerned about the Buddhists than he was about the Communists.

One method which has traditionally been used a good deal in this case was for the ruler, whether a king or dictator, to take personal control of the military. There are several problems here, not the least of which is that the man may not be a very good general. It permits him to feel somewhat more secure than he would if he were not in command. Note that only somewhat. Losing a serious battle while he is in personal command may have very negative effects on his future, both in the standpoint of foreign policy and the standpoint of having one of his subordinates rise in rebellion against him. Secondly, this of necessity means that he must devote a good deal of time to the army, which will be taken away from his other governmental duties. Lastly, simply being in command of troops does not mean he will be popular with them. Patton was, on the whole, a good commander in World War II and very unpopular with his troops.[53] The same can be said about MacArthur.[54] The politically adroit Eisenhower managed always to be popular with his troops. Whether he was a really very good commander is still an open question. He never fought without immense odds on his side and he was not responsible for the creation of these gigantic forces that he commanded. The question of whether he was a good general or just a brilliant politician is an open one.[55]

But basically this chapter points to serious problems. The dictator can be overthrown from outside and must maintain military forces to protect himself. These military forces can be used in offensive activities to improve his power, but even more important than that, they can be used in the balance of power to prevent neighbors from becoming too strong. He can, because of the balance of power, expect outside assistance if he is attacked by a strong neighbor, but only if he has a force large enough and powerful enough so that his neighbors regard him as a worthwhile potential ally for future wars. The military force so developed can, of course, be used domestically against his domestic enemies, too, but unfortunately it is a standing menace to him. Again, the life of a dictator is not an easy one, but there is no reason we should feel particularly sympathetic. No one is compelled by law to be a dictator.

NOTES

1. In 1978 Taraki and the Afghan Communist Party took power with Russian support. In September 1979 Taraki was deposed and replaced by Amin, in December 1979 units of the Societ Army eliminated Amin, installing Karmal in his place. For a detailed chronology, see Dunnigan and Bay, 1985, pp. 122-25.

2. *Ibid.*, p. 133.

3. *Ibid.*, p. 136.

4. Johnson, 1983, p. 529.

5. They performed the almost impossible task of producing a worse government than Amin's. The situation has continued to deteriorate with the result that some citizens are beginning to look back on Amin's regime as the least of all possible evils. See, *The Washington Post*, Sunday, August 5, 1984; pages 1, 32, and 33.

6. Johnson 1983, p. 657. It is notable that although the government of Vietnam in Cambodia is a vicious and oppressive one, the populace on the whole are not willing to try to overthrow it because it is so much better than the government of Pol Pot which it replaced.

7. Dunnigan and Bay, 1985, p. 73.

8. The Fulani Empire of Masna (1818-1862) which extended across the interior delta of the Niger River was the result of a Moslem crusade which forced conversation to Islam at sword point (Mair 1979, p. 71). The Empire of Mali existed from the later thirteenth century A.D. to about 1468. At its greatest it controlled both banks of the Niger River as far south as Kukuya (today Bentia), while in the west the kingdoms along the Senegal and Gambia rivers to the Atlantic coast became its vassals (*Ibid.*, p. 5).

9. *New York Times*, February 3, 1985, p. 16.

10. It seems likely that Hassan himself was, to a considerable extent, responsible for the selection of their very bad strategy and tactics.

11. In 1984, Iran's total population was estimated as 41,280,000, of which total defense forces constituted 2,200,000. The corresponding figures for Iraq were 14,200,000 and 515,000, respectively (*Facts on File*, March 23, 1984; p. 201).

12. Some of them seem to be better than their Iranian opposite numbers. This is, of course, weak praise.

13. Excluding South Africa, Ethiopia, Angola, Zimbabwe, Somalia, Mozambique, Uganda, Chad, and the Congo (all of which are currently involved in wars of various intensities), the average african nation devotes less than 2% of GDP to military spending. (Dunnigan and Bay, 1985, p. 373 [chart]).

14. Previously it succeeded in taking another bit from Mauretania. *New York Times*, April 23, 1984, p.5.

15. *New York Times*, December 21, 1984, p. 5; and January 3, 1985, p. 5.

16. The 1983 OAU meeting in Ethiopia collapsed after Morrocco refused to negotiate with the Polisario, backed by fellow OAU member Nigeria (*New York Times*, September 23, 1983, p. 5).

17. Johnson, 1983, p. 674-5.

18. According to Dupuy and Dupuy (1977, p. 124): 'There was no basis, constitutional, moral, or physical for assuring the subserviency of the Guard tothe state. They had little to occupy them, and so they were frequently idle, profligate, and vicious...possessing the means to influence policies and the succession to the throne.' The Praetorians power to make and break emperors led to an era of permanent military despotism' beginning with the reign of Septimus Severus in 193 A.D. (*Ibid.*).

19. While at its height (in the second century A.D.) the Empire included England, France,Germany west of the Rhine, the Iberian Peninsula, Italy, the

Balkans, Asia Minor, the Middle East and North Africa, there were no more than 174,000 legionary troops at any one time after 70 A.D., although if local auxiliary troops are included, the number would be somewhat in excess of 300,000 (Luttwak 1976, p. 16).

20. On January 1, 1941 (six and a half months prior to the German invasion) Soviet armed forces numbered 4,207,000 men (Fugate 1984, p. 317).

21. During the later eighteenth century, France maintained a peacetime standing army which averaged 182,000 (Goldhamer, 1977, p. 40).

22. During the period 1740 to 1786, Britain's standing army comprised only 21,000 men (Goldhamer 1977, p. 40).

23. In Nobember 1688, William of Orange landed at Torbay in England with a small force, causing James II to flee on December 11; William assumed the crown in 1689 (Langer 1972, p. 465). In March-April 1689, James II (accompanied by a small French force) landed in Ireland, and was narrowly defeated by the forces loyal to William at the Battle of the Boyne (June 11, 1690) after which James again fled to France. In December 1715, James II (the 'Old Pretender') landed in Scotland with a small force but was soon defeated. Finally, in 1745 Charles III (Charles Edward Stuart, son of James III, called the 'Young Pretender') invaded Britain and following Culloden (April 16, 1746), he, too, returned to France (Dupuy and Dupuy 1977, pp., 558, 638, 639).

24. Major Irish rebellions occurred in 1649-50, 1689, 1914, 1916-21, 1956-57, and 1969-74 (*Ibid.*, pp. 553-4, 683 994, 1261).

25. The events surrounding the removal of Louis XVI and the Paris Revolution of 1848 represented the only serious outbreaks of anti-monarchical violence in French history. The Fronde did not actually jeopardize the life of the King.

26. In this, as in many other ways, the relationship between the United States and those countries which are referred to as its allies is historically very remarkable. The causes are interesting, but too lengthy to go into here.

27. For a more through discussion of the balance of power, see my *The Social Dilemma*. pp. 126-38.

28. Lewitter 1965, pp. 338-39.

29. Gulick 1965, pp. 646-655.

30. *Ibid.*, p. 660.

31. The Emperor charles V of the Holy Roman Empire ruled from 1519-1556. On the complexities of his shifting alliances, see Langer 1972, pp. 428-430.

32. The alliance remained in effect from 1795-1808 (Carr 1965, pp. 443-44).

33. Dupuy and Dupuy 1977, pp. 667-68. Despite these seemingly long odds, Frederick characteristically struck first and won a great victory at Lobositz (October 1, 1756).

34. Bemis 1957, p. 9.

35. The League of Armed Neutrarlity was founded in 1780 by Russia, Sweden and Denmark, the United Provinces of Holland joined later in the year (Mahan 1957, pp. 359-60).

36. In addition to the thirteen colonies, Britain gave up Florida, the island of St. Lucia, Senegal in West Africa and the island of Minorca (Muir 1924, p. 72).

37. All of this is absolutely terribly reported in the standard American history of the Revolutionary War. I recently asked a historian who, is a specialist on the

Revolutionary period and who has received a Guggenheim fellowship, what was the largest battle in the war of the American Revolution [It was the Saints in the West Indies. The largest campaign of the war was Spain's unsuccessful effort to take Gibraltar]. She didn't know. A little further questioning indicated she was totally ignorant of the non-American part of the war. Since the war was primarily a war between England on one side, and France and Spain on the other, this was Hamlet without the prince of Denmark. [The Battle of the Saints (April 12, 1782) took place between Dominica and Guadaloupe and involved 34 British and 29 French ships-of-the-line. The siege of the British fortress of Gibralter by the Spanish lasted fromJune 21, 1779 to February 6, 1783 (Dupuy and Dupuy 1977, p. 717, 724)].

38. He fairly regularly won fair elections and normally faced a legislature which was dominated by his opposition. Henderson 1968, pp. 290-308.

39. *Ibid.*,

40. *Time*, Vol. 114, November 5, 1979, p. 46.

41. According to a table listed in Tapsell (1983, pp. 158-161), of 98 Roman emperors only 36 were relatives of preceding emperors. Almost all of the 62 remaining emperors were installed by means of violence.

42. For example, in 6 A.D., out of a total of twenty-eight legions, four were in Spain, five were on the Rhine or beyond, two in Raetia (modern day Southern Bavaria and Switzerland), five in Illyricum (modern day Yugoslavia), three in Moesia (modern day central Balkans), and nine in North Africa, Egypt and Syria (Luttwak 1976, p. 47).

43. *Ibid.*, pp. 80-85.

44. In 1775, only 19 of a total of 78 British Army regiments were located in England (Kushler 1976 [chart]).

45. They retained a number of contacts to their regiment, and would normally tell you the regiment they belonged to. It was, however, more a social matter than a formal structure. Bruce 1980, p. 152.

46. Youg an Lawford 1970, p. 101.

47. Lloyd 1965, p. 176.

48. In peacetime the East India Company's Marine was especially popular, and many officers even served temporarily in foreign navies (*Ibid.*, p. 179).

49. Charles Edward Stuart was defeated decisively at the Battle of Culloden only after attempting a surprise attack on the British army commanded by Cumberland which failed to surprise (Dupuy and Dupuy 1977, p. 639).

50. This in fact, scuppered the July 20, 1944 plot (FitzGibbon 1956, pp. 210-11) and fear of it evidently prevented at least two earlier plots from coalesincge, in August 1941 and March 1943 on both occasions while Hitler was visiting Army Group Center on the Russian front (Clarke 1966, pp. 121, 339).

51. Francia was appointed by the Paraguayan Congress to a five year term in

1811 and ruled as dictator until his death in 1840 (Weil, et. al., 1972, pp. 39-40).

52. The American overthrow of Diem, of course, took the form of organizing a military coup. Halberstam 1965, pp. 266-99.

53. Farago 1982, p. 281.

54. Griffeth 1980, p. 262.

55. The emerging concensus appears to be that he was a brilliant manager of a coalition army, with no detectable skills as a field commander (Weigley 1981).

CHAPTER IV

"POPULAR" RISINGS

In the mythology of revolution, the people rising to throw off a tyrannical ruler is the dominant theme. There is, it is true, a minor right wing mythology in which the people, misled by vicious and corrupt demagogues, rise and throw off a benevolent ruler and put the demagogues in power, but this is a minority. Most of the mythology concerns a people driven beyond endurance by the vicious oppression of their masters rising up and establishing a noble and just republic.[1]

I regret to say that this myth is mainly myth. I don't want to swear that there have been no cases in history in which the people have risen and disposed of a tyrannical ruler, but I have never come across a clear-cut case. There are, however, two not historically uncommon scenarios in which the ruler is removed not by other members of his own government or by foreign governments, but by members of the local community who do not make up part of his governmental machine. I'd like to talk about these two cases before I turn to the reasons why actual popular overthrow is as rare as it is. In the latter section I will also discuss a number of cases which are normally recorded in the mythology as popular overthrows of a tyrant, and point out that although they may indeed have been popular, they don't fit the myth.

Let us begin, then, with a situation which led to England having such a disturbed crown in the years before and after the Wars of the Roses. There was, in this case, a king and also local governments, spreading throughout England. Local government was primarily not royal, but government by local nobles.[2] Further, when the king went to war, he did so by holding a sort of levee en masse in which all of the nobles were supposed to rally to his standard and follow him to war.[3] There was no professional army, and almost nothing that could be regarded as a professional police force under royal control.[4] It is true that during this period the power of the king over internal policing matters gradually grew. His courts became supreme[5] and his ability to collect taxes and uphold the peace through his sheriffs gradually increased.[6] Until Cromwell's time, however, there was no professional army and if there was a professional navy, it was normally very weak in peacetime and depended on something roughly like the levee en masse to man ships in wartime.[7] Indeed, the English navy in time of war was largely merchant ships that had rallied to the royal standard.[8]

Under these circumstances, it was not surprising that some rival raising his standard might be able to rally as many or more men than the king. A rebel, Simon Montfort, Earl of Leicester,[9] is sometimes listed as the founder of the House of Commons. He summoned knights from each county and city in England. These representatives, so far as we know, did nothing except ride with Montfort to disaster at Evesham.[10]

One can, in such cases, refer to uprisings against the king, although in most cases, there was real doubt in many people's minds as to who was the king. There was not an uprising against an established governmental mechanism of force. Indeed, the established mechanism of force was, in essence, a call for people to gather together and defend the king, and it was just as easy to call for a group of people to gather together and attack the king.

A similar phenomenon, although in general not quite as vigorous, will be seen in the rest of Europe. As I mentioned above, the end product of this in Italy and Germany was that the central government gradually faded away. In England, France, and Spain, a firm central government was eventually established which, in the case of France and Spain, was a despotism, and in the case of England, what we would normally call a constitutional monarchy, although this term in those days meant something radically different than it does today.[11] It is clear that one can, if one wishes, call these matters popular risings, but it is equally clear that the popular myth does not basically refer to such things as Edward IV replacing his cousin Henry VI.[12]

In England, the victory of Henry VII at Bosworth Field put in power in England a clever and cold-blooded man who decided to stop this system.[13] His method was first to kill every single person who had even a remote claim to the throne of England and, secondly, to weaken the territorial nobles.[14] As part of this weakening of territorial nobles, he moderately increased the power of the House of Commons, and greatly increased the power of the royal courts.[15] These two policies were followed undeviatingly by his Tudor successors.[16] Whether it would have eventually led to a powerful central government in England we cannot say. Certainly there was no permanent regular army before the time of Cromwell. The House of Tudor , however, ran out on the death of Elizabeth and the throne went to the Stuarts who were less efficient.[17]

Now, this kind of thing will be found to have occurred fairly often in the history of the world. The Jews, in pre-Davidic times, had no central army and, in fact David acquired the throne to a considerable extent by raising his own army at the same time the then existing king Saul was raising a similar army. Saul's suicide occurred after a defeat by the Philistines, not after a defeat by David, but David's possession of a powerful band of followers is what put him in a position to succeed Saul.[18] More examples can be drawn from the history of many other countries.

All of this assumes that the central government does not have a powerful apparatus for its defense in the form of a professional army and, preferably also, a well organized professional internal police force. This is, in fact, a truthfully descriptive statement in a number of cases, but it is probably a fairly small minority of all governments of history. Indeed, it's only common in feudal societies and, as we have pointed out before, feudalism is a rather unusual form of government.

There is a good deal of romantic literature written around the Wars of the Roses, but I don't think anybody regards this kind of thing as a likely prospect for overthrowing a modern tyrant. Indeed, after Cromwell established a regular army, there were no cases of the government being overthrown by someone landing and asking people to rally behind him. The Duke of Monmouth and two Stuarts tried it, but failed. Charles II came back to England in spite of the existence of a professional army and navy, but in his case, Parliament had neglected to pay them for a considerable period of time, and their morale was not in good condition. Furthermore, Monck[19] the senior military officer after Cromwell died, organized what amounted to a mutiny of the navy against Parliament and in favor of the king, and the regiments of the regular army were either absorbed into a new royal army or disbanded without much difficulty. The king was, in fact, welcomed by parliament.[20]

William of Orange entered England from outside, but he came with a sizable military machine, and once again, made preliminary arrangements so that, in essence, he had parliamentary support.[21] In the case of George I, he peacefully succeeded Queen Anne.

In connection with all of these changes after the execution of Charles I, it should be pointed out that most historians think that the House of Stuart remained more popular than the Hanoverians.[22] It is a little difficult at this distance in time to say whether this opinion is correct or not, but in any event, it is clear there were very many people in England who favored the king across the water, and that the lower classes were particularly of that opinion. Nevertheless, the fifteen and the forty-five both failed because there was a regular army to defend the king.

So much for our first scenario. The second scenario revolves around the House of Parliament which played a minor role in the last few paragraphs of my discussion of the kind of rising which led to the Wars of the Roses.

As a start, I must talk a little bit about 'constitutional monarchy'. The original meaning of the term 'constitutional monarchy' was vastly different from its present meaning. Today we think of somebody like the current King of Sweden. He performs ceremonial but not substantive functions in his government.

When Montesquieu wrote the 'L'Esprit des Lois' he was referring to quite a different type of government.[23] The balanced structure, which also was admired by Locke, involved a king who actually had the executive power and a good deal of legislative power as well, balanced in part by assemblies. These assemblies were not, from our standpoint, very democratic. Indeed, the House of Lords or the Parliament of Paris which, up to Louis XIV, performed a somewhat similar role in France, were hereditary.[24] The House of Commons, while not hereditary, was in any event, selected by methods which we would today not regard as particularly democratic. There were seats in the Parliament which were owned by individuals. The two Pitt prime ministers actually owned six.[25] Other members were elected but from very, very restricted franchises.[26]

Further, the method of election was what we would today call corrupt. The term is not a very good description in terms of the morals of the day. There was nothing concealed about the purchase of votes, nor was it thought to be illegal. There were actually lawsuits by people who felt that they had been double-crossed after having paid good money down.[27]

The term 'limited autocracy' seems better than 'constitutional monarchy' for such governments. We are going to talk about such limited autocracies a good deal below. They are a sort of compromise between autocracy and electoral systems or, perhaps, a weak form of autocracy. Further, when we talk about methods of becoming an autocrat we will have to talk about the ways of reducing the power of such an assembly if the autocrat finds himself stuck with one. For the time being, however, we should simply note that this kind of an arrangement is by no means uncommon either historically or in the present day. To make a brief list of current examples, the Philippines under Marcos, Mexico, South Korea, Taiwan, and Thailand, are all examples. In each case we have a ruler who clearly is much more powerful than any democratic president. But we also have some kind of an assembly which acts in part as a check on his power.

The exact relationship between the ruler and this assembly is complex and difficult to explain or even to understand. If we look back at the England of George II, we find that the members of this legislature tended to literally sell their votes on most measures, and these votes were purchased by the king. The purchase was normally in the form of offering a job to a relative, but sometimes in other forms, of course.[28] The same kind of thing goes on in the Philippines or Mexico. Thus, we have the combination of a ruler of great power, and a representative body 'elected' by rather irregular methods, which has somewhat ill-defined powers but which clearly is able, to some extent, to check the ruler. Once again, we will discuss this in more detail later. For the time being we merely wish to point out that one type of 'popular' rising can be a split between the ruler and this assembly in which the normal stress and quarreling between them degenerates into actual fighting.

Splits between the king and this assembly are obviously actually a difference of opinion within an existing government. It is not the people rising against the government, but part of the government attacking another part. Indeed, the first of the major cases in which this kind of thing occurred in modern times, was what we would now think of as backwards. Charles I, as we have mentioned above, left London, went to Oxford, and raised his standard against the

House of Commons. The Commons retained control of the bulk of the tax revenues, and the only professional force, the navy. Charles was leading a (unsuccessful) rebellion. His eventual execution for treason was, in a way, quite merited.[29]

Something similar to this can, of course, be found in Roman history where the republic was originally overthrown[30] by its own military officers. Councels and procouncels in charge of armies were the people who were dangerous to it, although of course, there was a popular opposition to the Senate which eventually led to its losing most of its power to the Assembly. Eventually both the Assembly and the Senate lost their power to the Caesars.

We've seen various other examples of this kind of thing in history, but most of the ones that I am familiar with are cases in which the representative group disposed of the monarch, or autocrat, rather than vice versa. The American 'revolution' can be taken as an example of that, although by the time that it occurred, the king of England was already pretty much dominated by Parliament. Indeed, in the early days of the revolution, the revolution was nominally directed against the House of Commons, and George Washington toasted the king after dinner every night in the Commander in Chief's mess.[31] Eventually they changed to opposition to the king also, probably because they discovered that they had a number of allies holding up military appropriations in the House of Commons.[32]

Nevertheless, looked at from the standpoint of the colonies, the government of each colony consisted of a royally appointed governor and a very tiny collection of other royal officials but checked by an elected legislature.[33] Further, local police activity, and indeed, most of the local government, were carried on by local elected officials. The 'revolution' consisted quite simply in the elected assemblies throwing out the royal governors everywhere where there was not a large British military force present. It was part of the government, in this case most of the government in the thirteen colonies, throwing out the rest rather than a popular uprising. This does not, of course, raise questions about its popularity. There seems to be no doubt that these legislatures who were elected and who were then re-elected during the course of the protracted hostilities, did represent public opinion.[34]

When I say there is no doubt about this, I should say that there is a good deal of historical opinion on the other side. In the first place,

John Adams is frequently quoted as having said that about a third of the people favored the revolution, about a third opposed, and about a third had no opinion at all. This statement was made some twenty years after the revolution, and in fact refers not to the American Revolution but to the French Revolution. At the time of the American Revolution nobody seemed to have any doubts that it was popular.

The second reason why it is sometimes doubted the revolution was popular is that we did not have universal adult male suffrage at the time. There were property qualifications. This was, however, a frontier society, and most of the adult male population could vote.[35] There is no evidence that it was a small minority who disagreed with a large royalist proletarian majority who ran the government at that time. I think the reason some historians tend to regard the war as having been unpopular was the extreme moderation of the statements and the eventual measures taken by the rebels. It's hard to think of George Washington as a romantic rebel. He was after all, like Jefferson, a large scale slave holder.[36] There was, it is true, one reasonably prominent rebel who was undeniably proletarian in his origin, Alexander Hamilton, but he does not fit in with modern left wing prejudices very well.[37] Franklin also came from proletarian origins, but by the time of the revolution he was wealthy.

The moderation and lack of utopian dreams of the American Revolution seems to me evidence that our ancestors were smarter than the French. Utopians are apt to feel that it is not a true revolution unless blood runs in the gutters and the mobs scream for equality. I don't want to quarrel about the meaning of the word, whatever happened in the United States it was basically popular, and it involved a change in the form of government in which the elected part of the government replaced completely the appointed part.[38]

The French Revolution is normally regarded as a much more fitting and proper revolution than the American Revolution. The fact that the American Revolution involved almost no executions and established a peaceful and more or less successful government which ruled without much domestic stress for almost 100 years is, if anything, I think regarded as a criticism of it. The French Revolution, with its bloody executions, wars with most of the rest of Europe, and rise of Napoleon is certainly a more exciting and romantic event.

Nevertheless, the French Revolution, too, was not the people rising up but part of the government throwing out the other part.[39] For a variety of reasons, most European countries including France, had come to admire greatly the British system of government as it existed under George II and III. Very likely, the major reason for this was simply the military success of British arms. Voltaire in particular was an admirer of English institutions.[40]

The Englightenment was to a large extent an effort on the part of various Frenchmen to transmit a 'misunderstood' English philosophy and system of government to France. It would appear that Louis XVI was among the people who thought that this was a good idea.

In any event, Louis organized a government which was modeled after that of England, with an elected House of Commons and a segmented upper house, ie., a house representing the peers, and a house representing the Church.[41] Louis, however, was not a very bright man, and matters very rapidly got out of control. One of the reasons they got out of control was that not only Louis and most intellectuals, but apparently most of the officers of the French army and navy, favored restrictions on the power of the king.[42] The result was a period of time in which, quite literally, the Paris mob dominated the government of France by physical coercion of the elected legislators. The end product, of course, after the temporary conquest of most of Europe by France was the restoration of the Bourbon dynasty with a genuine constitutional monarchy modeled, more or less, after that of England.[43]

The story of the Russian Revolution is much the same. After the defeat by Japan in 1905 and some rioting in St. Petersburg, the Czar decided to established an elected legislature with a prime minister and government selected from the legislature. The Czar did not provide for universal manhood sufferage, but he did turn over the bulk of the power to the elected representatives of (a portion of) the people. His deposition in 1917, after a long and disastrous period of fighting in World War I, was carried out by that parliament.[44] It was not the people against the government, but part of that government, admittedly the part which had the greatest popular support, against the Czar.

The overthrow of the Russian republic by the Communists was essentially a coup d'etat by a group of determined men opposing badly muddled democratic politicians. The vital military force was provided by the sailors of the Baltic fleet. In this case, we have absolutely conclusive evidence that it was not a popular uprising because the coup occurred toward the end of an election campaign. In spite of the fact that the Communists were in power when the actual election was held, they lost disastrously. Needless to say, this made no difference in Lenin's plans.[45]

These are the most famous cases in which it is sometimes alleged that people overthrew an unpopular tyrant. All of them involved squabbles between different parts of the government, one of which could reasonably be called more popular than the other. They are an example of intra-governmental fights rather than an effort to overthrow the government as a whole. The overthrow of the Shah of Iran recently has become fashionable as a popular uprising against a tyrannical ruler. As time goes by, it becomes less and less fashionable because retrospectively the Shah seems much better than what replaced him. Nevertheless, at the time of the overthrow, the Shah was very unpopular in the west, and practically the entire western intellectual community cheered on the revolution.

It is not at all clear what did happen here. The Shah actually departed after a good deal of street rioting, when it began to be obvious that the military would not support him wholeheartedly. He had, to a considerable extent, brought this on himself, however, not by tyrannical rule - after all his father had been much more tyrannical than he was - but by a series of mistakes. Firstly, roughly eighteen months before his overthrow, he decided partly as a result of pressure from President Carter, but partly apparently on his own, that his secret police should stop torturing people. In order to see that they did, he brought in the International Red Cross, and after an interval, they did stop torturing. This greatly reduced the efficiency of the secret police.[46]

Secondly, he combined an inflation with a price control, which also made him unpopular with merchants, and last but not least, he was unable to either order his army to vigorously repress the rebellion or to decide to give in to it. His military officers found themselves sometimes firing at mobs, and sometimes ordered not to. It's hard to tell exactly what was going on because of the extremely biased nature of the reporting of the western press. I recall one occasion in which a general who had had some of is patrols cut off by the mob, forced his way through and removed the bodies of his men. These bodies, which were severely mutilated [it wasn't clear whether the mutilation was done before or after they died], he then displayed to his troops. This was regarded by all of the western reporters whose news stories I read as an example of unacceptable behavior on his part because it would make the troops likely to fight more vigorously in the future. None of the newspaper reporters criticized the mob for their action.

In any event, the Shah was not replaced by the people, but by government officials mainly drawn from his tame parliament. What followed was a series of rapid changes of regime, ending up with Khomeini who, it should be said, has on the whole been able to win elections without too much in the way of cheating. He has, of course, reintroduced torture as a standard police method.[47]

This incident is very confused and conceivably does represent a popular uprising against a ruler. The weakness[48] of the ruler, his lack of skill, the fact that he had not complete control over the military forces, and last but not least, the religious aspect of the problem, all were important.

There is, by the way, one other lesson we can learn from this incident. One of the reasons that the military were not well prepared for the whole thing is that the Shah had been deliberately keeping them divided. He was once before driven out of Persia by his Parliment and then returned with the support of the military. He apparently drew a lesson from this, that the military were dangerous to any ruler of Persia, and hence had followed the policy of preventing the development of any high level coordination within the branches of his services. As we have been saying before, weakening your army makes it less likely the army will overthrow you, but more likely that someone else will. The Shah found the truth of this.[49]

But why do we not see public uprisings against despotic and tyrannical rulers? There certainly have been enough tyrants in history, and there certainly have been many cases in which governments have been highly unpopular with their citizens. To take two recent examples, Albania and North Korea under their early Communist governments, seem to have established almost impossible levels of public opposition to the government. In the winter of 1951, the American army which had been beaten on the Yalu withdrew through Korea. Almost one quarter of the population of North Korea followed them south. Further, a good many more would have gone south had transportation been available. In most cases where there were naval evacuations of troops, large numbers of these northern refugees were taken with them, but in all cases, far more were left behind.[50]

Note the situation. These were a farming people. It was mid-winter and Korean winters are cold. Rather than come back under the control of the government which had ruled them for the previous five years, they were leaving their farms to follow a beaten army of foreigners. I can think of few more thorough votes of no confidence.

Nevertheless, neither in Albania nor North Korea has the government ever had any difficulty maintaining control against its domestic enemies. To take another collection of modern, unpopular governments, the East European countries certainly have extremely unpopular governments. In Poland, Czechoslovakia, East Germany, and Hungary, there have been extensive outbursts of anti-government rioting on the part of popular groups. In no case has this been anything more than an embarrassment to their Communist rulers.

Why do we find popular uprisings so rare? The answer, which I will present here, is available in much more comprehensive form in my *The Social Dilemma*[51] It is basically a simple argument, however. Suppose that we have our common citizen in a state with an oppressive and inefficient government. Suppose also that we have a group of noble people who propose to overturn this government and set up a virtuous and efficient government. Assume that some individual believes their promises, ie., does think they will establish and efficient and virtuous government. Should he join a popular uprising? The answer in general is no, and the reason is the simple old-fashioned economic argument of a public good.

The individual will have very little effect on the outcome. Note I say very little, not that he will have no effect. If he remains neutral, he will get the benefits of good government just as well as if he participates. Indeed, if he participates on the side of the government, perhaps because he is a professional policeman, and the revolution is successful, he will still benefit from the new and virtuous government. It is likely that any individual joining in the revolution as opposed to remaining at home and cheering will normally make only a tiny change in the likelihood of success, perhaps improving the likelihood of success from.53278 to.53279.

On the other hand, his chances of being injured are greatly increased. If he compares the benefit that he will receive from participating in the revolution with its cost to him, he's almost certain to find the payoff is negative. In other words, the private costs and benefits will fall on him: the public costs and benefits are spread over the society as a whole. He will only get a small fraction of them. It is obviously very unlikely that a careful calculator would join the revolution.

This argument has dealt, of course, with the actual fighting part of the romantic revolution. The conspiracy part, which we frequently talk about in connection with undergrounds, has somewhat the same set of odds attached to it. In the first place, at the stage of secret conspiracy the likelihood of success is always very low. Secondly, the likelihood of betrayal is high because the government will presumably offer significant rewards for anyone who reports such conspiracy. If the individual contrasts the likely benefit he will receive from the success of the conspiracy, granted the success of the conspiracy is very small to begin with, and second that it is a public good, with the benefit that he could get from betraying it, it is obvious which way he would choose. When you add that if the conspiracy is betrayed, the people who did not participate in its betrayal will be severely punished, the matter becomes almost a certainty.

A number of despotic, unpleasant, and generally deplorable governments are also corrupt. Such governments have great difficulties in offering rewards for information about plots against them. The reason is not that people are opposed to corrupt governments, but that people quite correctly suspect that the corrupt police will default with their rewards. A corrupt police commander is far more likely to pay the reward money to his cousin and simply grab some people off the street as potential conspirators than to actually use it to obtain correct information. Further, if a citizen does have correct information and reports it, the money is apt to disappear en route before it reaches him.

Under these circumstances such governments normally resort to torture. A corrupt police captain is not likely to torture his nephew. Torture is a markedly less efficient method of obtaining information than simply paying for it: You have to decide who you will torture, whereas the rewards lead people to voluntarily come in and sell you information. Nevertheless, torture if used on a wide scale, normally works. Stalin was, of course, a clear cut example.[52] Although the Gestapo normally preferred rewards to torture, they in fact used a mixture of the two types of incentive. Possibly Stalin's primary reliance on torture came from an intrinsic problem of any Communist state. If you give someone a million rubles for information, it's very hard for him to invest it in the Communist state in such a way that it is both even reasonably secure and will give a decent income. This, in essence, rules out the use of large incentive payments for information inside a Communist state, although the Communist apparatus has frequently used this technique outside Communist areas.

Democratic governments are sometimes unwilling to offer large rewards for information for essentially idealistic reasons. General Massu in Algiers, faced with a situation where he didn't have very much money to pay for information resorted to widespread torture and, in fact, broke the Algerian Liberation Forces in Algiers.[53] All of this was no secret, in fact he talks about it in his memoirs, but it did not in any way impede his promotion. He ended up as chief of the French general staff. It is dubious that this kind of a background would have led to similar promotion in the American armed forces. In any event, payment of rewards for information undeniably dominates the use of torture. The rewards technique is certainly more in accord with our views of human rights and is also more efficient, a fortunate coincidence.

Turning to another matter, one of the problems that the government faces in dealing with a conspiracy at high level, false denunciations, are not too important at the low levels. Firstly, people involved in these conspiracies are normally not subtle and skilled courtiers who are good at concealing their meaning. In general, they will talk openly and frequently leave written evidence around. More importantly, however, there is no great danger to the state from simply killing everybody who has been denounced. You may get some innocent people, but you'll get almost all the guilty people, and the people that you kill are not high ranking officials of your government so that this killing neither tends to weaken your government by eliminating potentially good officials, nor by lowering the incentives for becoming a high official. Indeed, if anything, widespread executions among the poor and powerless will increase the incentives for becoming a powerful and wealthy official.

There is an exception to all of this. There are undeniably individuals with strong public interest who are willing to take great risks or sacrifice their lives to benefit other people. This is particularly true if religion can be brought in. If you can promise that a Mohammedan who dies fighting for Khomeini will have twenty-two concubines in the next world, or that the martyr of Catholicism who kills Henry IV will stand at the right hand of God, you are more likely to get such people than if such promises are not believed by a cynical and agnostic population. Even among religiously agnostic populations, we do find individual zealots who are willing to make great sacrifices of their own well-being for other people. It turns out that such people are fairly rare, however.[54] Most people are willing to make some sacrifices for the benefit of the public or individual other people who are in a bad way, but these sacrifices are decidedly limited. What people actually do is rather sharply at variance with what they say. In analysis we should consider what they do and not what they say.

Thus, we have in this chapter, three different circumstances which can possibly be referred to as popular overthrows of the ruler. They can reasonably be dealt with seratim. Firstly, in the case in which the ruler does not actually have any professional forces at his beck and call and has to depend on some kind of levee to defend his country against both foreigners and domestic enemies, the problem is difficult. Traditionally, kings in this situation have attempted to play off different noblemen against each other, and to gradually switch the situation from essentially a feudal state to a centrally controlled state. As we have seen, the kings of France and the kings of Spain were successful in doing so, the Holy Roman Emperors were unsuccessful, and in fact, actually had the reverse process occur in Germany and Italy. In England, the rulers chose the rather unusual technique of attempting to create an opposition to the great nobles by turning to the lesser nobility, the squirarchy, and in the long run lost their own power to the squirarchy which, in our own days, has again lost its power to the common man. I have little to contribute to the discussion of this situation.

In the second case, where there is some kind of representative assembly which, to some extent, checks the power of the ruler, limiting the growth of power of that representative assembly, is once again, a matter of maneuver and devious plots. Historically, the rulers have tended to win these inter-governmental squabbles, but the success of the assemblies in the English speaking world has probably meant, for the world as a whole, more than their loss in most other places. In modern times, as a general rule, these assemblies, whether we're talking about the Mexican or Philippine case, have usually not had control over the forces of coercion. The army and the police force have normally been under the control of the dictator himself. This normally gives him an advantage, and there are, in recent years, no cases in which the representative assembly has succeeded in displacing the dictator, although there are a number of cases in which the dictator has been displaced by another dictator. In some cases, the new dictator has been allied with one of these assemblies. In all of the cases in which I am familiar, the ultimate outcome was no increase, and in some cases, a decrease in the power of the assembly.

The apparent reason for this difference between the present histories and the history of the development in England is, I believe, simple. The English House of Commons originally started as representatives of what we might call the lower officers of the army. The squires were not only the rulers of the local communities and the representatives in Parliament, they would also, in time of war, be the officers of the royal army. The king was dependent on them if he chose to call up troops, either to defend the country against foreigners or to defend himself against his domestic enemies.[55] Under these circumstances, if they were his domestic enemy, he was finished. In later days, potential military officers, as members of Parliament, became, if not rare, at least not dominant. All members of Parliament, however, were still closely related to military officers. The eldest son of a county family would manage the estates and go to Parliament, the second into the Church, and the third into the army. It was still true that the king could not depend on his army against Parliament.[56]

In most of the modern cases of this kind of thing, if we look around the world at South Korea, Taiwan, Thailand, etc., the officers of the army and the police are not eligible to be simultaneously members of the legislature. In those cases where a few of them may perhaps be in the legislature, it is just a few. Further, as a rough rule of thumb, these elected bodies have not been very favorable to increasing the wages of the military and police. Under the circumstances, the dictator has usually been able to depend on his police force and the military in squabbles with the elected legislature. The basic problem is not that the elected legislature, or for that matter the people, might rise again him, but that one of his higher officials, let us say a general in one of the army corps, may choose to overthrow him and may make temporary use of the legislature in that effort. This, as usual, means that he must try to keep his army sufficiently divided so that no general officer has that power, and that, in turn, weakens the repressive force. But all of this is another replay of what, by now, should be a familiar theme.

Our third way in which a democracy may be established after a dictatorship is essentially a retirement on the part of the dictator. Consider a typical South American dictator, he may after a time, tire of the game. His job is dangerous and time consuming if highly paid. Eventually however, some dictators decide that they would rather retire just as some heads of large businesses decide they would rather retire. Unfortunately, the dictator cannot simply ask the board of directors to elect a replacement because that replacement would, quite reasonably, regard the retired dictator as a continuing danger to him. It would certainly be true if the dictator chose to retire and continue living in his native land, but Somoza was assasinated in Paraguay because the people who had overthrown him thought he was plotting to overthrow them.

Under the circumstances, making up a democratic constitution and electing a new government is in general, a good idea. The new government is apt to be rather grateful to the dictator that established it and in any event, be busy with all sorts of political matters. If the former dictator simply lives in great splendor on his hacienda, they are unlikely to bother him.

It is of course true, that most democracies set up this way in South America have not lasted very long, but even if they only last four or five years, that permits the dictator to age enough so that his successor is not likely to regard him as a primary danger. It seems likely that this is the principle reason that a dictatorship has some tendency to alternate with democracy in South America. There seem to be some signs of a similar development in Africa, but so far it is not well established.

Preventing overthrow by the common people is, in general, quite easy if the ruler is only willing to repress vigorously and to offer large rewards for information about conspiracies against him. If his government is so corrupt that the rewards are likely to be intercepted before they get to the actual source of the information, he may find it necessary to resort to torture. On the whole, however, this is an inferior method.[57]

In addition, he should have a military machine which is capable of repressing riots, preferably without too much bloodshed, but if worse comes to worst, a good deal of bloodshed. He should also be willing to use it. Louis XVI, Charles X, and Louis Philippe of France all flunked this particular test.[58] Louis XVI first permitted the Paris mob to intimidate him into moving from Versailles into Paris,[59] and then when there was a fight between his Swiss guard and the militia of Paris, he ordered the guard to withdraw.[60] Charles X and Louis Philippe more or less were simply unwilling to engage in large scale fighting against their citizenry.[61]

As was pointed out earlier, the Napoleonic dynasty did not have any such scruples. The early republic was unwilling to use force against the Paris mob even when the Paris mob did use force against the legislature. General Napoleon Bonaparte received his first really high command after he had demonstrated a willingness to fire cannon into the mob.[62] The mob, discovering that rioting was dangerous, instantly ceased to be a menace to the government of France.

The second French republic, established after Louis Philippe's overthrow, was also menaced by the Paris mob and most of the French generals refused to actually use the maximum force against it. Napoleon's nephew converted himself from Prince President of France to Emperor, to a very considerable extent because he was not only willing to use such force, but personally led a cavalry charge into the mob.[63] Once again, on discovering that rioting was dangerous and unpleasant, the rioters stopped.

In general, this is the case. The riots in Eastern Europe against Russian control vanished quickly once it became clear that the Russians were willing to kill. The dangerous situation for a ruler is one in which he kills a few people and then decides he doesn't want to kill any more. This was, in essence, what happened to the Shah of Iran. A truly ruthless leader with loyal troops and a good internal intelligence service does not need to worry very much about popular uprisings.

Popular uprisings are probably most dangerous against democracies. In general, democracies do not have to worry about popular uprisings for the very simple reason that if the majority of the people are against them, they'll lose the next election, and hence, there is no need for rioting. If, however, there is a minority very strongly opposed to a given government, and that minority has little chance of growing to a majority, a situation which existed among college students in the western world in the 1960's, it can be dangerous. In general, democracies are not willing to use the kind of force that is necessary to put down such rioting. On the other hand, the students of the 1960's were neither centrally controlled, nor clear enough in their mind so that it was possible for them to take advantage of their opportunity. There have been earlier cases in which democracies have been overthrown by a somewhat similar means. The clearest example, of course, is Mussolini's overthrowing of the Italian government.[64] Lenin's subversion of the Russian republic, and Hitler's conversion of his perfectly constitutional parliamentary government into a dictatorship are further examples.[65]

The reader who has followed me so far is likely to have two objections. The first of these, which is I have said absolutely nothing about legitimacy or popular support for an existing government, will be dealt with in the next chapter. The second, which is I think, more serious, is to simply point to the undisputed fact that in the 19th century a great many monarchies of one sort or another in Europe and, for that matter, other parts of the world, were converted into democracies. As a rule, most of these democracies didn't last very long, but the ones in western Europe turned out to be quite durable. Indeed, all the west European countries are democracies at the moment. The two largest democracies, India and the United States, or course are not in Europe, and there are other democracies scattered around the world, but nevertheless, the dominant form of government east of the Elbe and south of the Rio Grande is some form of dictatorship. A quick count indicates that at the time of writing, there are twenty-eight democracies, and only five do not have their cultural roots in western Europe. Almost all of the present dictatorial countries at one time, quite frequently at their first independence, were democracies, but democracy has lost control.

But that is a remark on the fall of democracy, not its rise.

How did it rise in the 19th century? The apparent explanation is a combination of the continuing great success in most spheres of England, which was regarded as a model democracy and the fact that intellectuals of the enlightenment admired democracy. The result was that substantially everybody in Europe thought that at least some kind of democracy, in the form usually of the limited monarchy, was a desirable system. The czars of Russia held out until 1905,[66] but all of the other rulers set up some kind of representative assembly. The nineteenth century was a period of internal tension in most countries with the elected part of the government gradually gaining power. In most cases, the kings did not actually resist very vigorously, because they, too, had been convinced by the intellectuals and the example of England.

I don't want to give the impression that the change was entirely peaceful, although in most countries, as a matter of fact, it was. There was no significant internal fighting in Sweden.[67] In other places where there was fighting, the fighting did not, in general, have immense effect on the form of government. The ancien regime was almost everywhere restored in 1848, albeit in somewhat looser form.[68] The growth of democracy was, in general,[and I have to admit I do not know the detailed history of each and every country] a gradual process in which royal concessions were probably at least as important as popular pressure. The standard mythology about the overthrow of the emperor of Brazil is that the emperor himself was the primary proponent of a democratic government.[69] I don't know whether this is true or not, but it certainly is quite possible.

Note, however, that I have said that in many cases the rulers did not resist the democratization of their states, or even hurried it along. At first glance, this seems highly improbable because it clearly weakened their power. We will later have a chapter on this kind of mixed government which I call limited autocracy, and I will point out that it does have advantages from the ruler's standpoint. Whether these advantages are strong enough to overcome its disadvantages is not clear, but in a period of time when the dominant intellectual currents all were in favor of either democracy or constitutional monarchy, it would be very easy for a ruler to make a mistake on this matter. This would be particularly true with the hereditary monarchs who tend a) not to be terribly bright, and b) to be very, very confident of the loyalty of their common people to the royal household. Under these circumstances, following the advice of the intellectual community of your country to establish a constitution with elected representatives, etc., may well seem like a good idea.

Another pro-democratic characteristic of this period, however, and a very important one, is simply the composition of the armies. Large scale conscript armies have, in the past, frequently been used by absolute rulers both to defend their country from foreigners and to suppress rebellion internally. Indeed, the recent suppressions of democracy in Argentina, Brazil, and Greece all were done by professional officers commanding conscript armies.[70] Nevertheless, it has to be said that a large scale conscript army does have certain democratic overtones. A ruler does have to maintain a certain minimum amount of popular support if that conscript army is to fight for him. In this respect, it is different from a professional army, which may be hired for the specific purpose of keeping the common man down.

The strength of this factor is somewhat dubious, because historically kings and dictators have frequently used conscript armies. Nevertheless, the late 19th century and early 20th century were the heydays of the true nation in arms concept. Even if it is possible for a king or dictator to keep control over such an army, in the 19th century most of them thought they couldn't. Indeed, supporters of royal authority in the 19th century quite regularly were in favor of either professional armies or some very restricted form of conscription, such as that which was invented in the French monarchy after the Restoration in 1815.[71] Proponents of democracy, on the other hand, all favored an army composed of substantially the entire citizenry who were drafted. A ruler who, in fact, could have depended on his conscripts to fire into a mob if he had ordered them to do so, might have felt nervous about the matter, and made concessions when he didn't actually have to. Once again, this is particularly important, granted the intellectual climate of the time, and granted the fact that most of the absolute rulers were hereditary monarchs and not dictators. They were not the tough, aggressive, intelligent type we expect as a dictator, but the gentlemanly, not necessarily too tough or too intelligent type that we expect from the hereditary monarchy.

In any event, this rise of democracy has, in the 20th century, been succeeded by a decline. In 1905 all of Europe had some sort of electoral system , mostly constitutional monarchies. Most of the independent governments of Asia had at least some electoral institutions, and the gigantic empires were ruled by democracies, or consitutional monarchies even if they were not democracies themselves. The Indians were ruled by elected officials, although they had no part in electing them. South America was, as it has been since the Spaniards left, a continent in which some states are dictatorial and some states are democratic, and which changed from time to time. It was, however, true that the southern cone was both democratic and very prosperous in those days. This is, unfortunately, no longer true.

Except in South America, where much the same pattern persists, although the southern cone has now joined the rest of South America in being sometimes democratic and sometimes dictatorial, the situation has drastically changed. Firstly, considerably more than half of Europe, in terms of geography, is now firmly under an extremely strong dictatorial yoke. At any given point in time, one or two countries in Africa is temporarily,[72] a democracy. Normally, however, they are dictatorships. The same is true of the Arab lands, now that Lebanon has collapsed. Democracy never really struck root in any part of Asia except Japan, and granted the current status of Indian, Ceylon, and Malaysia[73] you could even say that democracy is at its high point there. Certainly, however, that high point is not very high, and granted the recent history of India, Ceylon, and Malaysia, one cannot feel very optimistic about democracy's future there.

This has been a digression inspired simply by the fact that many people feel that historic experience indicates that democracy can overcome the monarchy if it is supported by the people. These same people also think that the people will support democracy. The verdict of history is, as usual, ambiguous. But there do not seem to be any clear cut cases of an enraged people rising up, throwing off a vicious and corrupt dictator, and establishing a pure and noble democracy.

NOTES

1. Sometimes they establish a wise and just king, but this myth is normally placed in far-off lands and times.

2. Muir 1924, V. 1, pp. 174-175

3. Actually, each noble was obligated by indenture to contract with the king to provide a stipulated number of men-at-arms; in return for these services, the king agreed to pay wages. The men-at-arms remained in the employ of the nobles, not the king. See Newhall, 1940, pp. 3-4.

4. Until the reorganization of the metropolitan police in 1828 initiated by Peel created a disciplined professional force, 'absurd little bodies of watchmen under a variety of different authorities...played with the maintainence of order.' (Muir 1924, V. 2, p. 331).

5. But depended on juries composed of local notables from each district

6. Trevelyan 1953, Vol. 2, p. 21.

7. Hence the name of Cromwell's military force – the New Model Army – was quite apt. See Muir 1924, Vol. 1, pp. 448.

8. Muir 1924, Vol. 1, p. 218.

9. Who probably didn't speak English - he was born and spent his youth in France. This House of Commons was summoned by Simon de Montfort on January 20, 1265 (Jennings 1883, pp. 3-4).

10. Montforts power didn't last long enough for it to be known how he would have constituted the government of England, or whether the Parliament he summoned was any more than a congress of his loyal supporters. Prince Edward escaped from prison and led the armed opposition to Montfort. He won Evesham on August 4, 1265. See Muir 1924, Vol. 1, pp. 99-100.

11. A more general type of government, limited autocracy, which includes the old fashined constitutional monarchies as a special case will be discussed below.

12. Muir 1924, Vol. 1, p. 180.

13. Henry Tudor won at Bosworth Field (August 22, 1485) basically because he succeeded in convincing Richard III's two chief commanders to switch sides during the battle. See Dupuy and Dupuy 1977, pp. 422-423.

14. Muir 1924, Vol. 1, p. 211-212.

15. See Muir 1924, Vol. 1, pp. 212-213. By an Act of 1487 Henry VII established the Court of Star Chamber with extremely broad powers, which greatly increased the effective power of the royal courts (ibid.).

16. For the continuation of these policies under Henry VIII see, Gardner 1907, p. 463; for Edward VI, see Pollard 1907, pp. 476-477.

17. One of the reasons it went to the Stuarts, of course, was the above mentioned policy of killing off anyone who had a claim to the throne. The king of Scotland was able to protect himself against this activity and, hence, lived in spite of having a reasonably good claim to the English throne.

18. Shortly prior to the outbreak of war with the Philistines, David and his volunteer corps (of about 600) fled Judah after Saul's larger force moved against them. David actually joined the Philistines as a vassal, although his corps was apparently not involved in the struggle between Israel and the Philistines (in which Saul died at the battle of Mount Gilboa in 1013 B.C.) in any direct way. See Eissfeldt 1975,pp. 578-579.

19. Later the Earl of Albermarle.

20. Ashley 1977, pp. 201-205. Charles II secured Monck's services after offering him £100,000 a year following the Restoration (ibid., p. 160).

21. He was also supported by Princes (later Queen) Anne and Churchill (later the Duke of Marlborough). William of Orange landed in England on November 5, 1688 with a force of 15,000 (Tempoerley 1908, p. 245). But even before this force sailed, the majority of English peers had been convinced to support William (Prall 1972, p. 205).

22. According to one historian, George I was 'laughed at, sneered at, and ridiculed' (Redman 1968, p. 60). Another notes that ,'little sorrow was felt at...[the] passing' of George II (Garfield 1976, p. 92).

23. In 1748.

24. Hibbert 1980, pp. 27-28.

25. In fact, the House of Pitt controlled a minimum of six seats; William Pitt's brother Thomas controlled three or four, his cousins usually held two, and his relatives by marriage controlled several more (Namier 1961, p. 10).

26. Plumb 1963, p. 38.

27. See Namier, 1961. Actually this, of course, is simply what you might call the highest development of the system, and if you went back to 1660, things were no less disgraceful from the standpoint of present day morals but, nevertheless, somewhat different.

28. A special fund ('for secret service') was established and dispensed through the Secretaries of the Treasury, for purchase of votes. On average over £30,000 was spent for this purpose per annum (Namier 1961, p. 195).

29. On January 30, 1648 (Muir 1924, Vol. 1, p. 456).

30. Several times, it tended to get re-established for short periods of time after the early overthrows. Julius Caeser, the Roman Republic's chief general, successfully fought a civil war from 49-45 B.C., following the conclusion of which he assumed the title of dictator for life in 44 B.C. (Boren 1965, pp. 79-84).

31. Flexner 1968, p. 11.

32. Guttridge 1963, pp. 116-118.

33. The colonial legislatures controlled taxes, so that they were able to effectively check the power of the royal governors, despite the fact that the latter technically had the power to veto any legislation (Main 1923, pp. 102-103).

34. One historian maintains that the legislatures grew increasingly responsive to public opinion after the war began (Main 1973, p. 202).

35. Approximately 60% of the total adult male population could vote (Main 1973, p. 103).

36. Prior to Washington's arrival in Philadelphia to serve as President in 1789, Pennsylvania had provided for the gradual abolition of slavery. In order to prevent having to free his slaves, he provided for sending most of the household slaves he brought with him back to Virginia in the event that they subsequently sought their freedom (Knollenberg 1968, p. 154).

37. Hamilton was an illegitimate child and was raised by his unwed mother in St. Croix in the Virgin Islands. He became apprenticed as a clerk at the age of eleven, and was orphaned two days later. Brodie, p. 2.

38. Interestingly, one recent writer intent on redefining the American Revolution in quasi-utopian liberatarian terms insists that blood did in fact run in the gutters, and describes the War of Independence as a 'ferocious civil conflict' (Rothbard 1979, Vol. IV, p. 423). Most historians would disagree.

39. The best account of this, as in almost anything else upon which he wrote, is Tocqueville's *The Ancien Regime in France*.

40. Voltaire wrote a book entitled *Letters Concerning the English Nation*, (London 1733) which compared French institutions very unfavorably with English ones (Voltaire Foundation, 1979, p. 168).

41. Hibbert 1980, p. 40.

42. Montague 1928, p. 169.

43. Louis XVIII had spent most of the long period of exile in England. Fisher 1903, p. 563.

44. Fitzpatrick 1984, pp. 38-39.

45. Neither did the decision of the Russian supreme court, that his government was unconstitutional. In the November 12 election, which had been originally scheduled by the Kerensky government, the Bolsheviks won only 175 of 707 seats in the Constituent Assembly (Johnson 1983, p. 64).

46. In a CBS television interview on October 24, 1976, the Shah stated that he had abolished the use of torture (Hoveyda 1980, p. 94).

47. The Ayatollah had made it clear that he was going to do this before he came to power. In his book, translated to English under the title *Ayatollah Khomeini's Mein Kampf*, translated by the Joint Publications Research Service, and published by Manor Books, Inc., in New York, 1973. he said 'God's prophet, may God's prayers be upon him, was the executor of the law. He punished, cut off thieve's hands, lashed and stoned and ruled justly. A successor is needed for such acts.' [p. 15] 'If we attain power, we should not be content with improving the economy and ruling justly among the people, but must make these traitors taste the worst torture for what they have done.' [p. 88]

48. The Shah was literally dying at the time.

49. In 1953 the Shah briefly sought exile in Baghdad until a coup successfully overthrew Prime Minister Mossadegh (Forbis 1981, p. 59).

50. Ridgeway 1967, pp. 73, 95. In November 1951 the U.S. Navy evacuated 105,000 troops and 91,000 civilian refugees from Hungnam in Norther Korea. The average temperature at the time in the general area was 18 below zero fahrenheit (ibid., p. 70.).

51. pp. 26-86.

52. Tolstoi 1981, pp. 65-68.

53. Johnson 1983, p. 500.

54. For a general discussion of the limitations on the sacrifices that people are willing to partake for the benefit of people who are not members of their family, see my *The Economics of Income Redistribution*, pp. 49-72.

55. Newhall 1940, pp. 3-5.

56. Cromwell first emerged as the general commanding a substantial component of Parliaments army (in October 1642) in the Civil War with King Charles (Dupuy and Dupuy 1977, p. 550).

57. There are special cases, as even that great humanitarian Jeremy Bentham admitted, where torture might be used even by a ruler who generally abhors it. They are very special cases, however, and it seems unlikely that the average dictator would torture a single person in even a long reign if he stuck to Bentham's rules.

58. Louis XVI ordered his Swiss Guard to withdraw in the face of the mob on August 10, 1792 (Langer 1972, p. 631). Charles X ordered his troops to evacuate Paris after the mob had gained possession of the royal residence on July 29, 1830 (Bourgeois 1907, p. 476). Louis Philippe refused to employ either his regular troops or the National Guard on the mob on February 23, 1848, and abdicated

early in the morning of February 24 (Bourgeois 1928, pp. 100-101).

59. On October 6, 1789 (Langer 1972, p. 629).

60. Hence, the famous Lion of Lucerne. On August 10, 1792 (Langer 1972, p. 631).

61. See footnote 65.

62. Napoleon was responsible for suppressing the Vendemiaire uprising on October 5, 1795 (Knapton 1972, p. 76; Langer 1972, p. 634).

63. On December 4, 1851 (Langer 1972, p. 632).

64. Johnson 1983, pp. 98-101.

65. Johnson 1983, pp. 283-285.

66. Fitzpatrick 1984, p. 27. Nicholas II agreed to create a national elected parliament named the Duma.

67. There was in Switzerland, but since Switzerland started the century with an electoral system, the fight essentially was a religious squabble between the Catholics and the Protestants. It led to a quite major civil war in 1848.

68. In Italy, Germany, and Austria a new, more powerful king gained power following 1848. In France, the dictatorship of Napoleon III began in 1852 (See Massi 1928, 366-392; Ward 1928, pp. 202-233; Friedjung 1928, pp. 393-410; and Thomas 1928, pp. 286-308).

69. Fynn 1978, p. 30.

70. On March 23, 1971 the commanders-in-chief of the armed forces deposed the President of Argentina (Goldwert 1972, p. 209). In November 1968 the army high command of Brazil seized control (Flynn 1978, pp. 418-419). On April 21, 1967, a group of Greek colonels (with the apparent support of the high command) seized power in Greece (Theodoracopulos 1978, pp. 184-205).

71. Louis XVIII abolished the former system of conscription and replaced it with a voluntary system supplemented by a draft-via-lottery (Blennerhassett 1907, p. 55).

72. Excepting, of course, the Union of South Africa, which by our definition is electoral, but not democratic.

73. And possibly, in the near future, Taiwan.

CHAPTER V

LEGITIMACY AND ETHICS

The word 'legitimacy' has been given a number of meanings by various political scientists. I don't want to quarrel about definitions, and so I shall rather arbitrarily assign a very simple meaning to the term. It sometimes happens that there is popular or official support for a government, whether dictatorial, royal, or democratic, at a time when it does not seem to have a great deal of power other than that support. In other words, it is supported at a time when it does not seem to have much capacity, either to reward its supporters or penalize its opponents. We will call such a government 'legitimate'. But the word will extend further. A governement which does have power to reward and penalize will also be called 'legitimate' if the public attitude toward it is such that if it lost that power, it would still have support. Obviously the second meaning is of greater empirical importance than the first. Further, this kind of 'legitimacy' would be helpful to any government. How often it occurs in history is a matter to which we will turn below. Certainly there are at least some instances.

The other word in the title, 'ethics,' is not necessarily difficult to define. We should note, however, that it's specific content seems to vary immensely from time to time, and place to place. I've recently been reading Bodde and Morris's *Law in Imperial China*[1] This book is, to a large extent, a translation into English of a publication of the old imperial government. This publication, usually referred to as 'Exemplary Cases', consists of a set of brief reports of a large number of law cases which had reached what, very roughly, we can refer to as the Chinese equivalent of the Supreme Court.[2] These cases were put together with the idea of providing guidance for future low level courts dealing with similar cases.

The impressive thing about this, from the standpoint of an

American, is the deep concern that was given by this legal system to the status of the individuals involved, and the relatively modest concern which was given to such problems as evidence and whether the person was or was not guilty. Thus, a decision might turn on whether the accused was an older or a younger relative of his alleged victim.[3] This, we would regard, as a quite irrelevant and possibly even immoral consideration. They also provided lower punishments for officials than for private citizens convicted of the same crime. We would regard this as corrupt and probably perverse. And last but not least, they had some rather bizarre crimes. If I, in a quarrel, called somebody some bad names and he then committed suicide, in the United States we would probably take this as evidence that he was not of sound mind. Under the Chinese code, I would be executed.

All of this, however, was I believe, a correct expression of Chinese ethical code. The fact that it is different from ours is not remarkable. Recent readers of the newspapers have learned that under the Mohammedan ethical code, women can be severely punished for not wearing a long, shapeless garment that covers all of them except their face, for wearing makeup, and in general, for behaving in even a moderately liberated way. This is, from our standpoint, perverse as is the punishment for prostitution, which is stoning to death. Cutting off the hands of thieves seems to us as, no doubt, a treatment that has a good deal of preventive effect, but nevertheless, is undesirable. Once again, this is morally acceptable in pure Islam.

One of the intriguing features of Communist practice, both in China and in Russia, is a periodic upsurge of government concern about some particular type of crime, sometimes serious and sometimes minor. Thus, if the Russian police suddenly become concerned about speeding, they will indicate their concern to the populace by killing several speeders. Similarly, when China, under Deng Shaopeng, decided that there was too much crime in the country, they began executing people for such matters as petty theft.[4] All of this is done openly and in a way which implies that the officials doing it regard the matter not so much as one of terrifying the population, but literally, as something of which the populace will approve. Further, as far as I can see, the populace does not particularly disapprove and may, in fact, approve of it. Certainly, most Americans tend to think that our penalties for crime are too light, although they would hardly go to the communist extreme.

But all of these are simply efforts to point out that morals vary immensely from time to time, and from place to place. The Bible in the book of Joshua chronicles a war of extermination by the jews against the original inhabitants of the land promised them by Jehovah. This was genocide and today would be regarded as very wicked. Clearly it was regarded as moral at the time Joshua was written.

The relationship between legitimacy and ethics may seem obvious to the reader, but I should like to point out that a number of governments which, I'm sure, he finds very depressing have pretty clearly acquired legitimacy in our simple meaning in the past. German soldiers did not begin freely surrendering even after it was clear that Hitler was beaten.[5]

Even more remarkable, among the Italians who were captured in the early part of World War II or interned because they happened to be in an allied country at the outbreak of the war, a number remained loyal fascists right up to the end of the war.

Communists can present an even more spectacular example of this kind of thing. The foreign Communists, in particular, have been willing to follow the Communist party, originally in the Soviet Union and then in China, in the most extraordinary changes of policy. It may be, in this case, that they look forward to being officials of a new Communist state sometime in the future, i.e., they think that the current inability of the Communist state to reward or punish them will not be a permanent condition. We shall see below that this may always be part of 'legitimacy' as we have defined it. But I think a lot of this, literally, is something which cannot be explained in terms of even potential rewards and punishments.

As an extreme example, Christian, after he had seized the Bounty and put Captain Bligh off in a long boat, proceeded first to Tahiti and then to Pitcarn. All of this time he was aware of the fact that if the British navy caught him they would promptly hang him. Nevertheless, he always raised the Union Jack on each piece of terrain that he occupied. When the British navy finally did hunt down the Pitcarin Island remnant, the one remaining mutineer there greeted them with 'thank God you're English'. As a matter of fact, they didn't hang him, but he certainly must have expected that

that is what they would do. He could hardly know the changes that occurred in England in the many years that he had been totally out of contact with civilization.

In all of these respects, this legitimacy characteristic behaves rather like specific parts of our code of ethics. There, again, you will find people carrying out ethical principles, even when there is no obvious gain to them and, in fact, where there may be a loss. Those people, and there were several in the American army during World War II who threw themselves on a grenade in order to protect their comrades from being killed, were not acting out of hope of reward. Neither were the Kamikazi pilots in Japan who were, of course, immensely more numerous than Americans who were willing to sacrifice their lives in this final way. It is true that they were promised that their spirit would stay in Japan, but that, as a matter of fact, would have been true of substantially any Japanese who died at that time. They were not guaranteed a higher status in the next world.[6]

Of course, the Mohammedans if they are believing Mohammedans, are indeed guaranteed a much superior status in heaven if they die fighting the unbelievers than if they just die. In this case, therefore, there is a reward in the afterlife for believers, which might lead them to commit suicide in the course of trying to kill American marines or heretical Mohammedans. Still, it seems likely that for many Mohammedans, other aspects of the Mohammedan legal system are followed even when there is no obvious reward system available.

The point of this discussion so far is to indicate that legitimacy is probably merely a rather general term implying that for a great many of the citizens, officials, generals, etc., of a given regime, continuation of that regime and obedience to it is part of their ethical system. 'Legitimacy' is a collective term referring to the existence of a particular ethical argument in the psyche of a large number of people within that country.

If this is so, then any examination of legitimacy can best begin by looking into the problem of ethics itself. The explanation why most of us would refrain from committing most crimes, even if we thought we could get away with it, is the same explanation why most of us would probably continue obeying the American government, even if we thought that disobedience would be not only safe, but to our advantage. In both cases note I only say most of us, and I do not imply that we would continue on this course of action under all circumstances. Indeed, it is my opinion, and something which will be discussed below, that if the moral code, or the state, loses its ability to punish and reward then, over time, its grip on the individual psyche will disappear. Faster, of course, with some people than with others.

Where, then, do ethics come from? Why do we observe people accepting and obeying ethical codes? The traditional argument in favor of ethical codes has been either that they are divinely ordained and people had better follow them if they don't want to go to hell, or that they are the result of some kind of logical deduction. A traditional Christian divine, like the traditional Buddhist, Hindu, Mohammedan religious leader, favors the former, and the traditional philosopher, Aristotle, Plato, the latter. In, at least, the Christian tradition, the two may be combined in such a person as St. Thomas Aquinas, who relied upon both the Bible and Aristotle in reaching his ethical conclusions.[7]

I shall not engage in dispute with those people who believe that the ethical code is divinely ordained. I will, instead, permit them to continue debating among themselves. Since they are not in agreement as to who God is, or how many gods there are, for that matter, they are certainly not in agreement as to what these gods have ordained, and a simple atheist like myself can be excused for not going into their theological debates.

The philosophers are more in accord with 'advanced thought'. The philosophic point of view is now penetrating the churches by a somewhat odd route. No longer is it, as in the case of St. Thomas, combined with Christian religion, but Christian religion is, in fact, being bent to the philosophers. This is not the ancient philosophers as represented by Aristotle, but modern thinkers represented, in a real sense, by *The New York Review of Books*.

Thus, a disbelief in miracles is now quite common, apparently, among mainstream churches. I heard a German professor of theology argue that the resurrection of Christ probably did not occur. When a philosopher of science who is personally an atheist said that this was a challenge to the whole foundation of the Christian religion, a whole group of other German professors of theology reacted with great indignation. As the theologian said, [in German], 'You are ignoring the work of the theologians of the last three hundred years'.[8] If I were a Christian, I would prefer St. Paul to the theologians of the last three hundred years, but since I'm not a Christian, I let the modern mainstream churches make their own decision in these matters.

There has, of course, been a movement in the opposite direction by what are called the fundamentalists in American religion. They, in essence, go back to the pre-Thomastic view of religion depending on the Bible itself (and to some extent, Augustine) as their principal authority. This has led them into some fairly violent conflicts with modern science.

But turning to the philosophers themselves, they characteristically attempt to ground ethics in some kind of logical reasons. Normally, however, the particular ethics that the philosopher upholds depends more on his background than on his reasoning. The Chinese philosophers and the Hindu philosophers, for example, reach different ethical conclusions than do westerners. Further, western philosophers themselves frequently differ. Lastly, it is an intriguing characteristic of the discussions of these points that the people introducing new methods of deducing ethical principles, or attempting to argue for old methods, normally offer as evidence that their method is correct, not that the foundations of it are sound and that the reasoning is accurate, but that the conclusions drawn are those which are conventional among philosophers. This would seem to indicate that they are more accurately described as rationalizing their existing ethical code than as deducing it.

But this is not a matter of great importance for our current purposes. Philosophers clearly disagree among themselves.[9] It is, in any event, absolutely clear that most people do not derive their ethical code from careful contemplation of philosophical arguments as in favor of one or another set of regulations upon killing people, for example. The common man, then, follows an ethical code for reasons other than its philosophical coherence. What these reasons are is important to our purpose here simply because, as I have said, the feeling of the common man that you should support the government, even though there is no compulsion to do so, appears to be similar to ethical rules, and the 'legitimacy' of the government depends on large numbers having that attitude.

In the case both of legitimacy and other parts of the ethical code, the performance of the code by an individual when there doesn't seem to be any concrete reason why he should, other than his feeling that it is right, may be illusory. It is possible that he has a good reason for doing so or, alternatively, that he thinks he has a good reason for doing so, as a result of erroneous calculations. Obviously, it would be fairly easy for a common citizen to mistakenly feel that the government of his country is much stronger than it is. He might feel that the existence of a military force in the capital city, which has seized the radio station and the television station is merely an evanescent phenomena. He may feel that the government will restore order, and if he supports this small group of military men, he is in considerable danger. This calculation could be correct or it could be wrong.

Contrarily, we might have a good deal of quick change of position after such a seizure of the communication means by people who mistakenly think that the people who seized the television station are stronger than the government and, in fact, this mistaken calculation might, if enough people made it, make the mistake a reality. This would be something which could be referred to as a loss of legitimacy by the government, although in this case, there is nothing except rational calculations. The problem would be simply the calculations were wrong.

The reverse can happen, also. People could feel that the government was strong enough so that it would come back and put down the military occupiers of the TV station at a time when the government was actually weak. Once again, if enough people felt that way, the government might recover.

In these cases, if the erroneous calculations were widely enough made so that they, in essence, reinforced each other and became true, you might well think that 'legitimacy' was the cause although it would actually be irelevant. If we observe this same phenomena but the calculation turns out to be wrong, i.e., not enough people make the mistake, then we will observe people either supporting the government when, strictly speaking, they shouldn't have or attacking it when they should not have done that. This would appear to be, by our definition, legitimacy or lack of legitimacy of the government, but the appearance would be deceptive. In this case, it would simply be rational men making mistakes. It should be emphasized that it is very difficult to make accurate calculations under these circumstances and, hence, errors do not indicate any mental defect on the part of the people who make them.

The second reason that we might observe people apparently backing a government which is weak is, quite simply, a correct probabalistic calculation in which, however, the dice fell out wrong. Thus, it might be that there is a coup in a South American city and I, as a junior official with some power to affect the outcome, feel that the odds are about 2 to 1 against the coup being successful. I, therefore, support the government. Assume that the odds are, indeed, 2 to 1 against the coup being successful, but that this, as it happens, is the third time. I have bet wrong, my bet was properly calculated and I have just been unlucky. This could be taken as evidence of a belief on my part in the legitimacy in the government, although, as a matter of fact, all I was doing was making a purely opportunistic calculation.

If it had turned out that the 2 out of 3 chances of the coup failing had eventuated, i.e., it had failed, it could be argued that this was the result of 'legitimacy' on the part of the government, even though everyone in a position to make decisions had made the same calculations that I had and had, in this case, simply been lucky as opposed to being unlucky.

Similar calculations can, in both of these cases, be a sort of precursor to the actual coup. A reporter visiting some South American capital may find a very large number of people who say that they think the government will shortly be overthrown, and go back and say the government has lost legitimacy. The people who told him this either feel the government is weak enough so that it won't punish them for saying it, or alternatively, that in any event he won't tell who they are. But, they have, in essence, made a calculation which is that the next coup to occur probably will be successful. If it is true that a large number of important people have made that calculation, then the coup will, in fact, be successful.

It should be emphasized here, that reporter's comments of this sort tend to be rather bad evidence as to the actual state of information among leading members of a given government. The reporters tend to talk to their opposite numbers, local newspaper reporters, and for that matter, the fringe of the intellectual community. This group is not, in and of itself, very important in making decisions and may be totally misinformed as to the attitude of the higher officials or the army.

This is particularly true since a great many of these intellectuals and newspaper reporters will regard it as a matter of virtue. In other words, if they think the government is vicious, they are likely to say it does not have legitimacy. This is a different usage of the word than the one I am using so far, although it is not incorrect in ordinary discourse. The deduction that a government which has this kind of lack of legitimacy will necessarily be overthrown is, however, wrong. Foreign armies of occupation almost of necessity lack legitimacy, in the sense of popular support, and yet, the long history of the world's empires indicates that they are normally hard to overthrow. I doubt that any east European government would be regarded as being legitimate in the sense of having true popular support and being in accord with the local moral code. Nevertheless, I don't think there is much prospect of their being overthrown by domestic uprisings. They may be overthrown as a result of external interference, of course.

But the cases we have been discussing so far are not the cases of what I have referred to as 'legitimacy'; in other words, cases in which people support the government even when it is not to their interest to do so or, essentially, reasons very similar to those of ethics. There are a couple of other situations in which this can occur. For example, suppose that I feel that the present government is likely to be overthrown, but that the odds are that sometime in the not distant future it will come back. Under these circumstances, I might play a long term strategy and support it quite rationally. I might also feel that although the present governemnt is apt to be overthrown, it is very difficult to see what will replace it, and the best strategy under these circumstances of uncertainty, is to support that government, or to carry out its orders, even though I can't feel much confidence that the government will be around in the immediate future. I might, for example, pay my taxes, even if I thought the government was going out, on the grounds that whatever government comes in will probably ratify the tax rules of the outgoing government.

All of this applies also to general ethical rules. I might, if there is a breakdown of order, continue carrying out the laws as they exist, even though I know that I will not be immediately punished for violations. Even if I can make considerable gains from violating them and this would not neccessarily imply any particular ethical behavior on my part. I would be refraining from bank robberies, not because I think it is wicked, but because I think, either correctly or incorrectly, that engaging in a bank robbery is dangerous because some government will eventually punish me. This is not, I think, the basic reason why most people don't engage in bank robbery, although it is likely that if the government stopped punishing bank robbers, over time, it would become a very common occupation.[10]

But the main theme of this chapter has been why we observe this legitimacy phenomena in some cases. And, for this purpose, I need true legitimacy, not people rationally choosing that policy which seems to have the best odds, or rationally not thinking about the matter too much and, hence, making a mistake. I am interested in cases in which people would, let us say, support a government even though, on the whole, withdrawing that support would pay more than giving the support.[11]

Recently, I heard a distinguished German biologist[12] say that human beings were 'readily indoctrinable'. He was, of course, pointing to a difference between human beings and most other biological species. Most of the other species can be trained to do some things, but not a great deal. Their behavior is quite heavily dependent on straightforward hereditary characteristics.

Nevertheless, presumably, the 'indoctrinability' of human beings is also hereditary. In other words, we inherit, instead of a set of behavior patterns, a capacity for learning behavior patterns.[13] But learning is not all that he was referring to. We observe that people follow behavior patterns under circumstances in which, if they thought the matter over carefully, they probably wouldn't. Hence, the term indoctrination.

We observe that different societies have radically different ethical patterns, but that they all tend to accept their ethical patterns to about the same extent. Note that I say to about the same extent, not perfectly. All known societies have deviant personalities that follow the basic ethical principles of the society rather badly, and almost every single person in any society has, at least once, violated the ethical principles of that society.

If we consider the matter introspectively, assuming that all of my readers have, like myself, on occasion violated our ethical code, we note that there is a sort of policeman. We feel guilty and ill at ease after we have violated such an ethical rule. Further, we are usually driven to carry out the ethics without much thought, so that they can't really be 'applied' in the sense that, let us say, I learn to apply certain mathematical rules in appropriate circumstances. They are, instead, learned in the sense that somebody learns to play golf, so that his behavior in swinging the club is almost the same as the instinctive behavior of an animal who had inherited it.

Thus, the indoctrinability of the human being means that we can be indoctrinated into a set of rules which we then follow, more or less, automatically, and for which, when we deviate from them, we feel guilty and ill at ease. Note that this indoctrination is never complete. We tend to think of inherited animal behavior as being completely dominant, that is, there is no way of deviating from it once you have the right genes. By observation, this doesn't seem to be true. Animals put in sufficiently extreme conditions will, normally, deviate from their inherited pattern of behavior, but this may simply mean that the inherited pattern of behavior carries with it a deviation in more extreme conditions. Perhaps, for example, a herbivore that normally eats only certain types of leaves, if it gets hungry enough will begin eating random leaves.[14] It should also be noted here that this kind of indoctrinability can have much the same effect even when there is nothing ethical involved. If, for example, I have learned a certain pattern of behavior in collecting quarters to use in automatic washers,[15] if I deviate from it with the result that I don't have enough quarters, I find my feelings about this are not just the inconvenience of not having the quarters, but a vague feeling very similar to the guilt I would feel if there was something immoral about this. Needless to say, since this is a minor matter, the feeling is very weak. If I had, however, developed a pattern of behavior in dealing with the stock market which I believed to be successful, and then deviated from it, I probably would feel guilty. This would be particularly so if it led to me losing a large amount of money.

But let us temporarily stick with ethics, because I believe the support for government is very similar to ethics rather than being very similar to these other types of calculations. How, then, can we explain the fact that human beings are 'indoctrinable'? We could, of course, simply say this is a characteristic of human beings. There are a number of aspects of human behavior which don't seem to be explicable from an evolutionary standpoint. I put these things down to two explanations, one of which is simply that we have not yet learned enough about human evolution to be able to explain as much as we will have in the future.

The second explanation, however, which is probably equally

unsatisfactory, is simply that the human being is not very well adapted. We grew very, very rapidly in terms of evolution. Our large brain was a very quick change, if we look at the rate at which most species grow. Further, during almost the entire time in which we moved from an erect ape to homosapiens, our ancestors were apparently dominant predators. They lived, as far as we can tell, rather like wolves or baboons today, i.e., in small tribes, and, in general, had little to fear from non-human predators.[16] On the other hand, the predators probably had a good deal to fear from them. As our ancestors became both bigger and brighter, the degree to which they could refrain from fearing other animals, and the degree to which other animals had to fear them steadily increased.

Nevertheless, during most of this period of time, the principal selective pressure on human beings[17] was exerted by other human beings. From what we know of animal societies, and the various primitive human societies that have been carefully examined,[18] indicate that you have within the society normally a relatively peaceful status, but occasional dominance clashes. The losers in these dominance clashes can be selected out either by actually being driven out of the tribe, or having their reproduction possibilities reduced.

The big selection process, however, was basically what we might call wars between different tribes, essentially over real estate. Like wolf packs, these groups probably had their own real estate.[19] If they did not, then the only explanation would be that the natural death rate was high enough so that they did not fully occupy the habitable space. This, more or less, requires some kind of a predator, and except for germs, there never was one.

It should be said here that most modern scholars find that most of the primitive tribes they examined are quite peaceful. The basic explanation for this modern observation simply seems to be that the extension of various empires in the 19th century put down all local fighting everywhere except in Afghanistan and other parts of the northwest frontier.[20] Nevertheless, there do seem to be some cases in which, as far as we can tell, the area was quite peaceful even before the arrival of Europeans.

We have to be careful here interpreting the facts. The human specie is a very slow growing one. Tribes in a given area might well grow at the slow rate of growth which we would expect for quite a while before any tribe began realizing that the existence of neighboring tribes was reducing the resources they themselves had available. Thus, considerable periods of peace would not be surprising. The actual history of places which we have real knowledge of, that is, areas where a European or, for that matter, Arab or Chinese civilization expanded into a basically small tribe society, were mainly quite war like. This was true in Africa, and certainly true in the United States and South America. Note I am not here referring to the Aztec and Inca empires, although heaven knows they were war like enough,[21] but to the smaller tribes who engaged in almost continuous petty raiding across their frontiers. *Under the Mountain Wall*[22] is an account of this kind of society as it existed in New Guinea, before the European peace was imposed.

This description of human life before the advent of civilization implies that there was a very, very long period in which the principal predator to which man had to adjust himself was other men. Further, this was a period in which, not only did human beings improve, but their technical equipment improved too. They began, apparently, using clubs and stones, and gradually, at first very slowly and later more rapidly, improved these tools. They, apparently, also improved their knowledge of the natural environment and being human beings, they tended to migrate.

Thus, the environment that any given group faced was one in which their principal restricting predator was, not only other human beings, but other human beings whose physical equipment methods of fighting, etc., was changing. Further, they probably gradually shifted locations.[23]

This slowly changing environment, together with the fact that human being are a long lived species, and in particular, that it is a long time from the birth of an individual until he finishes his reproductive life, means that it would take a very long time for any gene to be fixed. If we use, as a rule of thumb, a hundred generations as the time necessary to fix a gene,[24] and a generation as twenty-five years, then it would be 2500 years to fix a gene.

It seems unlikely that very many human reproductive strains would go 2500 years without suffering a fairly significant change in their environment, either through migration or, more likely, through technical improvements in the method of warfare by their neighbors. There would, no doubt, be backwaters where this was not true, but they would tend to get left behind in the gradual evolutionary change. It would be the humans living in the cockpits, the places where pressure was greatest, who would tend to move most rapidly toward a large brain size. As we have said, the movement was very fast by biological standards.

What all of this indicates to me is simply that human beings were evolving a combination of greater body size and strength, and a very much larger brain, but that this very much larger brain could hardly be a highly specialized brain. It had to be rather general, simply because there was no environmental constant to which it could specialize. Under these circumstances, we would assume that the human brain would not be carefully adjusted to any particular need. If we consider another dominant predator, the lions, it is clear that their behavior patterns are very heavily affected by hereditary genes. These genes, on the whole, have a high survival value. Human beings, insofar as they have hereditary patterns of behavior or drives, are probably much less tightly fitted to any existing niche simply because there never was any relative unchanging niche during the period of our evolution.

Note here that I am talking about both specific behavior patterns and basic drives, or if you wish, basic values. Surviving species have to have some kinds of mechanism which leads them to eat and which has at least some tendency to lead them to eat safer and more nutritious foods. Larger mammals, of which human beings are an example, usually have quite a wide spread of things which they can eat. Nevertheless, our taste buds lead us to avoid quite a number of readily available foods. We eat practically no tree leaves, for example. Under modern conditions, I don't doubt that we could eat tree leaves suitably processed by our food industry, and get nutrition out of them, regardless of the fact that we don't like their taste.[25] Normally, if we are to reproduce, there has to be some kind of mechanism leading to sexual contact. We have to have suitable drives either in the form of a direct instinct for it, or in the form of a set of built in preferences, which lead us to move in the right direction, to avoid getting too cold, to avoid exercising too vigorously in very hot weather, and a very large number of other similar survival characteristics. As far as we can tell, in human beings this is, to a very large extent, simply a set of tastes or drives. When we are hungry we like certain types of potential foods and not others.

Taste buds, under present circumstances, probably are not a

terribly good guide, because we process food so extensively. Nevertheless, I think we have to agree that the original function of the taste buds in distinguishing between pleasant and unpleasant food was to guide us in the direction of, at least, reasonably nutritous food. Since primitive humans probably moved from one environment to another the guidance would have to be very general rather than very specific, and would also have to be designed so that if we came in contact with a new potential food source, the chances were good that simply tasting it would give us a much better than random information as to whether it was safe and nutritous.

This discussion of the human preference structure which drives our behavior, is, I think, fairly noncontroversial although the language is different from what is normally used. I don't see any reason why, in a book not intended for biologists, I should use the technical terms that biologists would use.

The important point here is that we are, to a considerable extent, an efficient animal, and that this efficiency is, to a considerable extent, the result not of our having built in behavior patterns, but that our having a built in set of tastes, values, drives, whichever term you wish to use. They are, of course, not identical from person to person, but they are quite similar. No one eats copper sulfate out of choice, and we all like things sweet, although the degree to which we like things sweet varies from person to person.

There are some fairly clear cut cases of things that we do which have negative evolutionary value, that is, they reduce the number of our descendants. These are so natural to us that we have difficulty believing that they are somewhat surprising. The one that I usually mentioned is our tendency to have decorations around us, i.e., pictures on the wall, etc. This clearly lowers our number of grandchildren and great grandchildren if contrasted with using the same resources more directly for improvement either in number or in quality or both, of our offspring.[26] Another is the peculiar human pattern of altruism. We have no great difficulty in recognizing our relatives.[27] The economic theory of altruism perhaps better referred to as nepotism, explains at least some gifts to our relatives. Many animals in fact make sacrifices for their relatives. Human beings however, make gifts to people who are in no sense relatives. Beggars for example. We also make gifts to house hold pets and to animals in the zoo.

All of these are cases where it would appear that we have a set of tastes, drives, or values, you may use your own word once again, that are not tightly in accord with the usual rules of evolution. We do not live solely in order to maximize the number of our descendants. My explanation for this is not that we are not the product of evolution, but that our evolutionary situation was peculiar. We did not adjust tightly to a specific niche because there was no unchanging niche in existence for us to adjust to. In consequence, we developed a fairly good general purpose computer.[28]

We also evolved a set of tastes or preferences which, granted the general purpose computer could tell us how to maximize survival. It is possible that in addition to this we have genuine built in behavior patterns, but so far, there's no unambigious case of such a behavior pattern in adults. Basically, the model which we seem to have developed is a set of tastes or preferences for things which in fact have survival value in the old stone age together with a rather efficient computer which permits us to choose behavior patterns likely to achieve these preferences. Some of these preferences seem to lead to behavior patterns like making gifts to complete strangers which have no obvious evolutionary value. Presumably, as I mentioned above, they come from the fact that we are not tightly evolved.

The reason for all of this evolutionary background of human behavior and human thought processes may not be immediately obvious to the reader. It is, however, necessary to explain why I believe human beings are, as Professor Markl said, readily indoctrinable. We turn now to three patterns of drives or values which are characteristic of human beings and which would lead to a tendency to accept indoctrination. Note that these three could be explained either in terms of evolution, which had given them to us, or in terms of our having rationally figured out a pattern of behavior and following it, or in terms of our ancestors having rationally figured out this pattern of behavior and indoctrinated us with it while we were small children. For our current purposes there is no reason to distinguish these three possible origins. People do behave this way. But all of this indicates that there are individuals who do not maximize their own well being in terms of careful calculations at the time of taking some action.

Note however, none of these reasons would give a motive for an individual to take action which benefited the group that he was in while injuring himself unless the relationship to other members of the group was close enough so that biological altruism became a feasible characteristic. This would never be true with a large group such as nations, states, or even most cities and villages. The reason that its never to his advantage is simply that although such behavior would increase the survival potential of that group, it makes it likely that his own descendents will be a smaller portion of that group. Careful calculations by biologists indicated that under most circumstances the effect of the reduction in share more than counter balances the selective effect of the increase in survival of the group. Thus, we should not expect the rational calculating individual making decisions which maximize preferences built into him by evolution for their survival value would make significant sacrifices for any large group of which he happened to be a member.

But the human mind is not of infinite size. It is not possible for the individual to engage in infinitely large calculations. Further, in practice he can't engage in very much calculation about most things he does. If you consider your daily round, you will quickly realize that although you may engage in very deep and prolonged thought with respect to some things you do during the day, most of the time you make up your mind with very little thought, and in many, many of the cases, you don't even make up your mind. They are habitual activities which you have put into the unconsciuos. I find, for example, that when I leave my house in my car, I have to carefully think where I am going if I am not going out to the University. If I don't concentrate on driving, I will take off for the University without thinking about the matter. This is, of course, a fairly complex set of actions, and a set of actions in which I must make many minor decisions, but I find that I can do it without conscious thought. It is a convenience, since it permits me to think about something else at the time.

All of this is simply one example of the necessary economies in computing power. The existence of a finite brain with a finite memory requires such economies. The possibility of turning certain parts of our behavior over to automatic or semi-automatic control leaving part, of course not all, but part of the brain free for more complex operations is merely one example. Indeed it is not an example which is of much use in explaining ethics or legitimacy, except that both of these have a rather distant resemblence to habit.

Another important economy is simply accepting other peoples

word. It is utterly impossible for all of us to learn everything about the world. Indeed the human race as a whole does not know everything about the world. If we go back in time, human beings knew even less. Nevertheless, we do find it easier to accumulate most of the knowledge that we have by either listening to what other people say or by reading things that they have written. This is obvious but when one thinks about it, one immediately realizes both that it is an immense economy and that there are some at least superficial mysteries about it.

To begin with the mysteries, one is why we tend to assume that other people are not lying and a second is why most of the time they aren't lying. We do normally assume that people are telling the truth but we don't always. We know that sometimes they lie. The new Soviet man, the new Chinese communist man, the new Cuban man, to name but three examples, are all great disappointments to the propagandists who tried to create them. It turned out that the Russians, the Chinese, and the Cubans, although they could successfully be cut off from all knowledge of alternatives to what their government was saying to them, nevertheless, tended to be very skeptical of it. They learned to repeat the approved slogans, indeed the Chinese were able to repeat long speeches by Mao Ssu Dung by memory.[29]

This ability to repeat them did not mean that it effected their behavior very much. There were active black markets, high officials who took advantage of their offical position, and low ranking individuals who just didn't work very hard.[30] All of these are unsurprising examples of people disbelieving what they are told.

The explanation here is fairly simple and proceeds along two lines. Firstly, all of these communist governments have simply said too many things that were known by their auditors to be false. Take for one example reference to superior Russian production etc., when it is a sign of status in Russian society to be able to use capitalist products[31] is pretty hard to sell. Also they periodically make great claims as to their ability to provide various consumer goods which rather quickly turn out not to be true. Many Chinese who lived through the great leap forward remember the immense efforts put into the back yard steel furnaces and the absolute nill output.[32] Those who lived through the great proletarian cultural revolution, no doubt remember the gigantic move to have everybody write poems and the very poor quality of the literary output.[33] Mao Ssu Dung has moved from being a god to being a villian and is now back to a sort of unperson.[34]

Thus the first rule is that you don't trust liars and when the only information you have are statements from a liar you distrust it. We should not exaggerate here however, the Chinese, Russians, and Cubans who have no access to other information are not likely to have any organized view contrary to that which their masters want them to have. It's just that they distrust what has been fed to them. In *1984*[35] the Prols were fairly immune to the Prolfeed which the hero was engaged in producing.

The second rule is to distrust people who would benefit from what they are saying if what they are saying were false. This is the old latin rule 'cuibono, who gains'. The Roman jurists and indeed all jurists ever since have regarded testimony by somebody who has nothing to gain from it as much more reliable than a statement by a man who has something to gain. Indeed the reverse rule is followed, a man who makes a statement which will injure him is regarded as an exceptionally accurate witness.

Note that this set of rules provides us with at least weak answers to both of our questions. In areas where telling a falsehood does not benefit you, it's probably less trouble to tell the truth, if you know the truth. Unfortunately, as we shall see below, what you think is the truth may simply be something that you've heard someone else say and the origins may not be scientific research but an exercise of imagination.

When the people who utter a given statement have frequently have been found wrong in the past or would benefit from your believing the statement, you would be well advised to give careful consideration to it and not necessarily accept it as true. This being so, individuals have some incentive to develop a reputation for honesty and accuracy. Still mostly the statements which are accepted without any question and regarded as true are those made under circumstances in which the person who makes them does not have anything to gain from lying.

Now all of this, once again, fits into our ideas of brain economy, i.e., it provides a way in which the brain can economize on its computation space. Faced with the infinitely large collection of possible computations it economizes by accepting as true, a large number of statements made by people who do not seem to have anything to gain from lying.

The individuals who make these statements unfortunately are not quite so well restrained here. In general, there is little in the way of an accuracy check. Thus if I am asked a question on which I think I know the answer, but I really haven't done any serious investigation, I am still likely to answer. There is little or no cost to me in carrying out this pattern of behavior. Further, if there is little or no cost to me, a professor and the man who does a good deal of writing of a scientific nature, costs for many many others are much lower.

Anyone who has had any serious contact with modern journalism or with the type of non-fiction which sells 100,000 copies is immediately aware of the fact that it isn't very accurate. In general this lack of accuracy is not the result of any conscious desire to lie. Normally, it is simply that the person who is writing it is economizing on his own time by not engaging in serious checking. Indeed in the case of newspapers, t.v., radio, etc., if the media did engage in serious checking of their information it would be delayed several days at the very least with the consequence that probably the readers would not be interested. Apparently the readers prefer to read current 'news' which is let us say, 85% correct, to reading a month later information which is 95% correct.

All of this is presumably sensible. Its not obvious that we have any evolutionary reason for wanting to know what is going on at the Olympics or in international affairs, but if we do have some reason for wanting to know what is going on, normally we need to know what is going on now not what went on sometime ago. Henry Ford thought that history was bunk. This is not true, but it certainly is true that history normally has no great practical use in the affairs of the average man. What is going on right now is far more likely to be something to which he should adjust than what went on a month ago.

This fact, that reports in the media are not necessarily accurate, is supplemented by the existance of a genuine motive to simply make things up. This is not a motive to make things up in such a way that it benefits yourself, but to make them up in such a way that you have something to say and that that something to say is interesting. Almost all societies have at least one, sometimes several creation myths, i.e., explanations as how the world started.[36] All of them, so far as we know, are false but there doesn't seem to be any obvious reason why they should have been created at all. The explanation presumably is that the person who invented them gained credence from his hearers because he had nothing apparent to gain, and he chose to make them interesting. The gain he got was in a primitive way the same as the gain that a modern writer gets writing something like *In His Image*[37] The human being wants to be entertained[38] and will pay for entertainment. Normally when he is dealing with information which he finds entertaining he doesn't check its truth. In most cases it would be extremely difficult for him to do so. *In His Image* of course turned out to be false but I doubt that few of its many, many readers were in a position to make any judgement on its accuracy at all. Presumably, they found it entertaining and believed it to be true, but were unable to check its accuracy.

This kind of 'information' is found through out almost all societies. Further, there are a number of areas where some one has apparently made up things without very much entertainment being involved. Lastly, but by no means least, there are many many cases in which people appear to have believed something, for example most folk medicine on the feeblist possible evidence. The witch doctor goes through some ceremony and some of his clients recover, which is inevitable since most people do recover from most diseases. As a result the belief that the ceremony works is likely to become wide spread. There were also, of course, a vast number of medicines which were given by doctors before the advent of modern science which we now know are worthless or in some cases very decidedly negative in value.

This is not a criticism of the way the mind works. It is very important that we economize on our use of the mind because we simply cannot conceivably hope to think about everything in a finite length of time. Thus, stopping our calculations at a point where it looks like we won't get very much further is necessary. Note my statement, 'it looks like'. We cannot know for certain what would happen if we engaged in further thought or further investigation of any sort. Some people are better at making these guesses than others.

What has all of this to do with our problem, first of ethics and secondly of that special subsection of ethics dealing with governmental 'legitimacy'? The answer is that in my opinion these characteristic of the human mind which I have been describing help explain both of these matters. Any human being has certainly been bombarded during his life with statements about various ethical principles which are dominant in his culture. You are trained not to take vengence because 'vengence is mine sayth the lord' or that you have an absolute duty to engage in feuds if your family has been injured by other people. It all depends on the culture in which you're in. As far as we can tell, individuals are about as easy to indoctrinate in one of those two principles as in the other. If anything the feuding one seems to be a little easier.

Indoctrination is not the whole of it. It is true we tend to believe things we are told, in particular, to believe things many different people have told us. But there is more to it than this. There is also the problem of stopping our calculations when it appears that nothing will be gained. This is a very well established psychological proposition. In the case of ethics and political matters also, we should stop our calculations and accept things at some point in time. In general, the motive behind this stoppage is not that it assures that our conclusion is true, but that we think that nothing very practical can come out of further consideration.

Thus, let us suppose that I am a citizen of Albania and it is obvious to substantially everyone who thinks about it that various improvements could be made in the government. The first thing to do obviously for any well intentioned Albanian would be to kill all the higher officials of the present government. On the other hand, it's equally obvious that he can't do this, they're very well guarded and efforts to kill them would likely lead to his own death. Under the circumstances, the standard human being is likely to stop thinking about this obviously impossible solution to the problems and turn to things which are in fact within his reach. Instead of killing the local officials he may make some effort to improve his relations with them. The first program is clearly impossible, hence it's ignored, whereas the second program is within the bounds of possibility. It is therefore a higher payoff activity to think about methods of possibly improving your relations with the local government than thinking about methods of killing some official when, as a matter of fact, if you succeeded he'd only be replaced by another equally bad.

Note once again, that this could be explained either in terms of a genetic disposition, a set of calculations aimed at minimizing the amount of time one devotes to worrying about problems which one could do nothing about, or indoctrination by your parents in your early life. All three lines of reasoning would lead to the same conclusion.

There is now another characteristic of the human mind which may help explain the matter. This is the phenomenon known as reduction of cognitive dissidence. In general, people are happier about their present situation than we would normally expect them to be. Let us suppose, for example, that you are interested in buying a car. You spend a good deal of time investigating the advantages of various models. If the Psychologist asks you to list those advantages and disadvantages you can do so of course. If however, he waits until after you have actually bought the car and then compares what you have to say about the advantage to the different cars with what you said while you're still making up your mind, he will normally find that you regard the car which you in fact bought as much more superior to the others than you did at the time you were making up your mind. In other words, now being stuck with the car, you are changing your opinion so as to be happy about your choice.[39]

Note in this case, there's no reason to believe that you have made a mistake, you may in fact have preferred the Chevrolet on the whole while you were making up your mind, now that you have it however, you will prefer it much more than you did before. It's obvious why human beings would be happier if something like this were built into their psyche. It means that they tend to be relatively satisfied with their current situation. Clearly once again, they are happier with this mechanism than they would without it. One can perhaps see the point most clearly by considering the possibility that they had the reverse reaction: that is that after they bought the Chevrolet their feeling, with respect to Chevrolet, fell. This would make them in many cases think that they had made a bad mistake and make them unhappy with their choice.

But although this is easy to see why this particular phenomenon does make people happy, it isn't exactly easy to see why this would be the outcome of any particular mechanism. Surely the point of evolution is not to make people happy, but to make them survive. As I mentioned above, it seems likely that human beings are not indeed tightly selected for optimal survival so that this doesn't prove that this is not genetic, but it does indicate that in any event we cannot argue for a genetic support. It may be genetic or not but it clearly does not have any particular survival value.

Suppose that people thinking the matter over would like to have this particular trait because it would mean that in the future they would be happier. You can imagine people deciding that they would be better off if they felt this way than if they did not. Unfortunately, we don't have that kind of control over our own feelings. The mere fact that I am thinking about a particular trait as something desirable for me to have, is apt to deprive me of it. I cannot decide that I shall make a particular logical error since it is good for me because once I recognize that it is a logical error I am no longer able to make it. Thus, a decision on my part to in the future believe that decisions I'd made in the past are better for me than they actually are would in an of itself probably make me unhappy because I would realize that this decision was a decision based on something that was untrue and hence, since I do realize that, I could not believe it.

It would, I suppose, be possible for parents to indoctrinate their children in this attitude in order to make them happier through their lives, so far as I know there's no evidence that parents in fact do so.

The result of all of this is that we undeniably have this particular trait, but there doesn't seem to be any strong reason why we should. Nevertheless, in the field of both ethics and legitimacy it is important. Once again, the citizen of of Albania is apt to come to the conclusion after some time that the Albanian government isn't as bad as it seems on the surface. He may begin finding advantages to it and becoming reasonably happy with it. If this is so, the political scientist would say that the government had developed legitimacy.

Thus, in this case, there seem to be only two possible roots from which we could develop this feeling of legitimacy, or acceptance of any other ethical principle which is not, in fact, in our best interest. These are a genetic predisposition and parental training. In any event, we observe that human beings do act this way, and it has some effect on the retention of power by a dictator. Firstly, he may find that he is benefited by this 'legitimacy', or he may find that he isn't and should do what he can to build it up.

Now, in dealing with this issue, it must be kept clearly in mind that the fact that this kind of 'legitimacy' exists does not mean that the government is a nice one. Indeed, historically I suspect the strongest cases of this kind of legitimacy have been hereditary monarchies in which a dynasty has been in power for a period of time. The House of Ming, in China, is notable in Chinese histories both for its great glories and strength, and for the fact that apparently almost all of the emperors were degenerate. There were generations of emperors in which the emperor never saw his high officials, dealing with them exclusively through eunuchs. One of the emperors, in an outburst of idiocy, succeeded in getting himself captured by the Mongols. The emperor was able to return to his throne because of his strong legitimacy. The junior relative who temporarily replaced him, and who certainly was as competent, was unable to hold the throne.[40]

The Chinese are, by no means, unique. English history is a history of revolutions and attempts to overthrow the government. The British throne was far less secure than any other in Europe. Nevertheless, with the sole exception of Henry VII, all of these people who attempted to overthrow the crown were blood relatives. An individual might, if he was closely related to the reigning king, attempt to overthrow him, but not anyone else. Surely, these were not those Englishmen most suited to rule.

The case of Henry VII, mentioned above, is a particularly intriguing one, since his accession not only ended the very destructive Wars of the Roses, but it brought a man who had no blood connection with the royal line to the throne. The Wars of the Roses, between Lancaster and York, in essence, broke out because Henry VI went insane.[41] The result was that for a considerable period of time, not Henry VI but his wife, was the actual leader of the Lancastrian House, and in fact, Henry VI for much of this time, was a prisoner in London.[42] The objective of the House of Lancaster was freeing him and restoring him to the throne. The importance of legitimacy is obvious here, since it is very hard to see any other reason why a lunatic should be restored to rule. Eventually, however, Henry VI died.[43] At this point, his wife, an exile in France married a Welsh soldier of fortune named Tudor. Their son had no hereditary claims on the throne, but through his mother he was head of the Lancastrians. With the aid of the French king, he was able to overthrow the Plantaganet Dynasty and establish his own Tudor.

Having considered seriously the history of England, he adopted a policy followed by his descendants, of killing all possible rivals to the throne.[44] As I have said above, the kings of Scotland were out of reach, and hence, when Henry VIII's syphilis and his children's sterility led the Tudor line to die out, the king of Scotland became the king of England.[45]

We could go on with this. Terrible governments have not

infrequently been able to acquire serious support from people because of 'legitimacy'. However, any form of government may get this kind of support. I wish to turn to democracy below, but let me begin now with dictatorship. South America has had, in most of its countries, a record in which dictatorship and democracy are intermingled. In most of the countries, dictatorship is commoner than democracy, but there are democratic interludes. Although the dictators are, by no means, always military men, they always have military support.

The point here is that for a great many South Americans, one of the signs of legitimacy of a government is military support. This is true for democracies as well as dictatorships. In other words, it is thought by most South Americans that not only is military support necessary for a government, but that a government which loses military support *should be* overthrown, not only *will be*. This point of view is shared by relatively few South American intellectuals, but South American intellectuals are a rather rare breed, and they are also are very frequently only intellectuals by virtue of a sort of ascription process. The output of some South American universities is rather like the output of the New York City public schools.[46]

It should be said, however, that indoctrination is also important in legitimacy, and in some cases, severe indoctrination of a particular type has tended to create a legitimacy even against the existing government. Needless to say, this occurs only when an existing government permits the indoctrination to go on.

An obvious case of this occurred in France in the reigns of Louis XV and XVI. At this time, the *philosophes*, deeply under the intellectual influence of England, favored a constitutional monarchy like that of England. Apparently, this point of view was so widespread, that even the last king held it. As a result, in general, the king could not depend on his army when it finally came to a showdown and he, himself, clearly was in two minds about opposing the desires of the newly created legislature.[47]

The same situation appears to have been true in South America during the time when South America became independent. Most historians are[48] of the opinion that the common people were royalist and it was the upper classes who favored republics. This meant that, of course, there was no prospect whatsoever of establishing a true republican form of government, and may have been one of the reasons for South America's rapid collapse into a series of local dictatorships.

In the 19th century, we see this feeling that democracy is the only legitimate form of government spreading throughout much of the world, although South America always tended to be rather resistant. In the 20th century, it has turned out that dictatorships can take advantage of this kind of legitimacy by simply announcing that they are democratic.[49] It is extraordinary how widespread this illusion can spread. I have had several major political scientists tell me that Russia has elections. Indeed, one of the characteristics of the modern day world is the strong tendency to feel that socialist governments somehow are legitimate no matter how they came into power or how apparently unpopular they are. This 'legitimacy' does not seem to protect them from their own people, only from the foreign press.

But, if legitimacy has these characteristics, it surely is something that the dictator would like. Obviously, when he first comes into power, he is not in a position to claim legitimacy on the grounds that he's been around a long time. This is probably the reason that new rulers almost uniformly announce that they are firmly in favor of whatever happens to be the current mystique. The Ching Dynasty, overthrowing the Ming, announced their firm devotion to Confucianism, although they had to announce it in rather bad Chinese because, after all, they were Manchus.[50] Similarly, if one looks back at the Wars of the Roses, one finds strong statements about how the previous government had not only been corrupt, but had failed to be respectful of the Christian religion.[51]

In recent years, dictators have usually announced that they are going to have a democratic government shortly after a few minor problems have been cleared up. Since, after a few years, the dictators are beginning the develop the other kind of legitimacy, they usually quickly forget their initial promises.[52]

Note that the dictator should, of course, try to avoid doing things which will unnecessarily annoy the people. If he is in a Mohammedan country, he should make a display of piety and avoid eating ham in public. His press should be prevented from reporting anything which might cause general distaste for him, etc. I do not think, however, that any of these things are of major importance. The really big way of getting legitimacy is simply to stay in office for a period of time. The psychological traits that I have described above will then take care of the matter.

But simply staying in office is not quite enough. He must always give the impression of being strong enough so that he will continue staying in office. Once the common man, or the officials, begin thinking he is in danger of being removed, this thought, in and of itself, reduces his legitimacy, although not necessarily to zero. Legitimacy is a help, and in particular a help in that it eliminates a lot of minor opposition; it is not, however, a major dependence. It is true that if a major effort to overthrow you starts, the legitimacy argument will lead a good many people to support you who, if they thought the matter over carefully, probably wouldn't. But a few defeats and this feeling will largely vanish.

My above statement about the ending of legitimacy, of course, is primarily true of dictators. There is no doubt at all that royal families can retain a certain hold on the affections of the populace and, for that matter, the officials, long after they have been thrown out of power. Charles II was welcomed back into England; most historians seem to think that James III and Charles III were actually more popular than the Hanoverians ruling in England, and were kept out primarily by the shrewd political maneuvering, and military and police strength of the Protestant ascendancy.[53] They can be said to have retained a good deal of legitimacy right up to the ascension of George III.[54]

But, if legitimacy is of some value to the dictator, and it is, it is more of a value to him in dealing with the junior officials of his regime than in dealing with the common people. The junior officials of the regime can, in the first place, cause him more damage, or benefit him more than the common people; and secondly, they are more likely to appreciate his regime because they have, presumably, gained from it. He should also always, however, worry about the junior official who just hasn't done very well.

Penkovsky, was a loyal and energetic servant of the Soviet regime, married to the daughter of a lieutenant general, and rising rapidly in their foreign intelligence branch. It was then discovered, rather by accident, that his father, who he had not only never seen, but who was dead before he was born was a white officer. This stopped his promotion at the rank of full colonel. At about the same time, his father-in-law, the lieutenant general, was retired and suddenly discovered that rewards offered by the Soviet Union to high officials did not necessarily apply to retired high officials. The combination led to what is, at least as far as the open literature is concerned, the most important betrayal of the Soviet Union to the west.[55]

This kind of thing can happen in any regime. Of necessity, when you promote a man from lieutenant colonel to colonel, there are several other lieutenant colonels who feel that they deserved the job. This is, incidentally, from the dictator's standpoint, the strongest possible argument for straight seniority appointments. If everyone knows it is a matter of seniority, then no one will be disappointed. Your time will come if you don't die. Seniority, of course, carries with it immense other disadvantages.

Unfortunately, legitimacy, in this meaning which I have given it, is a hard thing for a dictator to get by any means other than simply staying in power. Since staying in power is his basic problem anyway, all one can really say here is that the longer he stays in power, the more legitimacy he has, and hence, the more likely he is to stay in power. Once again, power begets power.

All of this is rather different from the standard account of legitimacy. Most people have mixed legitimacy up with their own personal moral code. In practice, as I have said before, the most vicious governments have sometimes clearly acquired this kind of legitimacy. Further, it can be more readily explained in terms of certain traits of human psychology than in terms of any virtue on the part of the rulers. Nevertheless, legitimacy is of some importance to the dictator, and if he is wise he will cultivate it. Unfortunately, although if he is wise he will cultivate it, there is not really a great deal he can do about it.

So far I have said nothing about ideology because I generally tend to think it is relatively unimportant both in the control of the dictatorship, and in the problem of legitimacy. Nevertheless, it is related to the legitimacy issue. Most dictators have taken the view that their government is, not only their government, but also, virtuous. For this purpose, they frequently create their own set of rules for virtue. I should say that, as far as I know, there has never been a case in which these rules are particularly coherent. Qaddafi's *Greenbook*, and Peron's 'Justicialism', will do as examples. All of them have made strong appeals to people who are gaining from their application, but have not had great impact elsewhere.

It is true that Marxism, like the other great religions, Christianity, Islam, Buddhism, and Confucianism, has had some export value. That is, people who are not directly under it have become convinced that it is true. In general, however, these are people who very much want to know the truth and aren't very critical, or people who are simply trying to get ahead. Probably the former are the largest single category. The average person would like to have some kind of explanation for the world. He is not very well informed or very critical, nor does he engage in lengthy thought about the specific systems offered to him.[56] The likelihood that he will be caught by one of these systems is, therefore, pretty good.

This is particularly true if there is a large and rather confusing literature which has as one of its themes that the system, whether it's Buddhism or Marxism, is true, but which otherwise, is quite hard to understand. The Trinity, a doctrine so obscure that St. Thomas took the view that one could only understand it as a result of divine guidance,[57] is probably one of the attractions of the Christian religion. Similarly, the extreme difficulty of fitting any society into the Marxist set of classes is probably one of the reasons that it works. It is awfully hard, not only to fit the society into those classes, but to prove that any particular fitting is improper.

Marxism has, of course, had the characteristic that it changes rapidly from time to time and, indeed, from place to place. The Ceylonese Trotskyite, the loyal follower of Deng Shao Peng, and a New York Marxist intellectual, have almost nothing in common except that they will all tell you that they are Marxist. Nevertheless, they are apt to be allied against outsiders, even if they fight vigorously internally. The same can be said, historically, about Christianity, Buddhism, etc. Currently, the Islamic world is rent by a revived version of the split between Shia and Sunni.

As the reader has no doubt discovered already, I, myself, have little patience or interest in these ideologies. But no one who considers the growth of the Islamic empire from the time of Mohammed to the fall of the Ummayid dynasty, can doubt they have been influential in human history. Further, although the Ummayids were, undoubtedly, the great spreaders of Islam, it continued growing at a somewhat lower rate and with various schisms and divisions for a considerable period of time thereafter.[58] Today, although it is no longer spreading,[59] it is clearly an extremely important influence in the lives of a large part of the human race. I think it is foolish. Nevertheless, most human beings seem to have felt a need for Christianity, Islam, Buddhism, etc. Atheists like myself are unusual.

Purely secular religions, i.e., religions which pay relatively little attention to the afterlife, such as Confucianism, Marxism, the pagan religions of Greece and Rome, and, for that matter, Judaism, have traditionally been almost as strong as those religions like Christianity, Islam, and Buddhism which offer rewards in an afterlife for a virtuous life here. Hinduism falls somewhere between these categories. It is certainly true that a good Hindu expects to go up in the caste structure if he lives a virtuous life here, but the virtue is defined in terms of whatever caste he happens to find himself in. The prospect of a Brahman being reborn as a worm in the stomach of a spotted dog because he's mispronounced one word in a sacred chant once in his life, seems to us excessive.

But to return to the main theme of this book, such an essentially non-material motive for supporting a dictator can be very valuable to him. He can also be damaged very severely if there is such a non-material motive for overthrowing him. The Moslems seem to have convinced the Byzantine governor of Egypt that, somehow or other, God was on their side. Since he was a Christian, it is very difficult to understand how he came to this conclusion, although it is true that his army had, at the time he reached this decision, lost a series of battles. In any event, this was a major step in their further success.[60] Of course, here again, success begets the belief that you have something on your side, in this case, divine providence, and the fact that people think you have that on your side makes it more likely you will win again.

To repeat an earlier theme of this chapter, what I have had to say is not very much like the standard account of legitimacy. I have said that it is a feeling on the part of individuals that a certain government is likely to win. Not that it is in accordance with a divine order of some sort. The problem is - why do they come to that conclusion and what, if anything, can a dictator do to encourage it? Certainly, it is to his advantage if he can encourage it, and if they come to the conclusion that the reverse is true, it is to his disadvantage. But having said this, I should go on to say that I am fairly convinced that it is a relatively minor factor. In the first place, the common people and the lower officials are those who are most likely to be influenced by it. They are less important than the higher officials. Many governments thought by their subjects to be legitimate have been overthrown. The Ming, after all, were replaced by the Ch'ing;[61] the Stuarts by the Hanoverians; the governments of Lithuania, Latvia and Esthonia by Russian conquests,[62] the Senatus populesque Romanum[63] by Caesar,[64] the more or less democratic constitutional monarchy in Egypt by Nasser.[65] Legitimacy is a help to any dictator, but it is hard for him to get it in the early part of his reign, and he'll get it almost automatically in the latter part. Further, although it is a help, it is by no means a stable support.

NOTES

1. Dirk Bodde and Clarence Morris, (Harvard University Press: Cambridge, Mass., 1967).

2. In fact, it resembles much more closely the adjutant general in the American army before the enactment of the uniform code of military justice. A defendant in a criminal case did not appeal his conviction, but the case was automatically sent on to the imperial court, where a body of legal officials would look at it for legal sufficiency, perhaps the emperor himself would express an opinion.

3. Note elder or younger here does not mean chronological age. It means status within the Chinese system of relationships in which, as a rough rule of thumb, senior members were older than junior, but where there could easily be exceptions.

4. Mosher, 1983, p83

5. According to Keegan (1982, p.323) at as late a date as April 1945, when the British and Americans were capturing 30,000 German prisoners *daily*, 'those Germans still at liberty battled on, fighting and dying at every river line between the Rhine and the Elbe, counter-attacking when they could and compelling the enemy to turn into rubble every other provincial town he approached'.

6. While it is unclear what the exact total number of Kamikazi pilots who actually sacrificed their lives was, it was certainly in the five figure range. In the period April 1 - August 13, 1945 in the Okinawa area alone there were about 2,000 Kamikazi sorties against U.S. Naval vessels, which sank 20 and damaged 217 ships (O'Neill 1981, pp. 169-170). The Bushido code was not the only apparent motivation behind Kamikazi volunteers; collections of the last letters of these personnel reveal a wide variety of ostensible motives, including the Christian religion (O'Neill 1981, p. 143).

7. In fact, Russell (1945, p. 452) claims that in most respects '[Aquinas] follows Aristotle so closely that the Stagyrite has, among Catholics, almost the authority of one of the Fathers [i.e., saints]; to criticize him in matters of pure philosophy has come to be thought almost impious.'

8. The most prominent recent proponent of this view of the divinity of Christ among theologians is Hans Kung, See Kung 1980.

9. 'That the truths dealt with in ethics are more certain and definite than those dealt with anywhere else is a point upon which all philosophers will agree. It is,

unfortunately, the only point upon which they will agree.' Annon.

10. It would also lead to various substantial changes in the design of banks.

11. The following discussion has been veted by a trained psychologist. The psychologist has become involved in active politics with both an increased authority in this field and a need for anonymity.

12. Hubert Markl of the University of Konstanz

13. There may be some inherited behavior patterns, too. The problem in the present state of knowledge is an unsolvable one. Hence Young (1978, p. 9) argues that 'programs in man are largely written by a process of learning' but that patterns of programability are inherited.

14. The degree to which animals deviate from their inherited patterns of behavior differs, of course, from animal to animal. The insects vary little, the great apes a great deal. In a way, the human variation in this area is simply an immense extension of the trend.

15. This example is taken from life.

16. *Sociobiology*, (Abridged Edition), Edward O. Wilson, Belknap, Cambridge, Mass., 1980, pp 290-6.

17. leaving aside here the selective pressure of parasites such as the malaria germ

18. They've all been carefully examined at a time when they were contemporaneous with civilized societies, and hence, the examinations may not have very much to say about our ancient ancestors.

19. See Ardrey 1976, pp. 102-128, and Wilson 1975, p. 565.

20. In both 1839-42 and 1878-80 the British attempted to establish puppet rulers in Afghanistan, and each time failed in the face of Afghan guerrilla resistence. See Fieldhouse 1982, pp. 195.

21. One historian explains that the Aztecs tended 'to think that it was the Aztec's business to make war, and other people's business to work for them' (Saustelle 1970, p. xxiii). Another historian summarizes the Incas' activity by concluding that '[either] the Incas were conquering new peoples, or defending what they had taken,' adding that many wars 'were undertaken to keep the professional army occupied' (von Hagen 1957, p. 198).

22. *Under the Mountain Wall*, Peter Mattheissen. Viking Press, New York; 1962.

23. As far as we can tell, wolf tribes or baboons, etc., do not actually remain in the same location forever. There are gradual shifts having to do with successful or unsuccessful wars on the borders, just like the shifts in the tribes across central Asia which depended on the relative success of the civilized peoples in China, the Middle East, and Europe. See Kraak, *Innocent Killers* A very successful tribe would tend to split, with the result that a new border would be set up. All of this does not mean very much moving in a period of, let's say, fifty years, but in a period of a thousand years, a very considerable movement could be expected. A given tribe might experience quite different natural conditions than its ancestors that far back.

24. As far as I can see, biologists use this number largely because it's a nice round one. At best, it should be regarded as accurate only to an order of magnitude.

25. Or possibly have some other kind of hereditary aversion to eating tree leaves. In any event, no human group has spent much of its energy in collecting tree leaves for food purposes.

26. Whenever I mention this point, I find an outburst of rationalizations offered

for pictures on the wall, etc. I shan't go through these rationalizations, but I suspect that most readers, on reading the above section, will immediately invent at least one of them. I merely suggest that you think about it carefully for awhile.

27. Recent research indicates that a number of animals can recognize quite accurately a degree of relatedness, too. Apparently, there is enough genetic similarity between different members of the same family so that their body odors are related. This may be true in human beings, also.

28. It does have various defects. We are prone to certain types of logical errors. These errors, however, do not seem to be of the type that have great effect on the survival of a Stone Age man.

29. Or at least they were when I was in Communist China in 1950. I was in Korea in the later part of the war and Chinese prisoners of war had the same ability. The speed with which they forgot one speech and learned another when the line changed was truly remarkable.

30. In China, black market operations are refered to as the 'art of going in the back door.' See Mosher 1983, pp. 76-103.

31. Smith (1976, p. 63) notes that although 'few Western goods are available, even goods from Eastern Europe and Third World countries have a certain snob appeal and Russians will readily pay exorbitant premiums for them even when Soviet goods are adequate.'

32. Over 600,000 coke-and-coal burning furnaces were hastily constructed in 1959, only to be abandoned six months later (Mosher 1983, p. 265).

33. When I was in Peking, his tomb was still there in the square in front of the imperial palace but it was closed to all visitors. Indeed, it was interestingly enough, quite clearly copied from the work of the american architect who has built so many embassies. The building in which the supreme soviet meets in Moscow is also a copy of his work. During the period 1979-81, statues and posters of Mao were torn down and the formerly ubiquitous Little Red Book was withdrawn from bookstores. In 1982, the Centeral Committee of the Chinese Communist Party restored Mao (mostly) to respectability, although it accused him of numerous 'practical mistakes'. See Mosher 1983, pp. 297-298.

34. George Orwell's *1984*....

35. As even a very good artificial one, see the *Sillmarilion*. Greatly simplified, this myth maintains that Eru, the One, made the world by giving physical substance to music. See Tolkien 1977, p. 25.

36. Rorvik, David, *In His Image: The Cloning of a Man*. Philadelphia Lippincott, 1978.

37. Exactly why is not evolutionarily obvious.

38. The decline of the Ming Dynasty began with the reign of Ying Tsung, who ruled from 1436-1449, allowed himself to be captured in a minor battle on the northern frontier by a Mongol Oirat army. He was released in 1450 and began a struggle with his brother Ching Ti, who had assumed the throne during his captivity. He was ultimately successful and his second reign lasted from 1457-1464 (Dupuy and Dupuy 1977, p. 442).

39. In 1453, Henry VI suffered a mental breakdown which left him in a stupor for eighteen months, and from which he never entirely recovered (Aubyn 1983, p. 39). For the complex chain of events leading to open warfare this breakdown

precipitated, see Muir 1927, V. 1, pp. 177-178.

40. Aubyn 1983, p. 48.

41. On May 21, 1471, Henry VI died in the Tower of London. He was probably killed on the order of Edward IV (Aubyn 1983, p. 58).

42. Muir 1927, V. 1, pp. 211-212.

43. The common man seems to feel that there is an element of legitimacy in military rule. Granted the description I have given above of the causes of legitimacy, this is understandable.

44. Note that the legislature was elected by a very restricted group of electors. Further, the early history of the French republic was very largely an effort to make sure that the royalists did not get a majority in the legislature. Apparently, the members of the legislature thought that although they were firmly republicans, the king had overwhelming support among the common people. Of course, the disasters of the early republic had something to do with their fear of a royalist electoral majority, and the various rather unfair measures taken to prevent it.

45. Or perhaps I should say 'were' - recently Marxism has developed.

46. E.g., the German Democratic Republic, the Libyan People's Republic, and the Union of Soviet Socialist Republics.

47. Although the Ch'ing (Manchus) came from a section of what is today part of mainland China (central Manchuria) they were not Chinese. See Dupuy and Dupuy 1977, p. 512.

48. For example, an Act of Attainder of November 1485 under Henry VII (following the defeat and death of Richard III at Bosworth Field) accused the latter of 'unnatural, mischievous and great perjuries, treasons, homicides and murders, in shedding of infant's blood' and numerous other 'abominations against God and Man'. See Aubyn 1983, p. 242.

49. Reasons why a dictator may, in fact, be motivated to hold a perfectly free election were discussed above.

50. In fact, one historian argues that James Edward's chances of overthrowing George I in 1715 were quite good but that the Stuarts and their advisors were simply too incompetent to properly exploit the opportunity (Green 1965, pp. 81-86).

51. Witness the invasion of England by Charles Edward Stuart in December of 1745 – the eighteenth year of George II's reign – which generated strong support in Scotland and at least lukewarm support in England. See Green 1965, pp. 160-164.

52. Penkovskiy 1965, esp. pp. 229, 394.

53. Margery Seldon's *Poppies and Roses*,Economic and Literacy Books, Sevenoaks, Kent, 1985) is a biography of her father, who was a particularly clear example of a man who became a Marxist for these reasons.

54. Aquinas claimed that reason could prove the existence of God, but not the Trinity (or the incarnation or the last judgement). See Russell 1945, p. 454.

55. The Ummayid (or Omayyad) Caliphate ruled from 661-750 A.D., and by 732 it controlled the Iberian Penninsula, Southwestern France, all of North Africa, Arabia, the Near East (except Anatolia), Armenia, Persia and a large bridgehead over the Indus River in Northwest India. See Langer 1972, pp. 200-204.

56. Except for some missionary activity in Africa.

57. See p. 103 above.
58. See Rosser 1969, pp. 188-190.
59. This chapter is dictated in Rome.
60. Who still put S.P.Q.R. on his standards.
61. On January 26, 1952(Johnson 1983, p. 488).

CHAPTER VI

The uses of dictatorship

So far, we have talked about how the dictator keeps his power, but have said little or nothing about why he should want that power. What can he do with the power? The first thing to be said here is that the dictator is far from having absolute power. He is, undeniably, the most important single man in the society in which he operates. But he is far from being the mythical absolute ruler of all he surveys.

He must always remember that he can be overthrown. To take but one obvious example, he can hardly order his personal guard all shot while he is surrounded by them. The rise of the Turkish empire depended very heavily on the Janissaries, but by 1800, the Janissaries had become a severe burden upon that empire. The Padishah decided that they had to be eliminated, and succeeded in getting rid of them, but it took a long, careful conspiracy. Indeed, it is on the whole odd that he got rid of them rather than they getting rid of him.[1]

It is not only his personal guard, the dictator, after all, is only one man. He is surrounded by a large number of people, and if he succeeds in either annoying them or giving them the impression that he is weakening, he will probably be removed. Thus, his decisions are always subject to fairly severe constraints. These constraints are not of the sort we think of as constitutional, i.e., that somebody can literally veto his action without removing him from power.

The president is restricted in what he can do because congress may choose not to pass acts he suggests or appropriate money for things he wants to do. Further, the supreme court may decide that various of his actions are unconstitutional. These restrictions, however, are of a totally different nature from the possibility of throwing him out, and in fact the procedure for getting rid of the president is tedious, difficult and only twice in our history has been even tried. On the other hand, frustrating his policies by the various other branchs of the government is a common everyday operation.

The reverse is true with a dictator or king. It's very hard to prevent him from doing what he wants provided he concentrates on it.[2] A dictator can however be removed, and this has been the historical experience of most dictators. Further, removal is normally not into a peaceful retirement, although he may well escape abroad. There have been, indeed, some dictators who were able to return to their country after a period of time and be reasonably safe and happy there. On the whole however, the ex-dictator faces a major risk of being killed, imprisoned, or forced to spend the rest of his life abroad. Death by torture is by no means unknown.

Thus, everytime a dictator does anything, he must keep in mind the prospect that is will weaken his position. Note that this once again is not like constitutional restrictions in that his power is restricted by rules which are supposed, on the whole, to lead to it being wisely and virtuosly exercised. It is, of course, not at all obvious, that the restrictions which we impose on constitutional democratic officials have that effect, but that is the intent.

The dictator on the other hand, has to worry not about the policy outcomes of his decisions, but about their effect on other high officials and on other powers in his government. Returning to his personal guard, it may be large and overpaid but he is unwise to briskly reduce it or cut its salary. He may shift officials out of jobs for which they are well suited into jobs which they are not well suited simply because it is safer for him. He may in various ways sacrifice the welfare of the state for his own continuance in office. He can also find it necessary to 'invest' by reducing his own living standard in order to increase his tenure in office.[3]

With this much said about the restrictions on the power of the dictator, we can now turn to what he can do with what power he has. We should divide this use of his power into two categories. The first is the use of his power for his personal aggrandisement, his own living standard either while he is dictator or after he has been forced to flee the country. Securing the succession for his family is another 'personal' gain which many rulers have apparently valued. Secondly, there is the carrying out of government policies which he thinks are desirable. Both of these are areas where he can use his power. But, of course, as we have said again and again, he is limited by the fact that he may get thrown out as dictator if he does either one too vigorously. Lets begin with his own living standard. No one who has visited Versailles or that vast complex of palaces that dominates the center of Peking, will have any doubt that rulers have devoted a great deal of money to their own living standard. For another instance, Buckingham Palace is a massive building. Communist rulers seem to do very well by themselves. In the last case, they are very secretive about their conditions of life, but rumors hold that they live very well indeed.[4]

In one case, a communist ruler's living standard is known to have been very high. Marshall Tito, during the later part of his life deviated from the ordinary communist practice, by having a good deal of the budget of Yugoslavia published. The ministry which dealt with his various houses had a larger appropriation than the ministry of interior.[5] Since this is a communist country where the ministry of interior maintains the secret police this shows an extremely high consumption level. Arab rulers have, of course, also developed extremely high living standards in recent years and most South American dictators live well too. There are occasional exceptions in South America and indeed there are even occasional South American dictators who when they are overthrown appear not to have very much in the way of outside resources.

President Rhee of Korea, after twenty years of rule was finally overthrown. It turned out at this point that he had laid away so little in the way of resources that he and his wife in essence lived on charity in the latter part of their lives. This does not mean that they were poverty stricken. They lived as permanant house guests of a wealth Korean businessman in Hawaii. But they clearly had not laid aside vast amounts of money in a Swiss bank account.

The problem with a high living standard, is that it's not obvious that it helps a ruler stay in power. It has been argued many times that royal rulers surround themselves with pomp, ceremony, and luxury because in a way this gives people who meet them the idea that they're important and powerful. There is undeniably something of this sort of effect for royal dynasties and to a lesser extent for dictators. But the idea that the dictator is wasting the taxpayers money is a little hard to avoid. When he tells the army or his guard, or for that matter the higher ranking officials in his own government that it's impossible to raise their incomes, they are apt to at least subconsciously feel that perhaps if he had one fewer palace they could have more money. Further, the more money spent on the dictator, the more there is to be divided up among other high officials if they conspire together to overthrow him. Thus on the whole, personal expenditures are probably negative factors in a dictator's survival. This does not of course mean that he will not make them, merely that he regards them as expenditures in two senses. One they use the taxpayers money and two they to some extent reduce the period of time that he will be dictator.

A special form of expenditure is of course foreign bank accounts, foreign investments, etc.[6] Indeed many South American dictators seem to put a good deal of money into domestic investments. The apparent reason for the domestic investments rather than foreign is that the return, as long the man is dictator, tends to be very high because he can in various ways bend government policy so as to make these investments profitable. A road apparently built solely for the convenience of the current dictator of Chile's country estate is merely one of many examples.

It should be pointed out however, that this way of benefiting himself, i.e., building up his local investments by having the government do things which improve their value, once again has a cost in that it makes it less likely he will stay and provides greater rewards to anyone who throws him out. Indeed, investments in his own country are particularly likely to provide a reward to the individual or group who replaces him because they can always confiscate them.

Foreign investment is safe in the sense that the dictator is unlikely to lose it if he succeeds in getting out of the country. Further, foreign bankers are accustomed to this particular business and can be depended on to hold the money and keep the investments a secret. They hope to also have the business of the successor. Thus, the exact size of the funds the dictator has will not be known. It is thought for example, that Batista had about a quarter of a billion dollars[7] at the time that he was first removed. It is also thought that he stole relatively little during his second term as dictator, probably because he already had enough. Peron is thought to have taken off a full half billion when he left Argentina. Certainly in both of these cases they lived well in retirement. The Somosa and Trujillo families seem to have invested enough money within their country so that the amount they could take abroad was not in the same category as the two I have given above. Nevertheless, no one regarded them as likely to become objects of charity.

Lenin when he was ruling Russia, in the early days, apparently put aside a significant collection of jewelry which was to be used for the specific purpose of supporting the higher ranking communists in the event they were driven out of Russia.[8] Since this jewelry was actually kept in the Kremlin, it is not obvious they would have gotten it out, but on the other hand, a deposit in a foreign bank in his case was probably not feasible.

But these are merely a small smattering of examples. Anyone who even glances through the literature will pick up many, many more. One thing that dictators do is put money abroad, another thing they do is to use money to build up their current living standard in their country and they many times also invest money domestically. It's interesting that kings, emperors, etc., are less likely to do this. Apparently they feel sufficiently secure in possession of their offices so that they do not think it necessary to provide for the contingency of their being overthrown. This has meant that in a number of cases kings and their close relatives have been driven into poverty or found themselves dependent on the charity of either refugees from their own country or foreign governments who think that they may be useful for political purposes in the future.

But all of this is familiar, Though it may excite some indignation, it will not surprise. Any dictator would, of course, realize that he can make money out of the job, but that the job is risky and the more money he makes out of it the more risky it is. He must balance these various requirments against each other and different dictators have choosen different exchange rates.

Let us now turn to the other area: control over policy. The first thing to be said about this is that there is really relatively little evidence that dictators have very strong ideas about policy. Most of them have risen to their rank by a series of complex political manuvers either within the military machine, in which they had to get promoted, or in other parts of the governments. In a few cases they have been able to rise to positions outside the government from which they then overthrew the government, but in all cases, this rise in rank to the position of dictator has required the ability to adapt very, very quickly to other peoples views on policy.

There is a partial exception here. The ruler may have risen to power in part because of his espousal of some particular ideology. Khomenei and Lenin are examples. Such a ruler is unlikely to abandon his ideology, although Franco abandoned his original ideology when it became obvious it was a handicap rather than an asset. Usually these ideologies are flexible enough so that they put little real restraint on the dictator. Lenin and Khomenei are, of course, examples of this. In these cases belief in the ideology and use of it to stay in power are intermingled. Operationally we cannot determine which is the strongest.

This book is suppose to deal with both dictators and hereditary rulers. As we said above, the hereditary ruler normally feels a good deal more secure and he normally has attained his position without the necessary devious political maneuvering which has dominated the early life of the potential dictator. Thus, we might expect such kings to have more interest both in high living standards and imposing their policy ideas on societies. With respect to the high living standard, I don't think there is any doubt, hereditary kings do live better than dictators on the whole. But when we turn to policy, the matter is no where near so clear. Hereditary kings frequently do not seem to have as much control over their government as do dictators. I believe the explanation is the high living standard. A young man brought up in the extremely privileged position of an heir to the throne is likely to develop not only very expensive tastes in terms of money, but also tastes for entertainment which are expensive in terms of time. Given the choice between a day's hunting or a day in the office, a king is far more likely to choose the day's hunting than is a dictator. This is in part the result of his upbringing, but also in part the fact that he does feel more secure.

But turning to policy it's necessary to avoid a misapprehension. The fact that a king or dictator very commonly may be able to change policy does not necessarily mean that his government will be extremely oppressive.

Those who have read Shandy's *Sentimental Journey,*[9] know that the 'Journey' was undertaken by two englishmen in Ancien Regime France. They were mildly inconvenienced because a war between the two countries broke out as they were about cross the channel and hence the traffic was interupted for several days. On arriving in Paris, they set out to see the sights. Several days after they had arrived their landlord told them that the police had been around and wanted them to get the proper documents since they were after all enemy aliens. They went to Versailles and saw an official who they convinced should give them the documents because they were Sheakespeare's countrymen and then continued their sightseeing. This is not the kind of government that one associates with deep oppression.

Indeed had Lewis XVI been a more oppressive king he probably would not have had his head cut off. He actually organized the elective bodies which eventually executed him. He was in the process of further cutting restraints on public expression when the revolution broke out. There was not one genuine political prisoner in the Bastille when it was taken.[10]

Once again Francisco Franco is a fairly good example of the dictator and Lewis XVI a less than a normally intelligent example of the heriditary monarch. Neither ran good governments but neither can be regarded as terrible oppressors.[11]

Turning then once again, to the dictator, not the hereditary king, the first thing as we have noted is that he has had to climb the greasey pole to get to his position. This has normally occupied his full attention and he has risen not by good judgement as to what policies the country should adopt, but by good judgement as to what policies are likely to get him ahead and who can, and who cannot be trusted. It is true, that once he gets to the top he has a little breathing spell and more power. He can, if he wishes, implement policies which are different from those which he inherited. Most dictators do to some extent change previous policies and some of them change them quite considerably. Pinochet in Chile, or Lenin in Russia are examples. Lenin of course changed them farther than Pinochet.

But if we look at democracies, we find that they also sometimes change policies very sharply. Bismark's invention of the welfare state occured essentially because he wanted to win an election.[12] As I have said the difference between democracies and dictatorships in policy is hard to document, but this is partly because both democracies and dictatorships do follow very many different policies. James Madison and Franklin D. Roosevelt were both American Presidents, but it would be hard to find anything much that their policies had in common. For a more recent example, there are indeed similarities between the policies of the late Mao Tse Tung and Deng Hsiao-ping. Nevertheless, it's fairly obvious that Deng changed policies sharply when he took power.[13] But, then so did Abraham Lincoln when he became president. Clement Atlee and Margaret Thatcher were both British Prime Ministers and both instituted significant changes in policy. Atlee's were more severe than Mrs. Thatcher's still she too made significant changes.[14]

Thus, the fact that dictators may make considerable changes when they come to power does not mean that their policies are radically different from democracies. Democracies also may make considerable changes. New democracy, that is a democracy which is set up after the overthrow of a king or a dictator, in particular is apt to make significant changes as the former military rulers of Argentina are now discovering. Lincoln actually started a war by his changes.[15]

But in the average case, the policies don't seem to be very much different. Both dictators and democracies normally go along without too much change in policy although they sometimes make radical changes. In both cases, the policies pursued, both before and after radical changes, seem to be drawn from the same sample, at least statistically.

Why is this? We've already pointed out that the dictator has to be a person who is deeply concerned with rising in power, he has to be intelligent, he has to be ambitious. He doesn't have to be a profound scholar of economics, and so far as I know none of them ever have been. Plato, it will be recalled nearly lost his life because he thought that rulers should be philosophers.[16] There was indeed later a philosopher Emperor, Marcus Aureleus. It's rather had to find any great improvement in Roman policy that came from his philosophy.[17]

What we see then is an intelligent, ambitious man without very much background in the science of government in so far as there is such a thing. He has risen by a series of difficult maneuvers which prove he clearly is intelligent but not that he has firm ideas as to what policies should be. As dictator, he must always concern himself seriously with the prospect that he'll be overthrown, i.e., keeping power is highly important to him. This is true even if he is consciously attempting to reform the society because he can only do so if he keeps power. If we look at dictators we frequently find that they announce they have some kind of general reform in mind, but the reforms seldom seem to be even coherent let alone brilliant.

A dictator, then, will spend much of his time worrying about being replaced and much of his choice of policy will turn on just exactly that fear of being replaced. Almost any policy proposal is apt to be judged by him firstly in its likely effect on his personal security and only secondly in terms of it's ultimate success. Further, by training and experience he is very good at judging the effects of policy on his security and normally has very little ability to judge the policies in terms of their probable social outcomes.

For example, a proposal to permit private competition with a national airline with the national airline being permitted to survive only if it can meet that competition is apt to be judged not in terms of its economic efficiency but on its effect on his survival.[18] It may not seem to have much to do with a possible coup, but surely there will be officials who will be irritated by being put under competitive pressure and there will be employees who face at least a theoretical risk of losing their jobs and there will be socialist minded intellectuals who feel that per se the government run airline is better than the private one and hence the private one shouldn't be permitted to exist. None of these are likely to be major minuses to the dictator, but they are all minor minuses. Most dictators in fact have decided upon a nationalized airline rather than private competition.

There is here of course another matter. The private interests may be paying off the dictator or high officials. In the old days of royal governments this was done quite openly.[19] A guild, asking for monopoly of, let us say, paving streets in London, would point out that they were particularly loyal, competent and honest and that they were willing to pay the King a certain amount every year. Another guild would appear urging that it was also loyal, competetent, and honest, in fact, more so than the first guild, and that it was willing to pay even more. This in essence to put the matter up to bid. I suspect that a great many dictators do the same kind of thing although it isn't done in the open end above board way characteristic of Mercantalist England.

Note that in this case, the funds given are not necessarily used to build up the dictator's swiss bank account. The Kings of England used some of these funds to maintain the army and provide other public expenditures. Admittedly, a great deal of them were used to support the court.[20] It would be easy for a dictator who did not have a good grounding in Economics, practically none do, to believe that group of 'patriotic' men who proposed to, let us say, monopolize

Copra exports from the Phillipines and pay out of their profits a very large sum of money either to the government or to the dictator himself, were in fact public benefactors. The dictator may have great difficulty distinguishing between this institution and simply taxing copra exports. Certainly, the highly paid experts who are provided by the potential Copra monopolist will not enlighten him. Further, it is unlikely that the potential free market in Copra will be able to hire such expensive lobbyists.

In this, of course, the situation is much the same as in a democracy, or for that matter, hereditary monarchy. In all cases there will be highly paid and skilled lobbyists, different lobbyists for the three forms of government, of course, who are pushing for various policy changes which are in the private interest of special interest groups. If we look at history in all three of these cases such private interests have frequently succeeded.[21]

It should be noted that both with dictatorships and with democracy the lobbyist activity does not necessarily involve corruption but may. In other words, they may depend on persuasion or on payment. It is likely that payment is commoner in the case of a dictatorship than in the case of democracy. Leaving the moral issue aside, in both cases if there is persuasion it will partly take the form of indicating that the new policy is a good policy and partly that it is politically wise in the sense that it would lead to political support. The dictator, like the democratic politician must balance these requirements off against each other. There are direct payments to be made that also should be taken into account.

We have so far been talking about various pressures that influence a dictator in making policy decisions. If the policy decision is how much he should spend on his palace or on his body guard, then history indicates that on the whole dictators are apt to choose very large body guards and large palaces. Occasionally there are individuals with rather spartan taste like Stalin. In the case of Stalin, of course, his rather spartan tastes in furnishings was much more the counter balanced in budgetary terms by his paranoia which led to an extrordinary body guard.[22]

But this desire to use your power to benefit youself personally is a very natural trait and we need not explain it particularly. Further, the need to offset it to some extent in order to avoid giving too much temptation to other people to replace you is also obvious. Note that the procedure followed by most communist dictators, living very well but concealing their living standard from the bulk of their subjects is not really very helpful in this regard. The very elaborate special facilities that are available for the higher ranking communists in Russia for example, are firstly known to other high ranking communists the most dangerous enemies they have and secondly depend on a very, very large number of low ranking Russians as guards, servants, etc. Thus, although the average Russian probably knows nothing about them, the Russians who are most likely to be in a position to do something nasty to the dictator do know.[23]

Turning to general policy again, it has been pointed out that the man who rises to dictator normally does not have very strong policy positions. There are occasional cases in history Lenin and Khomeni come immediately to mind, where a dictator has been very deeply involved in one particular ideological position before he becomes dictator.[24] He's likely to stick to that ideology. It should be pointed out however, and once again Lenin and Khomeni are excellent examples, within this ideology they are likely to make a number of changes which benefit them in terms of power. Khomeni's political theory is quite unknown in previous Shia writing and indeed he seems to have actually 'modernized' Shia political thought partly to make it conform to some extent with democracy but even more to make it such that his position of power would be very much greater than any previous Ayatolla.[25]

Lenin was somewhat the same type of person. Reading his biography I cannot avoid the impression that he honestly believed that the world was going to eventually enter the great Marxist Utopia and hence that the only real issue politically was who would be head of it. He was always willing to do almost anything in the way of damaging prospects of Communist control, spliting the party, etc, lf it only benefited Lenin's position within the Communist movement.[26] Thus, even these two individual's who seem to have a fairly strong ideological positions clearly bent the clear ideology to their own ambition.

Nevertheless, there is some possibility of a dictator simply exercising policy judgement in terms of what he wants. After all, he probably is very interested in power and likes to exercise it for its own sake. He is likely to take advantage of his position, not only to build himself a spectatular palace, but to flatter his ego by giving orders which people have to carry out. He is unlikely to give orders that people have to carry out if he thinks that they have a possiblity, even a small possibility, of leading to his being overthrown. In many cases he can avoid that possibility. Further, he may think that it's necessary to occasionally run a bit of danger in terms of longer run safety.

It should be said here however, that not only does he worry about his own safety, as a rough rule of thumb, he's apt to also want to be liked. Most human beings do. He would like to be liked by the people immediately around him and by other people too. Thus the dictator would, other things being equal, prefer to be the favorite of public opinion. It is true that he frequently will have difficulty in determining whether he is or isn't, but he may try to improve his status with the public by doing things that he they will approve as well as by increasing the level of torture in his dungeons.

Hassan, the current dictator of Iraq has featured a number of times in this account, and we have here a clear example. After his ghastly miscalculation in the early part of the war with Iran, when he realized that he was in real trouble, he increased sharply the degree to which opponents of his were arrested and tortured. He also at the same time, increased his subventions to the Shia church in Iraq, the church which contains the majority of the population and which he had previously rather moderately supressed.[27] Both of these measures were sensible.

It has sometimes been argued, incidently, that a dictator who decides to make consession to public oppinion, i.e., do things he thinks will make him popular, had better increase his level of repression at the same time. The populace and, for that matter, members of his own government, are apt to take concession made by him to any group, and particularly the public, as a sign of weakness and hence try to replace him. In the long run, the concessions may pay off in terms of greater security, but their short run effect may well be the reverse. The short run negative effect can be cancelled out by increased repression.

The problem here is that the individual dictator attempting to use his power for policy purposes, may in fact, have little or no policy effect. There are several reasons for this, the first of which is that he may in fact be trying to increase his popularity with various groups. This would mean that he would tend to select policies that are favored by other people. As we have said above, its likely the dictator does not have very strong policy preferences of his own if he had he would not have risen to high rank so using his policy power to: a) get the satisfaction of giving orders and b) make friends, its likely to be something that he thinks is a good idea.

Further, when he does try to do something which is 'good', regardless of its effect on the people around him he has a problem that he probably doesn't know what is 'good'. He is normally not a trained economist or political scientist, he isn't even, as a general rule, capable of recognizing a good economist from a poor one. He is likely to simply pick up what ever ideas happen to be current and fashionable in his society and apply them. Thus he is very likely to adopt policies which would have been adopted by a democracy or,for that matter, the preceeding dictator who he overthrew. This is probably the reason that it is statistically so extremely difficult to tell dictatorships from democracies by their policy output. There is a great deal of variance in the policy output of both dictatorships and democracies and it tends to occupy much the same issue space simply because to a large extent it depends on the same collection of basic ideas, fads, foibles, etc.

As general summary, the advantage to the dictator of being dictator is that he is able to get his desires carried out to a quite large extent. His desire for security cannot ever be fully satisfied, in other respects he can have a very high living standard. Not as high as a hereditary monarch, but still very high. He has considerable power to see to it that the people around him at least express friendship and admiration for him and can do various things which will make it likely that the populace will like him, at least to some extent.[28] It can also have considerable effect on what we might refer to as the grand policy of his country. Normally however, he won't have very strong ideas as to what that should be and is apt to end up giving orders which are rather similar to those which would be given by any other dictator or for that matter passed by a democratic legislature. Looking at it briefly, its a good life but apt to be a short one.

NOTES

1. By the summer of 1826, the Janissaries were a powerful force basically independent of the Sultan. Mahmud II prepared an ambush for the Janissaries in which hidden cannons deciminated their ranks with grapeshot: This was the

culmination of an elaborate conspiracy which might easily have failed. See Kinross 1977, pp. 456-457.

2. Passing whims on his part can frequently be bypassed in various ways.

3. A dictator will normally have a living standard which is sharply higher than that of anyone else in the government. Conspicous displays of truely great wealth however, are unusual too.

4. On the very affluent life-styles of Soviet rulers – palaces, unlimited open bank accounts, etc., – see Voslensky 1984, pp. 225-228.

5. I do not read Serbo-Croatian, so I am accepting the word of Professor Svetosvar Pejovich here.

6. It is extremely interesting to make an effort to approximate the foreign investments by dictators in the modern era. Thus banks are unlikely to make their books open to the investigator, but examination of how well the dictators lives after he leaves, when he gets away, would be a suitable substitute.

7. In 1946 dollars.

8. In 1919 or 20, Lenin's secretary saw records of a large cache of diamonds secreted in the Kremlin for use by Lenin and his immediate entourage should they fall from power. See Tolstoy, 1981, p. 58. Fainsod (1958, p. 157) reports that in 1922 a large hoard of gold was hidden in Smolensk for use by the Bolsheviks should they be forced to flee abroad.

9. Sterne, Laurence, *A Sentimental Journey Through France and Italy*, London: Simpkin, Marshall, Hamilton, Kent and Co., 1937.

10. There were seven prisoners in the late Spring of 1789. Four were forgers, one was a mentally unbalanced Irishman who alternately believed himself Julius Caesar and God, and was accused of being a spy; another, also deranged, suspected of being involved in a plot to assassinate the king; and the last was a young man imprisoned at the request of his family for incest. See Hibbert 1980, p. 72.

11. On Franco's relatively benign dictatorship, see Johnson 1983, pp. 608-609. On Louis XIV, see Hibbert 1980.

12. Bismark instituted his national social insurance scheme to limit the political gains of the pro-union and pro-welfare state social democrats. See Hoborn 1982, pp. 291-293. He also may have wanted to provide some centralized structure to the German Empire which at that time was a very loose federation.

13. After Deng came to power in 1978, the Peking *People's Daily* apologized to readers for 'all lies and distortions' it had carried during the Mao era. On this and the movement away from central planning under Deng, see Johnson 1983, p. 566.

14. When Atlee came to power in 1945, he wanted Britain to disarm, decolonize, make friends with Russia and build a welfare state. See Johnson 1983, p. 966. On the policy changes brought about by Thatcher see Hare and Kirby, 1984.

15. Actually, the American Civil War was precipitated by secession of the Southern states in *anticipation* of Lincoln's policy reorientation.

16. Plato apparently incurred the wrath of the Syracusan despot Dionysius I by lecturing him on his philosophical responsibility. See Cornford 1945, p. xxvii.

17. Grampp (1960, vol. 1, p. 98) argues that the stoic philosophy of Marcus Aurelius offered no unambiguous principles of guidance to rulers or anyone else; its principal structure was basically 'do whatever is necessary'.

18. Pinochet actually adopted a somewhat similar program. He permitted any foreign airline that wished to fly into Chile and charge what ever fares they wanted. It turned out that the Chilean airline was in fact able to improve efficiency and meet the competition.

19. See Tollison and McCormick's work on Mercantilism. *Mercantilism as a Rent Seeking Society: Regulation in Historican Perspective*, Robert B. Ekelund and Robert D. Tollison, College Station, Texas: Texas A & M Press, 1981.

20. A great deal of money was spent by kings to bribe members of Parliament. For example, George II spend over £117,000 on bribery in 1734. See Namier 1961, p. 195.

21. I have a paper which will be published in an upcoming book in which I argue that the reason for the development of the general freedom in England was in essence that the English government was incapable of establishing these specialized monopolies, because of a constitutional weakness in its structure. This is of course for the period from the English civil war to let us say, 1800. For the next century they seem to have been convinced that an open economy was a good idea.

22. About 15,000 NKVD troops were permantly stationed in Moscow as Stalin's body guard. See Tolstoy 1981, p. 52.

23. Periodically the privileges of certain high ranking communists became publicized in the U.S.S.R., apparently by opponents in various power struggles. For example, a dramatic 'corruption' scandal took place in 1970 when the lifestyle and real income of the First Secretary of Azerbaijan were revealed by a rival, who subsequently received the lucrative post himself. See Voslensky, 1984, p. 190.

24. On Lenin, see Fitzpatrick 1982, pp. 23-26. On Khomeni, see Bakhash 1984, pp. 19-27.

25. See Bakhash 1984, esp. pp. 32-51.

26. See Johnson 1983, pp. 51-57.

27. On Hassan's various repressive measures, see Marr 1985, pp. 303-305.

28. The Shah after he was overthrown pointed out that the serious rioting against him had started in a town in which six months before he had been welcomed by gigantic and enthusiastic crowds.

CHAPTER VII

Becoming a dictator

So far we have devoted our attention mainly to what happens after the dictator gets in power. We now turn to how to get power. This may seem a perverse way of dealing with the problem since obviously they become dictator before they are faced with the problem of retaining power, but for analytical reasons it's easier. The basic problem faced by a young man who wants to be dictator is the existing dictator himself. Hence unless we are fairly well informed about the defenses that that dictator may have, we're not in a position to discuss the rise to rank of such a man as Sgt. Doe[1] of Liberia.

As I trust the previous chapters have convinced the reader, the life of a potential dictator is not an easy one. He runs a very large risk of being neutralized or even killed. Further, even if he is successful in overthrowing the dictator, the chances that some colleague of his will become the successor rather than he himself is by no means zero. We closed the last chapter on the dictator by pointing out that he lived an insecure life even if a luxurious one. the man trying to overthrow the dictator does not have a high current living standard to set off against the even greater risks. He is, in essence, making an investment, laying his life quite literally on the line in hopes of a better future.

Because of this extremely risky aspect of the matter, it is not likely that very many who eventually become dictator started out in life with that as a conscious objective. Probably they simply were attempting to rise to high rank in the existing system, but then later took advantage of opportunities that opened up.

A rise to high rank normally means literally rising in the governmental hierarchy, whether on the military side or the civilian[2] Sometimes, however, the rise can be completely out side the formal government. Granted the history of China, probably every single bandit chief in the last 500 years has dreamt at least faintly of eventually becoming emperor. Chang Tso-Lin in the 1920's came very very, close.[3] Historically Nurhachi and Genghis Khan both started out as something between a bandit leader and the leader of a tiny tribe, in both cases mustering less than ten fighting men.[4] Although neither himself became Emperor of China they both built powerful dynasties which eventually conquered China. In the case of Genghis Khan of course, it also conquered much of Europe and the Middle East.[5]

But these are exceptions. More normally, a potential ruler rises in a functioning government of some size. He may of course, eventually, like Napoleon, massively expand that government,[6] but it is rare that he literally starts with nothing and then acquires great status by military means. Rising within a government structure is a far commoner first step. It was of course the way Napoleon rose.

Although rising within the government structure is the normal route, there may well be a major deviation. The current dictator of Uganda, Milton Obote, was put in power by Nyerere the dictator of Tanzania.[7] There are a number of other people in the present day world who have achieved dictatorial power in the same way. Kim Il-Sung of North Korea entered North Korea in the baggage train of the Red Army.[8] With quite clever maneuvering between the Chinese and the Russians he has actually succeeded in obtaining a status of an independent dictator.[9] Such men as Jeralzuski of Poland on the other hand, although of course appointed by outsiders cannot really be regarded as dictators. He is more akin to a provincial governor.[10] At best his status would be that of one of the Indian Rajas in the days of the British Empire.[11] He has a good deal of power to deal with local matters as long as he doesn't do anything which offends his masters too much. Kim Il-Sung on the other hand really has a good deal of genuine independence.[12]

In the former French Empire, the French government has been keeping people in power, or putting them in power for some time.[13] Nyerere himself was temporarily overthrown a number of years ago but that was back in the days when the British maintained an aircraft carrier in the Indian Ocean and a British expeditionary force with great promptness put him back in power. The whole thing was over within twenty four hours.[14]

I've chosen to talk about this particular situation using only present day examples but anybody who is at all familiar with history knows that it is a fairly common phenomena. Further, people appointed from outside quite frequently have genuine independence. They're usually appointed by the outside power rather than the outside power directly taking over the government because there is some reason why the outside power does not want to take over the government. In the case of the Communist Empire in Eastern Europe of course, the Russians did want to control its Empire, but thought that for political reasons there should be at least some kind of thin camouflage over that control.[15]

Nyerere on the other hand, clearly does not himself, want to run Uganda. He'd be delighted to have a government there which is strong enough so that it doesn't require any support from him. Of course he does not want an unfriendly government there, but basically he doesn't care very much what goes on inside Uganda and is quite willing to establish an independent power.[16] But one must be careful not to exaggerate here. Milton Obote, the present dictator of Uganda, is the third one appointed by Nyerere who became unhappy with his two previous choices.[17]

More normally the outside power which has established somebody as dictator has at least some ideas as to what he should do and may take action if he doesn't but will give the dictator a great deal of freedom. The Communist puppet rulers are decidely an exception from the norm.

Note that the person who is brought in from outside to be a dictator, is in most cases somebody who has risen to quite high rank inside the government to which he eventually becomes dictator and then has had difficulties which lead him to flee abroad. The old fashioned international law prinicples of asylum under which political enemies of your neighbors were given protection within your borders started not out of humanitarian motives but precautionary. It was always helpful to have somebody within your borders who could get support within your neighbors country in the event you had difficulty with them. The younger brother of the Emir now ruling your neighbor was as much a part of your armament as a division of infantry.

A recent illustration of this concerns the Ayatolla Khomeni. He was expelled from Iran and promptly went to Iraq which had very, very bad relations with Iran. He had been there a number of years in a position of respect and with a reasonable income until Iran and

Iraq's relations improved. As part of his moves to improve relations with the Shah of Iran, Hassan dictator of Iraq, simply deported the Ayatolla. Khomeni has never forgiven him.[18]

All of this is typical and represents the traditional view of the asylum institution. It is not infrequent that an ambitious young man will rise to high rank in his own government find it necessary to hastily go abroad and later return to become dictator either directly with the support of a foreign army or by organizing a coup or revolution from his foreign refuge without much in the way of aid from the foreign country concerned.

To repeat this route to power normally requires acquiring in one way or another a position of considerable prestige and general importance within the country before taking off for foreign climes. Further, if the individual is to be an effective dictator he must retain considerable influence within the country so that when he returns (whether he returns with a foreign army or at the head of a group of his own supporters) he will be able to set up a government of which he in fact is dictator. He must both be effective inside his own country's governmental machine and a good diplomat in dealing with foreigners. Fortunately, as a rough rule of thumb the same set of personal attributes which will lead to success in one area will lead to success in the other so this is not too difficult a task.

The person who has fled the country and is now engaging in intrigues to come back has a number of disadvantages due to his foreign location. He has at least one advantage: He can openly state his desire to overthrow the government and install himself as dictator.[19] An individual who stays within the country and attempts to rise to high rank does, in general, conceal his ultimate ambitions. Since coups far more commonly originate from officials within the government than from exiles abroad, its obvious that this disadvantage although real is not overwhelming.

There is another way to the top which does not involve working one's way up through the bureaucracy whether military or civil, but it's a very unusual one. We have not yet turned to the problem of succession to the dictator, but as a general proposition rulers do not like to have anybody around them who is their official successor. The reason is that they quite reasonable regard such an official successor as a risk to themselves. In consequence, it is frequently true that there is no official 'Crown Prince' in any given dictatorship.[20]

Death of a dictator under these circumstances provides an opportunity for many ambitious men and it is by no means obvious that the one who wins will always be somebody who is a high official in the regime. The previous dictator may have been carefully weeding out all people who he thought were strong aggressive, etc., from his higher officials with the result that there's no one there who really is capable of holding his own against a strong outsider. Dr. Francia, of Paraguay, was in some ways the worst of a absolutely awful array of dictators that ruled South America in the early nineteenth century.[21] When he died, Lopez, a complete outsider turned out to be in a better position to seize control than anyone else.[22] There have been occasional cases where somewhat the same thing has occured while the dictator is still alive. This is however, though possible, not a very common phenomenon. In any event, the outsider who comes in by this route has to engage in much the same kind of behavior as an insider would.

Another kind of government outsider is the leader of some non-governmental but powerful group, most commonly, a tribe or possibly a sub-nation within a country. In this case his rise to power normally takes the form of actual fighting. This is on the whole uncommon historical simply because the existing dictator knowing that there are these risks does his best to see to it there's no one in that kind of position. I say it's uncommon, but that's not to say that it never exists. What I would call the romantic revolution, people rising up under wise and noble leaders to overthrow a corrupt dictatorship would be a special example of this kind of thing, but it seems to be extremely rare historically.

We're thus left with the normal way in which somebody rises to a dictatorship in South America, Africa, etc.; a coup or attempted coup which we observe in South America, Africa and Asia with such regularity. Note that this coup normally is set off by fairly high members of the regime. Note also, that they are more likely to turn out to be attempted coup than coup, if we look at the actual figures. There is another even more commmon phenomenon in which the dictator announces that there was a plot and punishes the 'plotters' but in which there is at least some doubt that anything happened at all. Dictators are apt to be extremely suspicious men and may well misinterpet completely innocent activity for a plot. They also may feel that they want to get rid of certain of their officials and find that inventing a completely false plot is a good way of doing it.

Certainly most of the high officials killed by Stalin were not plotting against him and the Doctors plot[23] which he apparently was in train of setting off when he died was also completely imaginary.[24] Since he was a paranoid, its possible he believed in the plots, but it's certainly equally possible that he simply regarded them as a convenienent tool.

Having risen to a high position, one might simply aim at succession to the existing dictator when he dies or as ocassionally happens retires.[25] Sadat, of Egypt, is of course an example[26] as is Joaquin Balaguer, President of Dominican Republic after Trujillo.[27]

It is notable that these two people, and as far as I know the other cases where the same kind of thing has happened, were in the position of official followers of the existing dictator[28] because they were thought to be harmless. They had risen to high rank as complete 'yes men' in the case of Sadat and Joaquin Balaguer. Moi as a member of a minor tribe was thought not to have an adequate political position.[29]

As it turned out, all three of these people were actually strong personalities. When the dictator was gone, they turned out to be rather competent and strong people. In the case of Joaquin Balaguer, this is particularly remarkable because after the death of Trujillo, he ruled as a democratic leader with the elections in which he was elected subject to very extensive foreign observation.[30] His previous record certainly would not have led most observers to expect this. He had been so completely devoted to Trujillo, that when Trujillo decided to spend two years as a Dominican Republic Ambassador to the United Nations he appointed Joaquin Balaguer, President of Dominican Republic.[31] This took a great deal of apparently completely justified faith on the part of Trujillo that Joaquin Balaguer was completely under his control.

This route to power is certainly one which could be successfully followed by only very very few people. Historically it is not particularly common. Sadat, Balaguer, and Moi are exceptions. Normally when a dictator dies there's no official successor and we have an undignified squabble for power. Once again, the problem of succession and ways of avoiding this squabble will be discussed below.

Normally, an existing dictator is overthrown in a coup or civil war. The people who overthrow him are high, although not necessarily the highest, officials of his own government. In most cases the dictator does not last a very long time, five years would probably be par for the course, although there are individuals who last twenty or thirty years. Sometimes they go on and set up a dynasty. In the more normal case, however, most of the high officials were also at least medium high officials in the government of the current dictator's predecessor and rose to their high rank as a result of the overthrow of the predecessor. Thus everybody, the dictator and all of his officials, are fully aware of the possibility of such a coup.

We will not here discuss the early period of the rise to prominence of somebody who starts in the government apparatus at the bottom. I've written a previous book[32] on rising in the bureaucracy and so I will assume that the reader can turn to that, or for that matter to any one, of the large number of books on this general topic, if he is curious. Rising in a dictatorship where the dictator is periodically removed by somebody else is of course somewhat different than rising in a more peaceful bureaucracy. The principles however, are the same, I will not trouble the reader here with repetition. It's only when the bureaucrat gets to a fairly high rank that the special problem of coup and potential coup begins to impinge on his career prospects.

A high ranking official in South America, Africa, or Asia can feel fairly confident that during his career there will be one or perhaps many cases of attempted coup, successful coup, and those cases where the dictator decides to denounce a plot even if there is no actual plot there. Further, he can feel fairly confident that the existing dictator will in any event be sufficiently nervous about his inferiors so that he shifts them around a good deal.

Under the circumstances, he has to develop a sort of general policy with respect to such coups and this policy of necessity must contain a fairly large component of opportunism. That he should not join a coup which seems fore ordained to failure, but should join one that is certain to win is obvious. The problem with this rule however, is that he is unlikely to be particularly rewarded for joining after it becomes clear who is going to win. The high payoffs are for the people who enter into a coup in the early days before its obvious who will win, or who loyally support the dictator against a coup when it is not at all obvious that the coup will lose. Thus, both careful calculation and a willingness to take major gambles are necessary for the successful official at this rank.

Once again the life is a luxurious one although, of course, not as luxurious as the dictator's life, and a risky one. There's no reason for us to feel sorry for these high ranking officials in such dangerous positions, because after all they've chosen their own career path. Nevertheless, it's easy to see why in most of these dictatorships there are a fairly large number of highly talented men who strenously avoid all political activity. The businessman who finds it necessary regularly to pay large bribes to government officials may rather resent paying the bribes. He is probably aware, however, that the government officials to whom he pays the bribes sometimes change abruptly. He is normally not personally interested in joining in this highly paid lottery.

There is another problem with respect to the coup which is that even if the coup is successful, it's by no means obvious at the time that it is organized and carried off, who will end up at the top. Prime Minister Ben Youssef Ben Khedda was the man who basically ran the revolution against the French in Algeria. He also signed the final treaty with them. He almost immediately lost power and eventually died in an Algerian prison.[33] Many, many people who have been involved in the kind of high politics that involves a coup, have had similar histories.

Note that there's no safe way out of this problem. There's no conservative way of simply holding your position without, either joining in the squabble on one side or the other. Even though you may have been neutral and hence made no enemies, whoever wins will want to reward his faithful followers. Thus, you may be removed, not because anybody particularly dislikes you, but because somebody else wants to be Secretary of the Treasury.[34]

As a rough rule of thumb, anyone who rises to really high rank must be planning on following a rather opportunist course of action. This may in fact be one reason for refusing promotion. I was told by a member of the British Intelligence Service that in Russia under Stalin, you normally found that the brightest and most competent man in any given factory was not the manager, but the deputy. He normally had refused several opportunities to acquire the much larger prestige and income of a manager because it also involved a much larger chance of going to Vorkuta.

But we are interested in the people who actually do make it to the top and that necessarily means we must be interested in only people who do try. Of course, many of the people who try don't make it and the man entering into this particularly risky way of making a living must be aware of the fact that the odds are against him.

The problem is, of course, particularly difficult because everyone will be watching him with the intent of guarding against him. The dictator is worried about cliques and powerful men immediately under him. The people immediately under the dictator are looking for allies but not for superiors. In other words, they hope to rise in the world by a coup and on the whole would like to become the new dictator themselves. They look for supporters, and in general, do not look for a position as a supporter of someone else. There is of course, an exception to the latter category among people who feel that at the moment in any event they have no chance to be dictator, hence simply a promotion either through helping install a new dictator, or eliminating a plot so that a number of their superiors are removed by an existing dictator is a sensible course of action.

One thing that is frequently discussed in this area and which I believe is almost never found in reality, is a carefully laid plot. The trouble with a carefully laid plot, is that too many people have to know about it. Even literally discussing a coup with one or two persons is dangerous. On the whole, the high ranking politician must try to get into a position where he can quickly assume a position of control or at the very least take a position on one side or another of a coup without first constructing an apparatus which could betray him.

There is an exception to the above rule in those cases in which coup and attempted coup are perfectly ordinary parts of life, as for example, South America. It seems likely that most South American armies are so accustomed to coup that the potential of overthrowing the government or supporting it would be a rather ordinary topic of conversation in the officers' mess. Although this is true enough, the very highest military officers had better not engage in this kind of conversation. It's not possible for the dictator to get rid of the bulk of the junior officer corp, but he can always make his chief of staff Ambassador to Australia.

What the ambitious man should attempt to do is to convince all of the other high ranking officials that he is a very competent man. Competence in this case does not mean necessarily, that they would regard him as a good lawyer even though his present position may be a legal one. It means that they think of him as a man who is good at intrigue, tough, aggressive, etc., and likely to win.

At the time that he is attempting to develop this reputation among his co-high officials, he should be trying to convince the dictator that really he is not a significant menace. This looks impossible and certainly it is very hard. Nevertheless, he only has to look like a man of average safety to the dictator and more likely to win to the other high officials than anyone else. All of whom have been selected by the dictator for having only this rather limited amount of ability.

If possible, the individual should develop relations with others such that they are apt to on the whole accept his leadership. Once again, this is a dangerous matter, because it may tend to frighten the dictator. Trying to convince the dictator that you are a complete 'yes' man and the other officials of the dictator that you're a tough man who is likely to win in a fight is an extremely difficult task.

Let it be said here, that success may be dangerous. The number of generals who have been removed from office and possibly killed because they have been conspicuously successful and hence threaten the dictator and king is very large indeed. This is the reason that traditional kings always led their own armies. They might not be very good generals, but at least they can trust themselves. The switch to using professional generals, first in France and then in the rest of Europe was one of the harbringers of the restriction of royal power. Hitler, Stalin, and Mao Su Dung all commanded their own armies.[35]

We earlier talked about the desirablility of rotation, collective responsibility, etc., on the part of dictators who are attempting to keep the possibility of a coup or revolution down. Looked at from the standpoint of the man trying to rise, they are clearly elements which impede his rise. It should be kept in mind however, that they also impede the rise of anyone else. He is competing with the existing dictator for power, but he is also competing with other higher officials for the succession. The measures taken by the dictator which make it harder for him to overthrow the dictator, handicap the others just as much as he. He suffers no differential disadvantage.

But if he cannot engage in plotting and if building up a personal train is difficult, what are the things he can do? Clearly, he must convince other people that he would be a suitable replacement without frightening the dictator. Since, everyone who he must convince knows the danger of frightening the dictator they are apt to calculate correctly that a man who appears to be a total 'yes' man may in fact be very strong and independent.

The final act in any plot to overthrow the dictator is a coup, or what is in South America called a Pronunciamento. It is simply a statement, apparently backed by great force, that the dictator is to be releaved of his power because he is corrupt, etc., and above all weaker than the man or group making the statement. The Pronunciamento, is almost of necessity, sudden and not very well prepared because preparations will almost certainly come to the attention of the dictator.

This last is not absolutely certain. There appear to be some dictators who come to the conclusion that they simply cannot win and hence don't remove the dangers to them. Caetano, in his memoirs, says he read Spinola's book, spending an entire night doing so and in the early morning when he put the book down realized that his dictatorship was going to fall. Why he did not take steps immediately to neutralize Spinola, and in fact made him Chief of Staff, is obscure. It may be simply that he, himself, was a rather weak man. He had of course, acquired the throne when Salizar became incapable.[36] But this is very unusual. Normally a dictator would have simply removed Spinola on realizing that he was a danger.

A Pronunciamento, is of course, dangerous. Normally, it requires seizing control of at least some part of the communication network and using this for the statement. Anything can go wrong at this time. The Duke of Essex failed to a considerable extent because the horses didn't arrive on time.[37] The General's plot against Hitler in 1944, terminated when a Lt. Colonel refused to believe orders from his superiors and made contact with Dr. Goebels, with the result that the appropriate orders were not transmitted.[38]

More commonly however, the Pronunciamento is at least made public and there is an immediate counter Pronunciamento by the dictator. If the dictator himself can be seized, which is sometimes possible, either through the conivence of his guard or the overwhelming of the guard by other military units this will normally finish the matter off although, there may be a counter coup by people who at least appear to be in support of the dictator, but who probably are more accurately described as enemies of the first group who want to have another man as dictator.

In all of this the odds are on the side of the dictator himself, simply because the communication procedures are always better on his side. In other words, its easier for him to give the impression that he will win than it is for his opponents to give the impression that they will win. To say that the odds are rather on his side does not of course mean that he will always win and indeed he doesn't.

Sometimes all of this goes wrong, but not wrong in the sense that the coup is simply put down; wrong in the sense that the coup succeeds in getting control of significant military forces, but not enough to take over the country as a whole immediately. The result can then be a long lasting civil war. This is the way the Spanish civil war of the 1930's started[39] and there have been a great many South American civil wars fought out along these lines. The English civil war of the 17th century was another example, the King left London, raised his standard in rebellion, and attracted enough military support to hold much of the country but not all and therefore too, there was a full dress war.[40] As can be seen, the problems from the standpoint of the man who wants to rise are very difficult. Further, so far in any event, I have been unable to find any good generalizations or testible hypothesis about the matter. Economists know the so called random walk hypothesis about the stock market, which holds that all available information is already incorporated in the market price with the result that that price or its recent movements have no predictive value. Something vaguely like it is important in the situation we have been describing. The dictator probably knows as much as anybody else does about his immediate inferiors. Thus if one of them appears to be in a position where he might be able to overthrow the dictator, this probably indicates that the dictator is about to get rid of him. Outside predictions of the future such as this are extremely difficult. The main point of my discussion above is to point out the predictions from the standpoint of an insider are at least as difficult. Further, if he wants not only to predict, but to take steps to improve his position it is even more difficult.

As we have said above, life at these elevated ranks is a risky business, but the compensation is apparently high enough so that many people are willing to take the risk. Looking at it,not as a competitor for power, but as an outside analyst however, we can rarely if every hope to know either what is going to happen, or even, in any certain way, what in fact did happen. Retrospective accounts of this kind of intrigue by different participants normally differ a good deal. It is likely that this comes not from any desire on the part of the various memorialists, to lie about the matter, but from the fact that they themselves didn't quite know what was going on. The situation is one where everybody is engaging in devious maneuvers and attempting to conceal at least part of his maneuvers from everyone else with the result that the true story is seldom known.

We've talked about this vague inchoate area where technical hypothesis are impossible I would like to now turn to one specific detail of the process where I believe I can make a prediction as to what will happen with quite a high level degree of accuracy. Sometimes the result of the overthrow of a ruler or for that matter his death will not be his immediate replacement by another dictator, but by a small group of people called in South America, a 'Junta'. The hypothesis which I think would survive most tests, is that this Junta will gradually change into a dictatorship by one person, normally a member of the original Junta although occasionally the process of change will involve the introduction of outsiders to the original Junta in replacement of various members who are leaving and one of those will win.

The historical evidence that this is what does happen in South America, is overwhelming. Indeed so far as I know, only the recent Argentine military government avoided this fate. In that case, the Junta remained a Junta right throughout the entire period with the result that strictly speaking one cannot call it a dictatorship. There was usually one member of the Junta who was more important than the others, but no one ever really acquired complete control and indeed members of the Junta retired in a rather routine way from time to time and were then replaced by other high ranking military officers.[41] This is an extremely unusual event and I know of no other case. A more common precedure is the shrinkage of the Junta to one man.

The same thing by the way will be found in communist countries. After the death of Lenin there was a period in which the politburo of the party actually was powerful and was only gradually replaced by Stalin.[42] After Stalin's death there was a small group, first three and then five members ruled collectively while Khruchev was maneuvering into absolute power.[43] When Khruchev himself was overthrown there was once again a collective leadership although not for very long since the Breznev in this case was able to establish complete power very quickly.[44]

Its hard to say what has been happening since the death of Breznev since Andropov and Chernenko died so quickly. Gorbachev has not yet ruled for very long.[45] One would suspect however, that with time, this custom will become one in which the period of collective leadership is extremely short indeed. This is simply because all of the members of the collective leadership will have noticed previous cases in which it became a single person dictatorship and hence will anticipate that and take steps to either become the dictator or become the supporter of the dictator right away.

Among communist states the phenomenon is not confined to Russia, of course. The same thing happened in China after the death of Mao.[46] Other communist countries are mainly not genuinely independent and who is dictator is presumably decided in Moscow. Provincial governor might be a better term than dictator. Albania and North Korea which are rather independent have not yet had a death of the ruling dictator,[47] and I regret to say that I simply don't know very much about the history of Yugoslavia since Tito died. Developements there are extremely complicated and don't seem to follow any particular fixed pattern.[48]

Empirically the Junta characteristically shrinks to one man,but how can we explain this theoretically? The following theory I actually developed on my own before looking into much of the empirical literature, although I must admit I knew that the Juntas became dictatorships quite commonly in South America. In a way it is thus half way between ad hoc explanation of previously known data and a hypothesis which I tested by looking up more South American history.

The theory is really quite simple. Suppose we have a group of five men who are currently ruling a country by some voting process. Each of them presumably would prefer to be dictator. Suppose that one[49] decides to take action to make himself dictator. Either he succeeds in which event the Junta has been condensed to one man or he fails. If he fails, the remainder of the Junta have their choice of removing him from the Junta[50] or leaving him in. If they leave him in they're obviously simply asking for further plots of the same sort either by him or by other methods of the junta who notice that there's no cost to such plotting. If they remove him on the other hand, they have shrunk the junta by one man.

This means that each of the others is now stronger, but it also means each of the others now feels he has a better chance of succeeding in becoming a sole dictator. It is true that they could remove the plotter and bring somebody else in from outside and occasionally that has been done, but this involves a failure on the part of the majority of the junta to take advantage of an opportunity of improving their power. To bring somebody in from outside who is intended to be merely formally a member of the junta but actually inferior to the existing members is a possibility. Historically however, such outside members have on occasion turned out to be strong enough so that they are a genuine risk to their sponsors. It can be seen that this process would tend over time to lead the junta into becoming just one man through the gradual exclusion of individuals who had failed in plotting or the success of an individual who had not.

There is another possible route to the same conclusion, suppose again a junta of five and suppose that three of them form a caucus. A caucus of course has to first make up its own mind as to what should be done and in essence if the group is still voting, it will itself become the dominant group. In other words, the real junta has shrunk from five to three. Within these three there are apt to be two who tend to vote with each other more often than each with the third and that involves a still further reduction in size. All of this once again, makes it more likely that some individual will either take over as a result of the gradual shrinkage of the effective ruling group within the junta or through taking advantage of the strong position to remove the remainder of the junta.

Altogether, a small voting body in control of the government does not seem a stable situation. Note that it is totally different from a committee within a legal structure. The board of directors of a corporation which appoints an executive committee does not jeapordize its own potential control since the courts would enforce any decision the majority of the board against that committee. Within a group ruling an absolute government however, there is no external court to enforce such a rule. Thus small groups tend to reduce to one.

Earlier I defined democracy in a situation where quite a large number make decisions by voting. I didn't give any absolute number, but discussion of the condensation of the junta will explain what I had in mind. A group of five or six hundred people voting can readily afford to throw out some subset which attempts to overthrow the voting body. This would be true even if that subset were quite large. Thus historically such large voting groups have tended to be relatively stable where as the small ruling group, the junta, has tended to rather rapidly turned into a dictatorship.

In this chapter we complete our discussion of the internal functioning of a dictatorship. I wish that I had been able to provide a more rigorously testable theory, but what you have now read is what I have. To repeat what I've said before, I hope that this will inspire other people to do the research which eventually will produce a really rigorous theory of dictatorship.

Regardless of that point, there are a number of aspects of dictatorship's dealings with society which we have not yet dealt with. In a way, we have been talking about the micro politics of the dictatorship and will now turn to the macro politics.

NOTES

1. General Samuel K. Doe assumed the presidency on April 12, 1980 following a pre-dawn coup by Army enlisted men. The existing regime was charged with the general crime of 'rampant corruption' by the attacking soldiers, and the raid produced the death of then Liberian Head of State Tolbert. *The New York Times*, April 13, 1980, p. 1.

2. Africian dictators who are civilians are commoner than those who are military men. In South America, the reverse is true. See Mair, 1977, and Pothelm, 1979; and for example Wheatcroft, 1983 respectively. In African societies, apparent control over environmental threats (drought, disease, etc) rather than military oponents has often served as the catalyst for a rise to power. In Rwanda, for example, tribal rulers have been popularly held 'to have ritual powers; they controlled the weather, causing the rain to fall at the right time and not in excessive quantities, and they combated disasters such as locust invasion. Such powers were... an inseparable element in the quality of chiefliness.' (Mair, 1977, p. 25, See also, Potholm, 1979, pp. 28-31.)

3. Chang Tso-Lin, a well known warlord of nothern China dominated the region of Manchuria from 1920 to 1928. At times he ran the area virtually as a distinct country, independently negotiating treaties with foreign governments. For example, he conquered Peking (1925-26) and claimed the title of 'Grand Marshall' of China, despite the fact that southern China was not under his control Revolutionary forces from the south toppled him from power in the 'Northern Expedition' (1928). (Sheridan, 1975, pp. 61-65. See also, Sheridan, 1966). It might be noted that there is some dispute about whether Chang himself was a practicing 'bandit', or was merely 'accused of banditry only because the local defense unit he commanded was not part of the regular military establishment.' (Sheridan, 1975, p. 63).

4. On Nurhachi's modest beginnings, see Morton, 1980, pp. 138-9; Rodzinski, 1984, p. 156; Wakeman, 1975, pp. 75-79. Temuchin (Genghis Khan's originally-given name) 'came from a family of hereditary leaders but had to work long and hard to reach a position of power, since his father had been killed [when Temuchin was] a boy.' (Morton, 1980, p. 116.)

5. See Dupuy and Dupuy, 1970, pp. 336-345; Bjorklund, Holmboe, and Rohr, 1962, Map ±42. So efficient were Genghis Kahn's techniques that they were carefully studied by German Staff officers prior to the Second World War. (Crofts and Buchanan, 1958, p. 39.).

6. 'Absolutism' is a term frequently used to describe the extent of government controls under Napoleon Bonaparte's rule as emporer of France (1804-1815). For details of the economic and social regulations he instituted see, Ward, Protero, and Leathes, 1907, pp. 141-2; Blum, Cameron and Barnes, 1970, pp. 494-7, 503-4. Napoleon went so far as to regulate for example, the numbers and types of theatrical companies each city and town was to be allowed. (Ward, Prothero, and LEathes, 1907, pp. 129-130.)

7. See *The New York Times*, April 4, 1981, p. 3; *The New York Times*, April 29, p. 5; *The New York Times*, June 14, 1984, p. 25; *The New York Times*, July 1, 1981, p. 5.

8. His return by rail followed a period (beginning in 1943) of extensive indoctrination in the Soviet Union. See Ridgeway, 1972, p. 9; Han, 1970, p. 499.

9. See Han, 1970, pp. 500-504.

10. See Nelson, 1983, pp. 290-291; Dziewandoski, 1977, p. 233-236; Davies, 1984, passim; Carrere d'Encausse, 1980, pp. 343-346.

11. On the British 'Raj' in India, see Gipson, 1942, pp. 231ff.

12. See Han, 1970, passim.

13. See Dunnigan and Bay, 1985, pp. 130-138.

14. See Johnson, 1983, p. 528.

15. *Ibid*, pp. 76-77, 710-711.

16. *The New York Times*, August 26, 1981, p. 1, provides a summary of the last three successive Ugandan regimes, Nyerere has had a hand in installing.

17. Iraqi President Admad Hasan al Bakr expelled Khomeni from his country (to Paris) in early October, 1975. (Nyrop, 1979, p. 215).

18. It might be better for him to say the he proposes to overthrow a government and install a democrac., I doubt that very many people are deceived.

19. There are of course notable exceptions to this rule. See *The Washington Post*, June 27, 1985, p. 1, on the relevant transfer of power in North Korea.

20. See Dupuy and Dupuy, 1920, p. 814.

21. See Dupuy and Dupuy, 1921, p. 910-911.

22. See Tolstoy, 1981, p. 354.

23. *Ibid*, pp. 51-57, provides an account of the extreme precautions Stalin took to avoid attempts on his life.

24. Sometimes when he retires he will apt to set up a democratic government rather than a dictatorial one. This will be dealt with below. President Omar Torrijos Herrera of Panama, for example, retired as head of government in October, 1978 and was immediately replaced by President Aristides Royo. (Nyrop, 1980, p. 136) Despite his official retirement, however, Torrijos retained a large share of supreme power in his country until 1980. (p. 133).

25. Upon his death by heart attack on September 28, 1970, Egyptian President General Gamal Abdul Nasser was smoothly followed by his successor a then vice-President, Sadat. Sadat was installed as president the following day. (See for example, Hirst and Beeson, 1981).

26. Rafael Trujillo resigned as president of the Dominican Republic on April 1, 1962, and was succeeded by his hand-picked vice president, Dr. Joaquin Balaguer in August of that year. (Crassweller, 1966, 00. 273,375-377.) Trujillo assumed the presidency of anohter institution, the Central Bank, during his reign. By no mere coincidence were outstanding loans of $38 million borrowed by Trujillo's sugar company suddenly 'repaid' at about the same time. (p. 380).

27. Also Moi of Kenya.

28. See Crassweller, 1966, pp. 375.

29. *Ibid*, p. 377.

30. The *Politics of Bureaucracy*, Public Affairs Press, Washington, 1965.

31. This is of course characteristic also of democratic politics, He who follows the policy of neutrality in a presidental election is unlikely to retain his job. Secretary Forrestal, of course, was a very, very prominent example. On the career of James V. Forrestal, Secretary of Defense (1947-49), see for example Batchelder, 1961, pp. 197ff.

32. In the case of Mao Su Dung, this was rather concealed. In China the position of a general is not one of great prestige, so he always maintained a opium sodden senile wreck of a professional general called Chu Teh, as the formal commander of the army. He, himself was chairman of the committee that dealt with the army. No one in the army however, was deceived by the arrangement. Possibly some intellectuals outside were. When Chu Teh assumed the post of Commander of the People's Liberation Army in 1969 he was 84. On Mao's effective control of the Army, see Domes, 1985, p. 113.

33. Professor Marcello Caetano took over as the new Prime Minister of Portugal on September 25, 1968, after Salazar suffered a stroke (September 6) and could no longer perform the duties of that office. (See Kay, 1970, pp. 413-416; Marques, 1972, pp. 223-224) Salazars condition and the subsequent change in power was brought on by a freak accident; a chair collapsed under him, and his head hit the ground, producing a blood clot in his brain. (Marque p. 224.)

34. On Robert Devereux, 2nd Earl of essex, his failed attempt at a coup to install himself as King (February 8, 1601), and subsequent exectuion by Queen Elizabeth I, see Blum, Cameron and BArnes, 1970, p. 171; or Harris and Levey, 1975, p. 893.

35. It's also sometimes said that the fact that General Beck turned up for the coup wearing civilian clothes rather than a uniform was of some significance. In any event, of course, the fact that Hitler had not actually been killed would probably have scuppered it even if these other difficulties had not occurred. See FitzGibbon, 1956, p. 210.

36. See Johnson, 1983, pp. 321ff.

37. Actually two full dress wars, there was an intermediate period of peace. On the other hand, the restoration of the Stuarts after the death of Oliver Cromwell, was a more classical and quick affair with substantially no military opposition. See Cantor, 1967, pp. 412-433; Trevelyan, 1953, pp. 184-198.

38. See Paxton, 1983, p. 90.

39. See Fitzpatrick, 1984, pp. 98-102.

40. On the development of the collective leadership between Stalin's death in March, 1953, and Kruschev's assumption of effective control in early 1955, see Dmytryshyn, 1984, pp. 265-273.

41. Although about a year and a half separated the coup against Kruschev in October 1964 and Brechnev's appointment as General Secretary of the Communist Party in March-April 1966, the latter had assumed an increasingly dominant position in the collective leadership beginning with a month of Kruschev's ouster, and shortly thereafter was for all intents and purposes sole leader. See Dmytryshyn, 1984, pp. 334-336.

42. Andropov died in February, 1984, after a brief 15-month rule. See *The Washington Post*, July 28, 1985, p.1, for details on the recent regimes of Andropov and Chernenko.

43. What was essentially a collective leadership arose after Mao's death in 1976, in which Hua Kuo-Feng emerged as 'first among equals' as the Chairman of the Chinese Communist Party. But by late 1980 another member of this collective leadership, Teng Hsiao-Ding, assumed effective control after defeating Hua in a bloodless power struggle. Interestingly, Teng refrained from naming himself Chairman. See Domes, 1985, pp. 116-176.

44. Albania's dictator, Enver Hoxha, did recently expire, and he hand-picked (before death, of course) his successor, Ramiz Alia. See *The Washington Post*, August 8, 1985, p. A27.

45. Since Tito's death, Yugoslavia has remained nominally without an acknowledged individual ruler, with the politburo ostensibly forming a collective leadership. On the decisions leading to this post-Tito organization, see Stankovic, 1981, pp. 104-110.

46. Possibly two.

47. Perhaps by that most permenant of methods, a firing squad.

CHAPTER VIII

The problem of succession

So far we have dealt with a dictator who is insecure with people who are trying to replace him. Dictators do grow old however, and their replacement through death or, rarely, through retirement, is a real problem. As we shall see below, the long run solution to this problem is usually development of hereditary rulership which we call 'king' or 'emperor' rather than 'dictator'. Before turning to this problem however, we should examine the more general situation in which a tradition of passing the throne through one line is not yet established.

Consider then a dictator who is getting elderly and realizes that he is not long for this world. We shall begin by assuming that he is not proposing to retire although he may wish to lighten his work load to some extent by shoving some of his responsibilities onto someone else. We also assume that he is in fact concerned about the status of his country after he dies. Note this concern doesn't have to be very strong. Most of us are, to some extent, interested in the public good, but more interested on ourselves. The dictator presumably, normally hopes that his country will continue running well after he is dead, but he is likely to give this hope and actions to make it likely that it will eventuate less priority than avoiding assassination.

The basic problem that the dictator faces here is that if he formally anoints a successor, this gives that successor both strong motives for assassinating him and reasonable security that he will get away with it. Obviously the sooner the successor becomes dictator in his own right the better from his standpoint and shortening the life of the current dictator is an obvious way of speeding up the succession. Secondly, and this I believe is more important, there is always the possibility that the current dictator will change his mind. A man who has spent the bulk of his life in one of these dictatorial polities and observed the dictator continuiously engaging in the type of protective activity we have discussed above would feel relatively little security in his position as an official successor. He may remember the time when he had been Minister of War and suddenly found himself Ambassador to France. A similar sharp change with somebody else becoming official successor is surely something which he thinks is reasonably likely.

Thus he has a strong motive to get rid of the current dictator. Assassination is the short way. It may be possible to arrange exile or even a forced retirement, but in any event, his anointed successor now has strong motives to get rid of the man who he will succeed. Let it be said here that he is not the only person who has these motives. If the other courtiers around the dictator are convinced that this particular man in fact will be the successor, then they begin planning their own maneuvers on the theory that they will spend much more of their life under the rule of the successor than under the rule of the current dictator.

The position of the current dictator in essence goes down and that of the potential successor rises and any sign of bad health or weakness on the part of the dictator is likely to make this even stronger. The brother of the current dictator of Syria was in a quite strong position although he had not officially been anointed as successor. The dictator then had a heart attack and spent a considerable period of time under medical attention. His brother apparently thought that this indicated that he would shortly be in power and it seems likely that many other people thought the same thing and took measures to insure his succession. The dictator then recovered and the brother was exiled to Switzerland.[1] He was lucky, a more common procedure, particularly in Syria, would have been to kill him.[2]

So much for the motives. I earlier said that the successor is safe in carrying out the assassination. The basic reason for this is simply that he will be in charge of the investigation. He will be in a position to either maintain that the dictator died naturally, was killed by somebody else, or killed by his successor under circumstance where that is justifiable. As a general rule, no one will say him nay.

This fact is the reason that one can rarely be sure that kings who are succeeded by one of their children have in fact died of natural causes. In my opinion, Louis XIV simply died, as an elderly man very commonly will, with collected diseases of old age. If Louis XV, actually a great grandchild, or one of the courtiers who hoped to benefit from Louis XV had poisoned him, however, we would never know.

Actually if you look over history, the number of times that a king is known to have been killed by his eldest son, is by no means trivial. I frequently say that this is the commonest cause of death of kings.[3] I haven't actually counted up the cases. If you could add in those cases in which the king is killed by his son or one of his confederates, but where the son then covers up the assassination we might get a much, much larger number.

Note that the designated successor is not the only risk here. Once the courtiers begin shifting their loyality from the king to his successor, there inevitably will be some of them who feel they will be better off under the successor than under the current ruler. They do not have protection from being punished from an assassination that the successor himself will have, but nevertheless, it is unlikely that the successor will track down with great vigor any rumor or report that his predecessor was in fact killed instead of having a heart attack. Even if he does know about the matter, he may decide not to proceed further, because after all he has gained a great deal by it.

It isn't even necessary for courtiers, etc., to do anything directly. Those members of the entourage of the dictator who are responsible for his personal security may simply become a little careless. It should be said that this technique might not pay off since if outsiders succeed in assassinating one dictator it is on the whole unlikely that the captain of his guard will become the captain of the guard of his successor. The captain of the guard is unlikely to be punished and he might well expect that the new dictator would be grateful and would eventually give him some job of importance that did not give him the opportunity to be careless with the new dictator's security.

Looked at from the standpoint of the dictator then, it's dangerous to have an official successor. Even if we look in democratic politics we observe this kind of thing. In the United States it is required that a president have a vice president. If the president dies and the vice president succeeds, then various proceedures (they have changed from time to time over the history) provide automatically for a further succession. It's notable that as a general rule, relations between the president and his vice president have been poor. This is not I think, because the president suspects the vice president of trying to assassinate him, but because both the president and the vice president are aware of the fact that the vice president will gain a great deal if the president dies. This is not the foundation for a firm friendship.

As a result of this, in other democratic countries usually either there is no official successor at all or there are efforts made to keep the official successor in a relatively subordinate position. Before Nixon, the vice presidency was normally thought of as a job which was given in essence to an unsuccessful politician. In the musical *Of Thee I Sing,*[4] the vice presidential candidate is a figure of fun. At one point, he says he doesn't want to be vice president because he thinks his mother will object, and is assured by the professional politican to whom he is talking[5] that she will never find out. Keeping the vice president in a position of subordination, as I say, has been the tradition.

In the case of the United States, this changed with Nixon and since then vice presidents have had a fairly good chance of being permitted to run for the presidency on their party's ticket after the president in office completes two terms. It is possible that this change simply reflects the constitutional amendment which made it impossible for a president to have more than two terms.[6]

Another possiblity is simply Mr. Nixon's ability to convert a dead end job into an important job. Certainly his relations with Eisenhower were never very close nor were those of Nixon himself with Agnew.[7] In both cases there was an effort by the president in office to get his vice president to drop out of the election for the second term. In both cases this took the form of offering him a high cabinet post and in both cases when that was turned down the president decided the political cost of forcing the man out was greater than the benefit.[8] Johnson, of course, kept Humphrey in a position of extreme subordination, but then that was his habit with all of his inferiors.[9]

In some parts of the world we observe the same kind of thing. President Rhee of Korea is frequently referred to as a dictator, but I think this is too simple. He did run elections in which on the whole the votes were honestly calculated, he did have a reasonably free press and the legislature normally was dominated by his political opponents.[10] It is notable however, that when I was in Korea he had as his vice president[11] the only prominent politician in Korea who was older and more dilapidated than Rhee himself. The only time I ever saw the vice president he had his hat on backwards.

Eventually of course, President Rhee becoming very old, did decide on a successor. Yi Ki Pung appears to have been fairly loyal and in fact killed his family and committed suicide when President Rhee was overthrown.[12] It is notable that in the other form of government, parlimentary democracy, where the prime minister is not compelled to have an official successor none of them have chosen to arrange one. There is no official successor to Mrs. Thatcher, Kohl of Germany, or whoever at the moment happens to be prime minister of Italy etc. Once again the danger here would not be that the successor might assassinate the prime minister but that it would change the structure of power so that the successor would be in a position where his replacement of the prime minister who appointed would be a real possibility. Most politicans in this circumstance have chosen not to take the risk.

This by the way is also true of most dictatorships. Appointing a formal successor is rare. Further, it normally only occurs very late in the life of the existing dictator. Even then, dictators frequently change their successors. It is notable that Hitler, when he decided to make a noble gesture at the out break of the war and appoint the persons who would replace him if he were killed, chose Hess who had substantially no chance of developing enough support within the machine so that he could replace Hitler.[13] Mussolini and Franco of course never had a successor.[14] It is rumored that in the early days of the Franco regime they were consciously modeling their government after that of facist Italy.[15] They asked the Italians what the arrangements were for the replacement of the current dictator (Franco had been a soldier and probably was willing to consciously contemplate his own death). They were unable to get either a specification of what would happen when Mussolini died or even a clear statement that their was no such provision.

As a somewhat amusing aside, in the late forties when I was a student at the University of Chicago, there were of course a certain number of students who were communists and a number of them were attempting to conceal their affiliation. This was also true in 1951 and 1952 when I was studying Chinese at Cornell and Yale. I discovered a simple test. Most of my aquaintences were much interested in politics and particularly foreign politics. I would ask who they thought would succeed Stalin. The 'secret' communists, were completely unable to even discuss the question. I don't imagine this would have worked with more serious communists who presumably would have been given some kind of dispensation, so I never suggested this test to the FBI.

If we look at people who have risen high in a dictatorship and have then succeeded in replacing the dictator when he dies, we are apt to find that there are people like Sadat or Moi who must have seemed to the dictator, completely safe. Sadat after all, was a total yes man as long as Nasser was alive.[16] Moi was a member of a minor tribe and did not seem to have adequate political backing.[17] Thus their apparent weakness was one of their qualifications for their positions.

But even here, they are exceptional. Most dictators do not even have a single person who is a relatively prominent candidate as their successor because they regard it as dangerous. Even an apparently spineless yes man can not be permitted to occupy this kind of position. Clearly, Sadat, Moi and Balageur, were all men of really great talent because they succeeded in concealing their ambition, determination, and intelligence from the dictator whom they served. They were probably put in their relatively prominent positions not because the dictator thought they would be suitable successors, but because the dictators thought that they, like Hess, clearly were not suitable successors but by their mere occupation of the prominent position prevented the more likely successors from being in a position where they could damage the dictator during his life.

So far in discussing the succession, in essence, I have been saying that the wise dictator doesn't make any arrangements for succession. He tries to avoid clear cut straight forward succession procedures. Thus the actual succession once he dies will be a quick outburst of intrigue with possibly some violence, in which a number of potential candidates maneuver for position. This maneuvering may possibly take the form of the junta discussed above, but it also may not.

Take an open variant of this kind of thing. In the first part of the T'ang dynasty of China, the death of an Emperor led to a small civil war fought in the capital city by the adherents of his sons. Sian was repeatedly burned down as part of this fight.[18] One of the sons won the others lost.[19]

A number of African tribes have this procedure worked down to almost a formal ceremony. In both the cases of T'ang China and these African tribes, the king is of course polygamous and has a number of children. This formal civil war has nothing whatsoever to do with efficient transmission of power, but it does mean that the current ruling emperor or tribal ruling chief has little to fear from any individual one among his children.[20]

A somewhat similar arrangement was used by Turkish Padishah in the latter days of the Turkish empire. In this case the Padishah normally executed all of his brothers and his sons were kept in a special palace-prison until he died. At the time he died there would be quick squabble in this palace prison from which only one son would emerge alive. This procedure initiated by Selim the Grim pretty much eliminated intrigues for the throne during the reign of any particular Padishah. It also of course, produced a rather bizzare collection of Padishahs.

All three of the above examples are cases of hereditary succession rather than the non-hereditary succession we have been discussing so far. All three of them however, show in an open and overt way the kind of struggle that does go on after a dictator dies when there is no clear cut procedure for replacing him. They are in a way, an open and rather exagerated model of what happens anytime when a dictator dies and there's no procedure for replacing him.

As we have said above, the most likely outcome of all of this is hereditary succession, perferably a hereditary succession that is more peaceful than the ones we have just described. There have however, been some cases of reasonably successful governments in which the succession problem has been solved for at least a period of time.

The oldest of these is the Roman adoptive Emperors. The reader will recall that Gibbon thought that the century of their control was the high point in the history of mankind. Eventually the throne became hereditary.[21] Normally the Roman Empire was strong, peaceful[22] and prosperous during this period.

The procedure was fairly simple and straight forward. Each of these Emperors except the last Marcus Aurelius had the misfortune to have no son.[23] They therefore associated with themselves as an adopted son a prominent official, usually a military man, to succeed to the throne. The procedure seems to have been quite peaceful and there are not even rumors of murders in order to acquire the throne. It must be said however, that in a number of cases the new emperor had rather resented his predecessor. This is particularly clear in the case of Hadrian with Trajan.[24] Also, it appears that the emperor and his adopted son were rarely in close physical proximity. Whether this was important or not I don't know.

It will be noted here that once the man had been legally adopted it was hard, even if not impossible, for his newly found father to get rid of him. Further, the procedure normally occured in such a way that with ordinary life expectancy it was obvious that the newly adopted son would have twenty years or so of reign even if he didn't do anything about his adopted fathers life expectancy. Nevertheless, this seems to be an exceptional procedure and as far as I know has never been copied.

There is something that looks vaguely like it, a new invention actually of this century. The Mexican government since the 1930's have had a dictator who reigns for six years and then appoints his successor and withdraws.[25] A priori I would have said that this was not a likely system to succeed but so far in any event it has. Further, this system was copied by Brazil. The only basic difference was that Brazil had a four year term instead of a six year term. Here again, it seems to have been quite successful,[26] although it has now been abandoned. The Brazilians of course had the system for a much shorter period of time than the Mexicans and also were never willing to go to quite such extremes in eliminating opposition as were the Mexicans.[27] Mexico hasn't followed the Brazilian precedent and abandoned the system, but the current president of Mexico was 'elected' in an 'election' in which the opposition was actually permitted to campaign to some extent.[28]

To repeat what I said with respect to the previous system, this does not seem to be in any sense a stable way of running a government and I am very surprised that it has lasted as long as it has. There may however, be underlying structures which have not yet been discovered which make this feasible. I think that it is worth serious thought by anyone interested in dictatorial governments.

The third system for peaceful succession has been successful for quite a long period of time. The dictator appoints a voting body which while he is dictator advises him. He is free during this period of time to change its membership if he wishes. Upon his death, this voting body elects someone, usually but not necessarily always, one of its members as his successor. This successor then acquires the same dominance over the voting body as the man who originally appointed it.

This system has been used by the Catholic church for a thousand years,[29] although one would be hard put to argue there have never been difficulties in this particular chain of rulers, it has worked fairly well. There have been a number of cases in which there was more than one pope elected by different colleges of Cardinals.[30] Although the succession on the whole has been peaceful, and has produced a group of fairly successful rulers, it does have a tendency to select very elderly men.

This system has been copied by the Soviet Union. Its not clear whether this is conscious or whether they simply accidently fell into the precedure.[31] In any event, since the death of Lenin, the politbureau has played more or less the role of The College of Cardinals. It should be pointed out that in the early days, for example right after the death of Lenin, establishing one man control took some time.[32] The same was true in the second succession crisis after the death of Stalin. When Kruschev was overthrown[33] there was an immediate successor who possibly had engineered the overthrow. On Brezhnev's death of course, the succession was almost instantaneous[34] and the same was true at Andropov's death although in the latter case apparently his death was concealed for a few days.[35] Chernenko's death, simillarly seems to have led to an immediate succession, by a much younger man.

The tendency to move towards gerontocracy is of course particularly conspicous in the Soviet Union because the early rulers Lenin and Stalin, were members of almost the same generation. Four of the rulers since then can be regarded as more or less contemporaries.[36]

Note however, that this tendency to move to a very elderly ruler is not invarying. The current Pope is by Papal standards a young man.[37] Further, Gorbachev is also a relatively young man.[38] Note in both cases however, that relatively young means somewhere in their 50's. In more competitive system, such as the other kind of dictatorship in which people fight their way up the greasy pole, or for that matter in democracy, the top rulers tend to be younger when they first take control.

The advantage of this system from the standpoint of the dictator who is interested in obtaining control thoughout his life and arranging a relatively peaceful succession so that at least to some extent his work will be continued, are obvious. The voting body can be made large enough so that the members of it can exercise, on an individual basis, supervision over all parts of the government and so that no one of them has very much power. In addition, the individuals within this group find some difficulty in conspiring because of the fact that they regularly, day in and day out,[39] discuss matters in an environment which would be very hard to conceal from the dictator any cliques that seem to be developing. The dictator is not absolutely secure under these circumstances, Kruschev after all was thrown out, but he is reasonably secure and the succession so far has not involved open violence.[40]

Note that the system works best when the members are indeed elderly. The reason for this is very simple. If the current dictator is elderly, it is obvious that one doesn't have to wait to long for his replacement. Thus the ambitious man has no strong motive for fighting his way up right now. Further. With this large collection of people, all of whom can anticipate some kind or promotion in the not too distant future through the death of the dictator, it's harder to promise promotion as a bribe for support. Last but by no means least, the dictator can remove a member of the politbureau and replace him by somebody else without significantly changing the dynamics of the process. We do not have to worry about the condensation of the Junta here.

But although this system does have advantages, as far as I know, the Catholic church and the Communist Party of the Soviet Union, are the only places where it is used. It is of course, quite possible that China will move to this system. After all, if we had observed the Soviet Union right after Stalin achieved power, we would not have been able to predict the eventual outcome. China has just gone through its first succession crisis in as disorderly a way as Russia its first succession crisis in the 1920's.[41]

The three communist ruling parties which are independent, North Korea, Albania, and Yugoslavia, do not seem to be following this process. Tito has been dead for quite a while now and Yugoslavia has not yet developed a dictator or this kind of politburo control.[42] Once again of course, this would be.the first succession crisis and we can't deduce too much from it. In the case of North Korea, the first dictator is still alive, but there seem to be arrangements for keeping the throne in the family.[43] In semi-independent Romania, the same thing seems to be taking place.[44]

Perhaps there are other ways of arranging a peaceful succession without jeopardizing the current dictator, but the number of instances which could be given of regular institutional structure for this sort of thing is very limited. I would not like to claim that I have discovered all of them, but I don't think there are any very conspicious examples which I have missed.

As we have said above however, commonly hereditary succession is the ultimate outcome. We as people of European ancestory, tend to think of hereditary succession as succession by the eldest son. This is not necessarily the system used in other cultures. You may recall Marco Polo went to China over land, but came back by sea. The reason that he did so is that in Mongolian law, the youngest son succeeded his father. Khubalai Khan, was not the youngest son and the youngest son living in Mongolia led a revolt which broke the gigantic Mongolian empire into halves. It was not safe for Marco Polo to return across the Gobi Desert as he had come.[45]

This is not, of course, the only case of succession by somebody who is not the eldest son. I mentioned above cases in which succession actually involved a sort of war among the possible successors (in the case of the Turkish institutions a very small war confined to one palace prison). There are other cases. The Ch'ing dynasty of China was perhaps the strongest dynasty that China ever had.[46] The basic reason for this, I believe, was the in the early days the succession was not to the eldest son. The Emperor selected from among his children the one that he thought should succeed. Since as a polygamist ruler he always had quite a large number of sons, the early emperors were all men of exceptional capacity. Unfortunately, they were living in China and the Chinese view that the eldest son should inherit was eventually adopted with the result of a set of weak emperors.[47]

I could name other examples. The basic reason the Pharaohs of Egypt normally married their sister was that succession in Egypt was through the female line.[48] The current Prince of Monaco succeeded his father while his father was still alive.[49] Altogether, hereditary succession is not necessarily eldest son to eldest son.

Even if we confine ourselves to areas where the succession is supposed to be eldest son to eldest son, uniform peace is by no means insured. In the first place, lines do run out. I.e., there is no son of the current ruling king and there is no near relative who seems a reasonable replacement. The Uffici, in Florence was a gift to the city of Florence left in her will by the last of the Medici.[50]

We could go on. Hereditary succession is certainly not a guarantee of peaceful succession. The obvious example of this of course is the War of the Roses in England. It started when a potential heir to the throne, although not necessarily the most likely heir, overthrew the existing king. It continued for years and years and years, being mainly a war between close relatives.[51] The end product, Henry VII, was a man who actually had no Plantagenet blood in his veins.[52] The long and bloody Hundred Years War between England and France was set off when the king of England decided that he was the legitimate heir to the recently deceased king of France.[53] Those of you who have seen Shakespeare's *Henry V* are familiar with the English claim that descent could go through the female line in France because the 'Salic' Law which banned such succession did not apply in France. Shakespeare does not tell you that if female succession was permitted, there were around a dozen people who had better claims to the throne than Henry V. All of them were French.[54]

All of this is merely to point out that hereditary succession does not guarantee a peaceful succession of the throne from father to son over untold generations. Nevertheless, it seems to be more peaceful than other methods. I can think of two examples, Byzantine history and the history of the Mamaluks in Egypt, both running about a thousand years.[55] It is clear that things on the whole ran better during those periods of time usually not more than three generations in which they did indeed have hereditary succession than in those periods of time in which they fought about the succession. Popular devotion to the 'legitimate' king may have been quite sensible. The common people had little or nothing to gain from a civil war and a great deal to lose. Unfortunately, there almost always is at least one person who can gain from it.

In any event, historically hereditary succession to the throne has been the commonest form of government. This does not means that every succession is undisputed, merely that most of them are. England, with disputed successions in roughly every third generation is an exceptionally disturbed country. Since most of us think of our history as English history this exceptional disturbance may appear to us to be characteristic of hereditary monarchy. Actually I think every fifth time would be a better rough average.

This has been a discussion of the historical record of hereditary monarchy and not an explanation of why it is indeed quite a common form of government. Why do hereditary monarchs tend to replace dictatorships which are not hereditary? Why do we observe today, dictators of North Korea and Singapore obviously planning for hereditary succession and the last dictator of Haiti as being in fact the hereditary successor to his father?[56] Why was the house of Somoza as successful as long as it was[57] and for that matter why did it take direct intervention by the American government after the death of Trujillo to prevent his son from remaining in control of the family hacienda?[58]

The first thing to be said is that from the standpoint of the father son pair, the situation is a little easier than the relationship between a dictator and one of his officals. Secondly, and this is actually an important matter, the son is apt to be at least twenty years younger than the father. Thus he has a reasonable chance of a fairly long personal reign even if he waits until his father dies. It is not of course, true that this has always worked out well. Louis XIV and XV both outlived their children.[59] Muhammad Ali founder of the dynasty of Egypt which was only replaced by Nasser lived long enough so that his extremely talented son and he had a relationship of almost mutual hatred at the end.[60]

Nevertheless, as a rough rule of thumb the eldest son is wise to simply wait for his father to die. He knows this, his father knows that he knows this and concern about assassination by son is less in a hereditary successional arrangement than if the designated successor is a high ranking official of the existing regime. Note I say *less*. I have already expressed by opinion that a careful count would indicate that murder by eldest son was the commonest single cause of death to kings in those areas where the eldest male succeeds.[61]

As another aspect there usually is a certain element of affection between father and son and that means that both would get at least some satisfaction out of the satisfaction of the other.[62] There is an interdependence of utility functions here even if it is very far from a complete interdependence. This also makes it less likely that the son will murder his father. The fact that this is less likely means that the father will worry less about the matter and hence this again makes this method of succession more likely.

As a final item while we are talking about reasons why sons may be designated as successor, its hard for the father to switch under these circumstances. He after all, has only one eldest son and many kings had in fact only one son. If he becomes suspicious or annoyed with the current crown prince, he can hardly simply appoint somebody else as his eldest son. It is true that if he has other children he could kill his son, many kings have. But this is an extreme measure.

The result of all of this is that the father has greater confidence in his son and that in turn means that the son has a much weaker motive for murdering his father than would the designated successor if the designated successor was simply a high official of the regime.[63] This again means that the father can trust his son more than he can trust other people.

As a final item, I mentioned above that the adoptive emperors and their adopted successors seem to have rarely been fairly close to each other. It is rare, but not an unheard of precaution for a ruler to appoint his son as viceroy in some distant and not militarily important province on the ostensible theory that he needs to be trained in rulership.

An even more common precaution however, and this may be one of the reasons that hereditary monarchs tend not to be terribly good rulers is simply to provide the son with a great deal of entertainment. The son can be provided with substantially any number of fine polo ponies, beautiful concubines, swimming pools, etc. This normally will not cost the king a very high percentage of his nations GNP and it may provide the child with enough distraction so he's not seriously concerned with immediate succession. Unfortunately, this kind of training is unlikely to make him a good king.

These are reasons why the king may prefer his son as a successor. We also have to explain why the son is able to in fact seize control after the death of his father. Indeed if we look at history we will find a number of cases in which a legitimate heir seized power even though he was not designated. When Queen Elizabeth died, she had not designated an heir.[64] James of Scotland was however, a clear example of a suitable king and took over with no difficulty. Similarily on the death of the reigning king of France which led to the Hundred Years War, in France itself a quite distant relative of the existing king was peacefully accepted as the legitimate successor.[65] These of course are cases in which a dynastic tradition already exists. Movement to hereditary succession when it has not previously existed is not obviously the same thing. We can however, find one very conspicious example of this. Julius Cesear was not king of the Romans but he certainly dominated the country.[66] On his assassination Augustus a young man who at the time must have seemed to have substantially no positive qualities except his relationship to Cesear immediately became a member of the Triumvirate, later partly because he was a member of Cesear's family, and partly because it turned out that he was a very talented intriguer, he of course became Emperor and established a dynasty.[67]

A number of Greek tyrants were successful in placing their sons on their throne. Usually in these cases, however, there was a more definate designation than had occurred in the case of Augustus.[68] Note that I've had to go back to very ancient history to find examples of this kind of thing. The history of the nineteenth century was the history of the replacement of absolute rulers of one sort or another by democracies.[69] The twentieth century has shown a good deal of movement in the other direction[70] but in general this, as of now, has had such a short running time that a general tendency towards a particular method of succession has not yet had time to establish itself.

But to return to our main subject, why is the 'legitimate' heir usually a son in particularly good position to succeed his father. In order to answer, we go back to our earlier discussion of the work of Schelling and the Schelling point.[71] Higher ranking courtiers all would of course like to be the new dictator themselves, but all of them are aware that only one will win. Thus, although they are looking at the main chance always they're also very interested in backing whoever they think will win. Under these circumstances as Schelling has pointed out conspiciouses is apt to be a strong argument. The Coalition is apt to form behind the son simply because he is a very conspicious individual. Being conspicious it is likely each politician thinks that other politicians will be attracted to him. Therefore, since other politicians will be attracted to him I had better join him myself. All politicians feeling this way, the conspicious person, in this case the legitimate heir, has a great advantage and will probably win.

Note that this would be particularly true if the legitimate heir were also a man of very considerable capacity. But that is by no means obviously true in most cases. Biologists are familiar with 'regression to the mean' under which characteristics which are sharply away from the average of a given specie tend to be less strongly represented in the next generation. The original dictator who climbed the greasy pole is undoubtedly of very considerable capacity, his son may not be. Further, his upbringing very likely has been one which gives him a strong feeling that he has a right to rule, but no great capacity to do it well.

Note that I am not alleging that hereditary rulers of countries are totally unfit, merely that in general, they are not that particular resident of the country whom a divine judge would select as the best ruler. Perhaps from the standpoint of the country as a whole, hereditary succession's principle advantage is that it avoids civil wars at the death of the dictator and indeed makes it unlikely that anyone other than his legitimate heir will make any effort to assassinate him. Succession is apt to be peaceful, at least most of the time, and that is surely a boon even if not an infinite boon.

But if this is, in my opinion, the likely outcome of the present situation in most countries, certainly is not the current situation. Disorderly succession, putches, coup d'etat, and in South America in any event, an alteration of dictatorship and democracy seem likely near term predictions, even if the long term prediction would be hereditary monarchs.

NOTES

1. By his actions at the time of his illness, President Hafez Al-Assad himself seemed uncertain about the desirability of appointing his brother (one of six) Rifaat, as his temporary successor. (*The New York Times*, May 17, 1984, I27:1.) Rifaat, a powerful figure in his own right, was later exiled to Switzerland. (*The New York Times*, July 17, 1984,I4:1; October 31, 1984, I6:3; and November 27, 1984, I8:4.)

2. For Syrian law on assasination attempts, see e.g. Kelidar (1976), p. 47; Nyrop (1979), p. 222.

3. At least of those kings for which there is a regularly established succession with the eldest son succeeding. There will be more on this below.

4. George Gershwin (1931). See Schwartz (1979), pp. 212ff; Chase (1955), pp. 628-629.

5. Who has previously mistaken him for a waiter.

6. The two-term Presidency limitation appears in Section 1 of the 22nd Amendment to the Constitution, and was adopted in 1951. See Abraham (1980), pp. 237-238 for a text of the Amendment.

7. The Nixon-Eisenhower relationship was not improved by Eisenhower's refusal to designate Nixon publically as his preferred running mate in the 1952 and 1956 presidential elections. (Larson, 1968, p. 8) SDee also Rather and Gates (1974), passim, but particularly pp. 74-75, on Nixon and Eisenhower. On Nixon's relationship to Agnew, see Evans and Novak (1971), pp. 312-313, 402; Rather and Gates (1974), pp. 128,255,281.

8. Greenstein (1982), p. 234 discusses the (reconsidered) attempt by Eisenhower to eliminate Nixon from the Presidential race; on the similar case of Nixon and Agnew, see for example, Rather and Gates (1974), p. 281.

9. See Bornet (1983), pp. 320-321; Caro (1982), pp. 230, 234.

10. The use of free elections and the extent of opposition-party power during Ree's Presidency in South Korea (1919-1960) are noted in Vreeland et.al. (1975), p. 28; Allen (1960), pp. 101ff, 205ff.

11. The constitution had been copied after that of the United States where Ree spent such a large part of his exile. Rhee's Vice President was Lee Si-yong. For a history of the modeling of the Korean constitution along the lines of the Constitution of the United States, see Vreeland et. al., (1975) pp. 143-149; Allen (1960), p. 218.

12. The President who had no children had formally adopted Yi's son. Rhee's immediate successor was Yung Bo-Son. His reign lasted only 9 months, and was cut short by General Park Chung Hee. See Vreeland et. al., (1975), pp. 28ff.

13. In September 1939 Hitler appointed Hermann Goring his first successor; Rudolf Hess, his second in line. (Bullock, 1964, p. 547-548.) A few years later, however, before his death in April 1945, Hitler asked Admiral Karl Donitz to succeed him in order to show 'his disillusion with his generals.' (Jarman, 1961, p. 304) (Hess had defected to Scotland in May 1941. See Bullock, 1964,p. 643.) With Donitz designated President and Supreme Commander, the Chancellorship went to Joseph Goebbels, and the position of Party Minister to Martin Bormann. (Jarman, 1961, p. 304; Bullock, 1964, pp. 795ff.

A 'weakest-successor' rule has apparently emerged (in a somewhat modified form) in the Soviet Union: '[I]n the struggle for power inside the Central Committee [over] the post of Secretary - General... the contestant with the best chance is neither the strongest nor the ablest. The prize usually goes to the least able and most harmless-seeming member of the politburo.'(Voslensky, 1984, p 255.) The possible motive?: 'Politburo members find it easier to have as weak a Secretary-General as possible. A quite human characteristic: Life is easier when you have a weak boss.' (p. 367) Voslensky notes however, that, 'In the countries of eastern europe, the rules of the political game and of making a career differ from those of the West. An ambitious Western politician must attract attention and try to stand out of the ruck, since his advancement depends on the favor of as large as possible a proportion of the active members of his party or the electorate as a whole. A rising politician in Eastern Europe must stake everything on the goodwill of the [current] Secretary-General, and, if not the support of, the absence of opposition from, other leading figures. He must therefore concentrate on not standing out of the ruck, on not drawing attention to himself; he must create the impression of being innocuous and even rather dumb in the eyes of his colleagues. That was how Stalin, Khrushchev, Brezhnev, and later

Chernenko rose to the top.' (p. 263). Gorbachaev may be an exception to the rule.

On the relative benefits (and costs) of appointing 'weak' successors see also, Tullock (1974), pp. 72ff.

14. Mussolini had three sons, Bruno, Romano, and Vittorio all of whom were for a time available as potential successors. Unfortunately, the first was killed in a car accident, while 'Vittorio had been interested mainly in films, Ramon in Jazz, and it caused their father much grief that they took after their mother and lacked serious intellectual interests. Vittorio was now egged on by various friends and relations to play a part in politics, and his father, by encouraging the ambition of these "princes of the blood", showed poor judement.' (Smith, 1982, p. 310.)

15. Blum, Cameron, and Barnes (1970), p. 943: 'In 1936 General Francisco Franco led a revolt against the government...Franco, who reorganized the Falange party, created by Primo de Rivera, on the model of Mussolini's Fascists and Hitler's Nazis, and proceeded to establish a reactionary authoriarianism that outlasted by far its model.'

See also Ben-Ami (1983), passim.

16. See for example Dekmejian (1971), on the relationship between Nasser and Sadat. On Nasser's relationship to his predecessor, Mohammed Ali, see Nutting (1972), LaCourture (1974).

17. Moi's tribal beginnings are indicated in Miller (1984), p. 28.

18. Sian also called 'Ch'ang-an,' 'Ching-chao-chun,' and 'Hsi-an-fu', was the western capital of China at the beginning of the T'ang dynasty (618-907 A.D.) See Langer (1972), pp. 145, 363.

19. The first emperor of the T'ang dynasty, Han Kao Tsu (originally Liu Chih-Yuan) was succeeded by his son, T'ang T'ai Tsung (Originally Li Shihmin).

The son ruled from 626-649 A.D. His reign began 'after a brief struggle with rival claimants [his brothers]' (Dupuy and Dupuy, 1977, p. 239). His battle for succession was won on July 4, 626, the day 'Li Shihmin murdered his brothers (Wright and Twitchett, 1973, p. 246). See also *Ibid*, p. 19; and Gungwu (1963), p. 203; Bingham (1970), pp. 119-120, Langer (1972), pp. 363ff.

20. 'In African kingdoms it was exceptional for succession rules to designate a single individual; in the majority of cases a choice was made between a number of eligible candidates, and in some of them the contest was expected to be one of armed force.' (Mair, 1977, p. 121; see also pp. 122-131.)

21. 'The superior prerogative of birth, when it has obtained the sanction of time and popular opinion, is the plainest and least invidious of all distinctions among mankind. The acknowledged right extinguishes the hopes of faction, and the consious security disarms the cruelty of the monarch. To the firm establishment of this idea we owe the peaceful succession and mild administration of european monarchies. to the defect of it we must attribute the frequent civil wars, through which an asiatic despot is obliged to cut his way to the throne of his fathers....The daring hopes of ambition were set loose from the salutary restraints fo law and prejudice, and the meanest of mankind might, without folly entertain a hope of being raised by valour and fortune to a rank in the army, in which a single crime would enable him to wrest the sceptre of the world from his feeble and unpopular master.' (Gibbon, 1909, pp. 182-183.) Sinnegen and Boar (1977) point out that the rule for hereditary succession was not formally instituted and imposed, but was

simply tacitly adopted and used by a succession of emperors during this period (p. 432). Starr (1982, p 38) offers a possible rationale for the adoption of such a rule: 'Such a pattern made it legally easier to pass on the ruler's personal estate or *patrimonium*, which was already extensive under Augustus and was enlarged by bequests and additions from the property of condemmed political criminals. Although later rulers sometimes made gifts of land to favorites, mistresses, or wives, the *patrimonium* of the emperor tended to become even larger as aristocrats were sent to the block.' C.F. Jouvenel (1962), pp. 327ff.

22. Peace was not universally enjoyed, however; and on occasion there was even some confusion about the identity of the peace keepers: 'Althought imperial literature has frequent praises of the imperial peace which safeguarded travel "from the fear of bandits" attacks,' realities did not always correspond; and travellers faced dangers especially if they strayed off main routes. Disguised by the conventional eulogies of the empire as bringing order and security there bubbled in reality a caldron of violence and sudden death as men settled their differences outside the law and preyed on the weaker. Lucius, the hero of Apuleius' picaresque *metamorphoses*, found brigands aplenty in Macedonia, and his group was almost attacked by villagers with fierce dogs and stones until it could prove that it was not a band of robbers. Marcus Aurelius, as crown prince, jestingly wrote...that he and his companions in the vicinity of Antoninus Pius' royal villa were mistaken as robbers by sheperds, whom they charged on horseback and scattered - the sheperds may not have thought it as amusing. (Starr, 1982, pp. 118-119.)

23. Marcus Aurelius had the misfortune to have a son. During this period (98-161 A.D.) of the Roman Empire (27 B.C. - 493 A.D.) 'Physiological accident produced the series of "good emporers" - Trajan, Hadrian, Antoninus Pius - none of whom had sons; the last of this group, Marcus Aurelius, however, did, and Commodus duly became emperor (at age 16), ruled badly, and was strangled on the last day of 192.' (Starr, 1982, p. 39.) See also Sinnegan and Boak (1977), p. 320.

24. 'Trajan and Hadrian were personally incompatible, since the late emperor had not distinguished the younger man by granting him much power during his own lifetime.' (Sinnigen and Boak, 1977, p. 314.)

25. Needler (1982), pp. 8, 85, 89-93. See also Camp (1980), esp. 15-66.

26. See for example, Roett (1978).

27. *Ibid*, pp. 76ff. See also Johnson (1984) p,. 12, on Mexxican opposition parties and their treatement by those in power. Fiechter (1975), offers an overview of the 20th century political developments in Brazil.

28. *The Washington Post*, July 16, 1985, Aiza; Needler (182), p. 58. But C. F. Scott (1964), pp. 297ff; and Hellman (1983), who notes (pp. 127-128, 129), for example, that 'even today, the [Mexican] president is rarely challenged publically. A ban on direct criticism of the president in the Mexican press is enforced by the state monopoly on the supply of newsprint. Since 1935, a government agency has set the price and allotted quantities of paper to each publication... Newspapers and magazines critical of official policy are often forced to buy paper on a black market or "borrow" from sympathetic periodicals against the day when those publications may incur the hostility of the regime....The Christmas season is made particularly jolly for both Mexican and foreign journalists by the arrival on their doorstep of huge baskets of liquor and gourmet foods sent by government and

party figures. But perhaps the most subtle form of control of the press is exercised through the use of the government's advertising budget, which constitutes the bulk of paid advertisement in many publications. For example, until government advertising was withdrawn in 1982, *Proceso*, a weekly mens magazine which attempts to maintain a clearly independent editorial line, received $117,000 from newsstand sales and subscriptions and $53,000 from the government publicity and propaganda carried in its pages each week... Historically, the relationship between the PRI (Institutional Revolutionary Party, headed by the President of Mexico) and its official opposition was so close that the parties were often referred to as a "kept" opposition. Indeed, in some cases opposition parties were financed by the government itself....Ballot stealing, strong-arm pressure at the polls, and electoral fraud of every description contribute to the offical party's electoral preeminence.... The corruption of the electoral process in Mexico is so well documented that few people take the final statistics without a large serving of salt...[O]pposition parties have never achieved more than the status of pressure groups.'

Another difference here is that the Mexican President and other higher officials seem to have stolen much more money than the Brazilian ones. I am at a loss to explain this difference.

(*The Washington Post*, June 8,1984, C15c; *The Washington Post*, September 8, 1984, E53c.) Johnson (1984) observes that 'in the colonial period of Mexican history there was less corruption and more respect for civil liberties than in present-day Mexico,' and concludes that 'people in Mexico accept fraud, terrorism, even bodies lying in the street with no public show of pity, as facts of life. This sounds very much like a war of all against all, in which almost everyone is certain to lose.' (p. 3)

Brazilian political corruption has of course also been widespread (e.g. Haring, 1985, pp. 170, 171); but bureaucratic waste and inefficiencies appear to be an even larger problem. Daland (1980) suggests that, 'The picture is not simple incompetence derived form clientelistic patronage appointments – though we should not minimize this element. There is a whole class of do-nothings (*ociosos*) in the bureaucracy. some do nothing because they are incompetent. some do nothing because they are protected by their patron, and have job security without the effort of working for it. Still others do nothing because they are not permitted to...

'A young lawyer obtained a technical position in the ministry of education upon finishing his studies. After some delay, during which he was given no instructions whatever as to his job, he sought out his supervisor and asked what needed to be done. The supervisor replied that he should wait and instructions would be forthcoming later.'

'After several repetitions of this exchange, the idealistic young man became restive about accepting his monthly check without earning his pay. He then went to his supervisor with various suggestions for projects which by law it was evident should be undertaken. The boss became positively threatening, and warned the employee that he should terminate the pressure to engage in actual work if he wanted to keep out of trouble. So the employee gave up, and decided to enter a career in civil engineering, which he did with a scholarship from the Ministry,...and went into the private sector as a successful engineer.(pp. 216-217).

29. In the early days of the church the pope was elected by popular voting in Rome. The College of Cardinals control is thus more recent than the papacy itself. (Lynskey, 1985, pp. 93-94.) See also Rank (1913), Volume II, pp. 5-19.) Bishops also were originally elected by the laity. See Chadwick (1976), p. 165.

30. The election of 'multiple' popes occurred in 1378 A.D., beginning a period of papal history known as the 'Great Schism' (1378-1417 A.D.). Following the death of Pope Gregory XI, the college appointed two 'Popes', Urban VI of Rome and Clement VII of Avignon. Such multiple appointments continued to occur until the early 15th century and were in each instance usually resolved by a meeting of the Cardinals to determine the 'true' pope. Occasionally, a 'pretender-pope' (or, 'Anti-Pope') such as Benedict XIII would persist in asserting his papal authority despite the Cardinals' decision. For a brief synopsis of events, see, e.g. Grun (1983), pp. 194-202; Langer (1972), pp. 299ff.

31. See for example Harasymiw (1984); Hill and Frank (1983). I believe that it has also been copied by a number of minor churches in various parts of the world, but I don't know enough about them to be certain. Many churches, such as the Mormans or the menonites are governed by a board of elders who do indeed tend to be very old, but most of them do not have a single ruler on top of that board. See O'Dea (1957), pp. 160ff, 176ff, for a discussion of the internal organization of the Mormon church; on the Mennonite system, see for example Hostetler (1968), p. 13.

32. Harasymiw (1984), p. 86; Blum, Cameron and BArnes (1970), pp. 923-294. As Volensky (1984, p. 255) points out: 'The public in the West often hears about "struggles for power in the Kremlin" and wrongly associates these with the idea of perpetual differences of opinion and dramatic debates similar to those that enliven Western parliments. Nothing of that sort takes place in the Central Committee. There is a long-drawn-out affair involving lying in wait for years, in the course of which intrigues develop of a subtlety probably inconceivable to Western politicians.

33. I know of no direct parallel to this in the history of the Catholic church.

34. See Volensky (1984), pp. 370ff. He notes (p. 377): 'The probability of Andropov's getting the Secretary-General job became significant; it was noticed even by a computer. In 1981 a computer at Iowa University predicted who Brezhnev's most likely successor would be. The result was, given the variables - age (sixty to seventy years) and nationality (Russian)...limited to one person. That was Andropov.'

35. Volensky (1984), pp. 381ff, discusses Chernenko's succession to Andropov's position as Secretary-General.

36. See Hough (1980), especially pp. 150-156; Velonsky (1984), pp. 263ff. Actually, there have been six rulers since Stalin: Georgi Malenkov who ruled for a brief and politically turbulent period (1953-1955); Nikita Khruschev (1955-1964); Leonid Konstantin Chernenko (1984-1985); and the current Secretary-General, Mikhail Gorbachev (at this writing).

Though 'contemporaries', recent Soviet rulers have tended to replace 'old' policies with those more reflective of their own 'political syle and policy preferences.' See Brown (1982); and Bunce (1981).

37. Pope John Paul II was 58 years old upon election in 1973. – The youngest

Pope to be elected in this century. (*The New York Times*, October 17, 1978, p. 16).

38. Gorbachev was a relatively young man of 54 when appointed at the time the youngest member of the politburo, (*The Washington Post*, March 12, 1985, A1c).

39. Actually there is only one official politburo meeting a week, on Thursdays (Volensky, 1983, p. 264) - perhaps to avoid scheduling conflicts with the Secretariat, an equally-powerful commitee partly composed of politburo members which meets on Wednesdays (Hill and Frank, 1983, p. 68). But the members do have a lot of outside contact: 'A less formal, but frequently used and vitally important communication channel is the telephone: it is in constant use at a local level, between officials and officers of the district or city committee and primary organization secretaries, economic managers, and so forth. Central Committee meetings are reported in summary to the press, but presumably these accounts for mass consumption are amplified in private conversation to party workers and, as appropriate, the mass membership, though the PPOs [Primary Party Organizations], where they may be discussed. Information internal to the party's affairs - on party finances, for example, or in how to conduct the party's affairs - is kept essentially private.' (Hill and Frank, 1983, p. 81).

40. Though of course not for everyone. In the Soviet Union, 'There is likely to be a rapid turnover of elite personnel. This will have a number of effects, including making certain categories of people very happy, others sad.' (Harasymiw, 1984, p. 190.).

41. See Chang (1984), for a discussion of Communist China's recent succession crisis.

42. 'One possible solution, which seems the most obvious to commentators accustomed to Kremlin-gazing, would be for a new strong man to emerge. There are however no obvious personalities in Yugoslavia today fitted to play this role. Party leaders have always tended to be identified with their republics, and the trends in party organization since the sixties have strengthened this attitude, so any aspiring heir to Tito is hindered by the likely resistance from other republics... There is no doubt that the army is an important force in Yugoslav politics, well represented in the party; and General Nikola Ljubici has been Minister of offices. If there were a really serious nationalist, crisis, then it is possible the army would back a strong man to reimpose and maintain order. There is not at present any evidence, however, that they army aspires to exercise controlling power. Therefore, it seems likely that the republican party bosses will be forced to resolve their disputes by compromise, as Tito envisaged, and to cooperate in a genuinely collective leadership. The virtually confederal nature of the Yugoslav state, and the federal elements in the party organization itself clearly conduce to this kind of solution. So it is possible that Yugoslavia after Tito will, as in many other respects, diverge from the standard comunist party pattern, and avoid one man dominance.' (Carter, 1982, pp. 256 - 257.) See also Burg (1983), especially pp. 326-335.

43. On current plans for the succession of 42 year old Kim Jon IL by North Korean president 73 year old Kim Il Sung (See *The Washington Post*, August 7, 1984, Azia: *The New York Times*, July 9, 1985, A1:5. According to North Korea's constitution (1972), 'Although he is to be elected every four years by the Supreme People's Assembly, to which he is theoretically accountable for his conduct in

office, there is no explicit constitutional limitation on his tenure, nor is there any ambiguity about the fact that he is not actually accountable to any governmental authority...the Constitution is silent on the question of presidential succession.' (Vreeland et.al., 1976, pp. 160, 161.).

44. See Gilberg (1984).

45. See Polo (1931); Blum, Cameron and Barnes (1970), p. 49: Langer (1972), pp. 383-384.

46. See e.g. Kessler (1976); Spence (1974).

47. See Langer (1972), pp. 575-579, 909-916; Kessler (1976), pp. 167ff.

48. As for example noted in Cottrell (1969), p. 14.

49. Prince Rainier II, current ruler of Monaco is in turn preparing *his* son Albert to succeed him in the not too distant future (*The New York Times*, February 17, 1984, II6:2.).

50. The Uffici, an art gallery containing a 'mass of pictures, statues, bronzes, rare gems, and other works of art' was donated 'to the state of Tuscany forever, in the person of the new Grand Duke and his successors' by Anna Maria Ludovia (1667-1743), 'The Last of the Medici,' Shortly before her death. (Young, 1930, p. 740. See also pp. 736-747.).

51. See, Fisher (1906), pp. 1-24ff; Cheyney (1918) pp. 269ff; Dupuy and Dupuy (1977) pp. 419-423.

52. See Mackie (1957), pp. 47-50, 656a; Fisher (1906), pp. 1-15ff.

53. Seward (1978).

54. See Blum, Cameron and Barnes (1970), p 225. On Salic Law, see Langer (1972)p. 296. Harrison (1952) reproduces Shakespeare's 'The Life of King Henry the Fifth' (pp. 732-772).

55. On the Byzantine Empire (324-1453 A.E.), see Mango (1980). The Mamaluks (or 'Mamelukes') of Egypt are discussed in Muir (1896), Passim; and Harris (1971), pp. 461-466.

56. Jean-Claude Duvalier succeeded his father Dr. Francois Duvalier ('Papa Doc') following his death in 1971. (*The New York Times, February 1971, 4.6; The New York Times*, April 23, 1971, 1:2). He occasionally expressed a nominal interest in democratic elections beginning in 1987. (*The Washington Post*, July 7, 1985, A14d.) In light of his father's brutal regime and practices (Diederich and Burt, 1969), these reforms were not considered serious proposals.

57. Anastasio Somoza Debayle finally resigned under fire as president of Nicaragua in July 1979. (*The New York Times*, July 18, 1979, 1:1).

58. See for example, Martin (1966); Crassweller (1966), pp. 261ff.

59. Louis XIV's death in France in 1715 'brought his five-year old great grandson Louis XV to the throne.' (Blum, Cameron, and Barnes, 1970, p. 390; see also, p. 454, Armstrong (1925), pp. 120ff; Krowenberger (1942), pp. 4-5.) Following Louis XV's death (of smallpox) in 1774, Louis XVI, his grandson, became king at the age of twenty. (p. 462).

60. Sayyid-Marsot (1984, p. 83) notes that Muhammad Ali and his son, Ibrahim (one of Ali's thirty children) 'closely resembled each other physically, although morally they were very different and clashes between father and son were to become frequent later on... Clashes over the promotion of Egyptians to the rank of officers broke out between the two men; [as well as] clashes over policy and

tactics.' (see also *Ibid*, pp. 223ff, 254ff; Lewis (1966) p. 167.) Ibrahim died in 1848, while his father was still living. (Mustafa, (1968, p. 300) On Ibrahim's military accomplishments see, E.G. Baer (1968), p. 139.

61. This would of course depend to some extent on how you classified other forms of death. I am sure it is not commoner than 'natural death', but if natural death is subdivided among the diseases my generalization, I think, would follow. Jaszi and Lewis (1957), for example, note that following the collapse of the Roman Empire (during which 'the practice or assasination became almost a political institution'), 'Political murder of this sort was characteristic also of the period that followed the German Migrations. 'The closest ties of nature are here disregarded; fratricide, the murder of the nearest relatives, becomes an everday event.' This situation lasted until the strong rule of the Carolingians enforced a certain order and unity.' (p. 152.) See also Langer (1968) p. 161.

62. Also disatisfaction out of the other's misfortune. Davis's son Absolom (not the eldest son) revolted against his father and drove him out of Jerusalem. When Joab led the King's army against Absolom he was ordered by David to see that no harm befell Absolom. Nevertheless he killed him, and David was thrown into deep grief. 'Samuel II' chapter 19.

63. Or, like Absolom, merely one son among the many of a polygamous father.

64. Blum, Cameron and Barnes (1970), p. 171. At her last illness she is reported to have placed her hands above her head and this was taken as indicating that she wanted the crown to go to the only potential who was already a king, James of Scotland. It seems likely to me that he people who interpreted her gesture this way were already partisans of James.

65. See for example Langer (1972), pp. 297-303; Seward (1978), passim.

66. See Mommsen (1928), Chapter XXXIII, 'The Old Republic and the New Monarchy, 46-44 B.C.,' pp. 362-396.

67. On the relationship between Juluis Caesar and Augustus, see Weinstock (1971), passim, but especially Chapter XIII, 'Kingship and Divinity,' pp. 270-286.

68. For a history of the Greek Tyrants, see E.G. Perrin (1968), Turner (1963).

69. See for example, Langer (1972), Part V, passim; blum, Cameron and Barnes (1970), Chapters 11-29; Ward, Prothero, and Leathese (1928). See also Moore (1966); Elias (1982), pp. 258ff.

70. Langer (1972), Parts VI and VII; Blum, Camoeron and Barnes (1970), Part 4; Johnson (1983).

71. Schelling, (1980), esp. pp. 113-115; See also Tullock (1974), pp. 75ff.

CHAPTER IX

Democracy and despotism

This book is primarly about absolute rule and hence I have given very little attention so far to democratic governments. In my other books on democratic governments I have normally paid no attention at all to despotic governments. Nevertheless, there are situations which are sort of between democracy and dictatorship and there are other analyzable situations in which a democracy is changing into a dictatorship or a monarchy into a democracy. This chapter will discuss these situations.

In current usage, 'democracy' is normally confined to systems where all adults are permitted to vote.[1] Historically this situation was almost unknown before the 20th Century. Governments in which there were voters, however, did exist in those times. In Athens, for example, the full citizens conducted their affairs in an extremely 'democratic' manner, but they were only a minority of adult inhabitants.[2] In the England of George II, the House of Commons clearly was an important part of the government, and carried on its affairs by voting, but it was selected by rather odd procedures, and was far from the most important part of the government.[3]

In order to deal with these cases, I am using the term 'electoral system' for all cases where voting is a significant part of the governmental process. Democracy in its modern meaning, thus becomes a special type of 'electoral system'. We can classify electoral systems in terms of how closely they approximate democracy, with the Holy Roman Empire at one extreme and the United States in 1900[4] very close to the other.

Before discussing electoral systems, however, I must make a brief digression to deal with a phenomenon which is frequently referred to as partially democratic but which in fact is simply an aspect of some dictatorial governments. This is the 'one party state'. Its origin is simple. A good many of our current dictatorships developed out of democracies or countries which were well on the way to democracy. In a number of cases, the dictatorship began as a party struggling for control in a democracy. Take Lenin for example. I'd not like to call Russia as it existed during most of his life a perfect democracy, but it had at least some electoral aspects and during most of his life before 1917, he was a party leader rather than an official of the government. All of his loyal followers were members of the party. That, when he seized control, he would put his followers, the members of that party, in all the positions of power that he could was of course obvious. There was also no reason why he should have formally dissolved the party and he did not.[5]

He simply made all the other parties illegal, retained his own party in power and called it a one party state. In so far as there was any direct motive in this, it probably was a desire to camouflage the dictatorship under a democratic patina, but a remarkably thin one. As time went by the Communist party in the Russian state actually developed independent power, not as a party but as in essence a personnel control arm of the state. It was in part a propaganda agency for the state and in part an organization which controlled, through the Nomenklatura, its personnel.[6] Presumably, its advantage for such dictators as Stalin, Kruschev, etc., depended largely on providing an alternative channel which could be used to divide the government officials below them. More traditional governments without such a single 'party' had used other methods for the same purposes.

Russia is the oldest 'one party state' in existence and there has been a rather intermittent tendency for membership in the party to expand.[7] I would predict that assuming things go on as they are, in fifty to seventy-five years they will make everybody in Russia automatically a member of the party just as eventually the Roman Emperors made every resident of the empire a citizen.

The Soviet Union is not the only one party state. Mussolini and Hitler both rose to power as political leaders and in both cases retained their former party. In neither of these two cases did this party have quite as much influence as the Communist party of the Soviet Union, but still it was in both cases part of the control apparatus.[8]

In Franco's case, he of course took over the government as a military man from the outside, but there was one party which proclaimed its devotion to him and which was given one party status. In this case it seems fairly clear that Franco never really trusted the Phalange which had no great real importance.[9]

The party in most of the other one party states are even less important than the Phalange was under Franco. Their history is usually the history of a party leader who led his party during a period in which the colonial power was withdrawing and who has like Lenin seen no reason for demolishing the party when he comes to power.

Nevertheless, the party in most cases is more decorative than anything else. A prominent man in the government, or for that matter outside the government, is apt to be a member of the party for the same reason that a businessman in a small town in the United States is a member of the Rotary Club. Further, it probably is as important and has somewhat the same function as the Rotary Club except that most of them do not have as much purely social importance as the Rotary Club.

In a small town in the United States we would be quite surprised to find anyone of prominence who was not a member of the Rotary Club; in a small African dictatorship we would be rather surprised to find anybody of importance who was not a member of the Party. In both cases, however, the actual levers of power lie elsewhere. Mugabe of Zimbabwe is currently attempting to cement his power and as part of that is talking about establishing a one party state. By one party state, he simply means he is going to get rid of all the political power of his opponents. Any member of that one party who thinks that the party is in control of Mugabe rather than vice versa will find that he has made a mistake.

Note that in this case, as in the case of most African one party states, the party itself is not an instrument of control. It is in essence a society which the people who exercise the control are normally members of. Once again, its resemblance to the Rotary Club is much greater than its resemblence to the Communist Party of the Soviet Union in let us say the 1920's.

But this has been a digression. The main point of this chapter is to talk about those situations in which democracies or dictatorships change into one another and to discuss a very interesting intermediate situation.

The first thing to be said is that autocratic governments changing to electoral systems, let alone democracies, have historically been uncommon. The average reader of this book whose knowledge of history tends to be concentrated on the recent West may not realize that this is true, because that was a period in which democracy spread over Europe. But nevertheless, if he looks at the long sweep of history, it clearly is a fact. Most autocracies are succeeded by other autocracies. Succession of an autocracy by an electoral system is much less common than a change of dynasty.

On the other hand, if we look again at the long sweep of history, we will find cases in which autocracy became electoral. We will also find cases in which electoral systems succumbed to dictatorship. The most common explanation in both cases, of course, is foreign conquest with a conqueror who imposes his own system of government. In the great days of Athens, it conquered a number of other greek city states, and in each case imposed upon the conquered city,[10] an electoral form of government.[11] This electoral government was, of course, in most cases subordinate to a super-electorate in Athens. In this case, the governments replaced, were in general, by the rather lax standard presented in this book, already electoral, but with a much more restricted franchise. The governments which replaced what the Athenians called 'democracies', when Sparta and later Thebes became dominant, were called at the time oligarchies.[12] Using the terminology of this book, we would call them 'electoral' but with a much smaller electorate. They were still governed by voting, but only a quite small group was permitted to voter.

To continue then with the foreign conquest matter, the Romans in general, set up electoral systems as the local government wherever their armies spread.[13] This did not mean that Rome itself was electoral, although at the time of its greatest expansion it was.[14] Macedonia, of course, never was even remotely democratic. Neither were the successor kingdoms which continued to use electoral local governments. The replacement of hereditary kingdoms in Gaul or Asia Minor, by self governing local structures of the over arching Roman Empire was presumably a movement in the direction of democracy even if the movement did not go very far.

Note that this would not have been true with respect to the former Carthagenian empire, since Carthagenians also were electoral.[15]

Indeed in the period just before the Roman conquest, the Mediterrian was infested with city states which had elected governments usually with a rather restricted group of electors. Rome, partially conquered and partially extended this system but converted it into a system of local self government.[16] As in the United States, with time, the local governments became less and less important and the central government more and more so. Unlike the United States, of course, the central government was by this time a despotic and frequently chaotic monarchy.[17]

More recently, the European states have had somewhat the same phenomenon. During the period of the French Republic, electoral institutions were imposed all over Europe and a good many aspects of them, elected parliments, juries, etc., remained in existence through the Napoleonic Empire.[18] As a result of this experience, and possibly of other factors, the nineteenth century was a period in which monarchies gradually shifted to what we will call 'limited autocracies' below and then became either republics or what I think should be called 'decorative monarchies', like the present situation in Sweden.

These 19th century electoral governments were among the greatest conquerers in world history.[19] They certainly deserve to be ranked with Rome and the Macedonians. Their empires were not originally electoral, but as time went by the European countries controlling them gradually began moving towards electoral institutions for their colonies. At the same time, of course, they were expanding the franchise at home with the result that most of them became full democracies with universal adult suffrage in the early 20th century.

The ultimate outcome in the colonies was depressing. They were all given independence with democratic institutions, but most of them switched back to autocracy fairly quickly. The degree to which they retained electoral institutions after independence seems to be roughly correlated with the amount of experience they had with such institutions under the colonial regimes. The prospect for democracy, or indeed, any kind of electoral institutions in these areas seems poor.

The most famous military extension of democracy, of course, was the imposition of democratic regimes on about half of Germany and all of Italy.[20] In Japan the existing electoral system was changed to full democracy by giving women the vote and lowering the voting age.[21] The house of peers was also abolished.[22] All three of these countries had had extensive experience with electoral institutions in earlier years.

These are all cases in which democracy came as a result of outside intervention and I don't think that we need to concern ourselves very much with them. Its obviously possible for a powerful military system to impose a form of government on nations it conquers. Whether these democracies will last a long time is not an easy question. In most cases the democracy established as the empires withdrew collapsed almost immediately. Nevertheless, I think we can simply recognize here that democracy can be spread by military force and historically has been on a number of occasions.

I ignore cases in which a democratic country simply expanded itself as for example, the United States and Canada moved into Indian areas which had previously been subject to a rather chaotic system which was not obviously either electoral or despotic and indeed was not obviously even a government. In Latin America, of course, the Spaniards seized a number of well organized kingdoms, but this did not change the form of government.[23] It was one autocracy replacing another.

But these are cases in which electoral governments have conquered other areas and imposed their form of government on it. There are also cases of course where despotisms have conquered countries with electoral systems and imposed their form of government. This is I think, rarer not because it's any less probable, but simply because electoral systems themselves are rarer. If Ligny had gone the other way, and the European kingdoms had re-established the monarchy in France, only one government would have changed form. Since Ligny was won by the French Republic and it then proceeded to win a number of other battles, it was able to change the government in many countries.

There are however, a good many cases historically, where electoral systems have been taken over. All of the Greek city states in Greece itself fell under the suzergainity of the Macedonians, who in general permitted electoral local self government.[24] Nevertheless clearly, such places as Athens, became in essence states in a larger despotic kingdom.[25] Similarly, many, although not all, of the electoral city states which were set up in the Middle Ages succumbed to conquest by autocratic neighbors. Mostly conquest meant they were annexed, but in some cases an independent dynasty was established.[26] Once again, this is not a matter of great interest. It is clear that for example, both Hitler and Stalin could impose their systems on Czechoslovakia once they had occupied it. Nevertheless, as I have said above,it seems most likely that the commonest single reason for a country ceasing to be a despotism and becoming electoral is conquest by a country which itself is electoral. Similarly the commonest reason for a country moving from electoral government to despotism is seizure by a neighboring despot. Although this is true enough, its not very interesting. Neither autocracy or electoral systems could have originated in this way.

As far as we know, the earliest governments, the ones we find in Mesopotamia, Egypt, and China[27] were all despotisms.[28] Further, as far as we can also tell the same situation existed everywhere else in the world, except possibly central Europe. Further, there seems to be no evidence that any of these governments ever became electoral except by foreign conquest.

We have mentioned that Alexander and his heirs imposed self governing city states all over their empire which included Mesopotamia and Egypt and indeed much else. In the late nineteenth and early twentieth century, of course these areas came, temporarily, under the control of democratic states from outside and in some cases this led to short intervals of domestic democracy.[29] Lebanon, where democracy was most successful, has for the last ten years been living through a genuine political nightmare They still have an elected government, but that government is not able to govern.[30]

There is one exception to this rule for early states. For reasons that are not clear, the Phoenicians seem to have lived in a set of city states. Their internal government was electoral, apparently with a very narrow electorate. Nevertheless, they did not, strictly speaking, have kings.[31]

Exactly why the Phoenicians and their great colony Carthage, had this form of government we do not know. It certainly was not in all ways a particularly pleasant government. Human sacrifice of children was in fact a major phenomena, just as their Roman enemies' propaganda said it was.[32]

To offer my own personal opinion here, I believe that the Phoenicians were descendents of the peoples of the sea, an invasion that swept over most of the middle east in about 1500 B.C. They were part of that same great wave of barbarian invasion which over a period of five or six hundred years made such a gigantic change along the northern coast of the Mediterrainian.[33] In my opinion and I emphasize this is merely my opinion,[34] they differed from the Dorian Greeks, or the tribes who eventually established Rome, mainly in the fact that the very dense populations in the middle east meant that in general they were absorbed by the natives and adopted native governmental techniques. The Phoenicians would then be a minor outpost that stuck to their older forms to at least some extent.

The rest of this wave which came in at about that time destroyed Cretan and Mycenean civilization.[35] It inaugurated the Greek dark age and these Dorian conquers seem to have set civilization north of the Mediterrian back very very sharply.[36] Nevertheless, when Greece comes out of the dark age, it is no longer a country of many petty kingdoms, but a country of many petty governments which were electoral. They are usually called oligarchies or aristocracies.

We don't know very much about what happened in the Italian penninsula. There do not seem to have been any literate people there when the invaders arrived. Once again however, this area does come into history about the same time as the Greeks recover from the dark age.[37] At the time there were a number of states with basically electoral institutions.

Note that in all of these cases, the electoral institutions might possibly include a king or in the case of Sparta, two kings.[38] These would however, either be people who were deliberately elected, as was the man who is carried in our history as the first king of Rome, or if they were hereditary their powers were sharply restricted. We don't know as much about this area as we do about the later German invaders of Europe, but it seems likely their institutions were similar.

We know a little more about the Germans partly because their institutions were described by Roman historians, and partly because remnants of them existed well into relatively modern times. Nizhni-Novogrod, for example, seems to have been governed by this traditional method.[39] Alexander Nevsky, who beat the Teutonic Knights and surrendered to the Mongols without fighting is an example of the kind of leader who was referred to as a 'king' by the Roman historians talking about Germany.[40]

The germanic institutions were simple.[41] The basic governmental agency of these German tribes was an assembly of the entire population. They of course were not gigantic tribes in general. This assembly might or then again might not elect a king. Normally, these kings were members of the same family, but there was no regular rule of succession within that family.[42] Further, there was no requirement that the tribe have a king.[43] If someone was elected king he remained king until he died, but the tribe might not decide to elect anyone else at that time. The basic role of the kings was as a war leader and they were completely subordinated to the volkmoot, but of course, during war time it only rarely met.[44]

The invasion of the Roman Empire meant that these tribes were in essence at war for very considerable periods of time. As a result, the kings appear to have been able to convert the institutions I have described above pretty much into a genuine kingdom in which they had hereditary succession and true control. Bits and pieces of the control of the volkmoot however, did remain. Further, of course, many bits and pieces of the former Roman structure which involved elected local governments remained and, of course, the church itself retained a number of electoral aspects.

Thus in the Middle Ages one found city states with electoral governments, 'national' voting bodies which might have some control over the king (usually very little) and the local Catholic Cathedral might have a 'chapter' which elected its own officers.[45] The Emperor was commonly an elected official, albeit elected by a very very narrow sufferage and the Pope was throughout an elected official originally elected by the people of Rome in a rather disorderly assembly and later by the College of Cardinals.[46]

It would be hard to argue that these electoral institutions were of fundamental importance until modern times. There were however, two reasons to believe that governments might once again become electoral. Firstly, education in Europe depended very heavily on Greek and Latin,[47] and hence almost all people who could read and write were aware of the existence of the previous electoral systems. Further, they tended to look back on these periods as high points of civilization and their current situation as in every respect except religion, inferior.

Secondly there was that rather mysterious state, England.[48] From the time of Simon Montfort onward, kings of England, rather irregularly called councils of their lords and of the country squires meeting in two houses.[49] In fact, the level of power of these groups was never very clear, but England was a very disorderly country in any event in those days, with the crown frequently in dispute.

Nevertheless, from the time William of Orange became king of England, England began winning wars and also apparently being the most economically developed country in Europe.[50] This led to a tendency to copy English institutions, particularly in France where Voltaire and Montesque led the intellectual movements which eventuated in the French Revolution. At the time of the French Revolution, substantially everybody in France apparently including Louis XVI, were in favor a constitutional monarchy modeled after that of England. Of course things didn't work out that way.[51]

We've been discussing constitutional monarchy, in the meaning which that term was understood by Montesque and George II. But in any event, with the American Revolution and French Revolution modern republican governments were born.[52] In the nineteenth century the electoral system, mainly with quite large, if not universal, electorates rapidly spread all over Europe,[53] partly of course due to the Armies of the French Revolution, and quite seriously also through the Armies of the French Empire since Napoleon also, at least in theory, believed in constitutional monarchy.[54]

In the meantime, in England, George III had gone insane[55] and the government of England had become almost entirely a parlimentary government with little or no royal influence. It was however, a parliment the upper house of which was purely hereditary and still very powerful and the lower house of which was elected by a set of bizzare institutions under which for example, the House of Pitt owned in fee simple absolute six seats.[56] Conversion of this system to modern English democracy was the result of a series of reform movements running from about 1830 on and its hard to say whether they were copying the United States, the Continent, or pioneering. Indeed, the motives which led the people in control of England at that time, to gradually give up their control step by step are not particularly clear. It looks very much like intellectual conversion to the democratic ideal as well as to free trade and limited government.[57]

In the twentieth century, democracy, which probably peaked in 1914, began a long slide which we hope will not continue. In 1914 there were only two countries, Thailand and Ethopia, that did not at least have some kind of an elected legislature with at least some power.[58] It is true, that in the northern part of South America and Central America, democracies tended to pop up and then pop down again as dictators overthrew them.[59] The three strongest countries in South America, Brazil, Argentina, and Chile, were however, electoral, and had been for a considerable period of time.[60] The other South American countries, at least paid lip service to 'democracy' systems and in fact were electoral from time to time.[61]

Note that our definition of 'electoral system' is one under which a colony owned by an electoral nation is counted as electoral. A resident of Ceylon in 1840 did not have any vote in the English elections, but the same was true of most Londoners. This can obviously be critized, but there is a difference between Hong Kong, where the government is appointed by an elected prime minister in London, and Canton, where the governor is not. Further, by 1914 a number of the major colonies had begun to develop electoral aspects in their local governments. There were local elections for example, in various parts of the British Empire. What there was of an American empire was obviously in the process of being converted into either independent countries or self governing parts of the United States at a reasonable rate.

The change since 1914, is of course, drastic. All of Eastern Europe is now ruled by despotisms. The bulk of the former French, Belgian, and Dutch empires have suffered the same fate and in the former English empire only some Islands in the Carribean, India and Ceylon, are democratic. The former French empire no longer has any elements of democracy except (residually) in Lebanon. In South America, Argentina, Chile, and Brazil, have joined the tradition in which countries are sometimes democratic and sometimes dictatorial.[62] All of this represents a significant setback for electoral systems.

This has been a historical account; can we do anything more than simply recount these things? Let me run through a few historical theories. The first of these, is that in times when infantry is the basic arm and when large numbers of troops are needed, democracy is apt to be the form of government. We must begin by pointing out that as a matter of fact, the times in which democracy developed are all 'infantry' periods. Greek city states depended primarily on mobilizing their adult male citizenry to fight as infantry.[63]

Similarly, the Roman Legions were essentially infantry forces.[64] The American Revolution occurred during a period when infantry was the primary arm[65] and the French Revolution which introduced conscription into the modern world and won its battles essentially by throwing vast numbers of men into the gun fire of the outnumbered royal armies it opposed was an almost perfect expression of this theory.[66]

Further, it should be pointed out that the fall of the Roman Empire was essentially a triumph of mounted warriors over foot soldiers. Adrianople, was the first time that the Roman Legions had been riden down by cavalry.[67] From Adrianople for another three hundred years, Roman armies consisted primarily of armored cavalry[68] and the restoration of infantry in the army of Byzantium[69] was not duplicated in Western Europe where cavalry remained the dominant arm until the British bowmen and the Swiss pikemen restored the older infantry predominance.[70]

Similarly, the slide of democracy in recent years has been accompanied by the developement not of cavalry, but of tanks, aircraft, etc.; weapons which are not really suitable for quickly trained conscript soldiers of the levy in mass.

But having said that there is this much truth in it, it is easy to find counter examples too. Greece fell not before cavalry, but before the Macedonian infantry.[71] In modern times, a great many democracies have been overthrown by conscript armies following their officers rather than their elected political leaders. Colonels in Greece and the Generals in Argentina, are merely specific examples.[72] I think there is something to be said for this theory, but not very much. After all, historically infantry has normally been the dominant arm simply because it is the cheapest arm. And the dominant governments have in fact, been despotisms of one sort or another rather than democracies. It is true, as far as I know, there have never been any democracies that depended essentially on cavalry for their defense, but granted the relative rarity of democracies and the relative rarity of cavalry predominance on the battle field, this may simply be coincidence.

We now turn to what I call the Aristotelian theory of the overthrow of democracy.[73] Aristotle had a sort of cyclical theory of government, although it was never very obvious why thc tyrannies would be replaced by oligarcies. Nevertheless, his theory of the overthrow of democracies clearly does fit at least some of the empirical evidence.

He thought that the basic reason for the fall of democracy was essentially what we would now call left wing politics. He hypothesized a 'popular' leader who succeeded in convincing the common people that he needed a professional body guard in order to protect himself against the wealthy. Once he had this private body guard, he converted it into a sort of secret police and controlled the city state.[74] There seems to be no doubt that a certain number of Greek tyrants did indeed follow this line of development.[75] Further, both Caesar and Lenin carried out what might be argued to be a sort of modernized version.[76]

Having said this however, it is, to put it mildly, easy to think of cases in which dictatorships have overthrown democracy where they represented not the people or the political left, but the political right. Once again the Greek Colonels and the Argentine Generals, are obvious examples. Thus, although the Aristotelian scenario, undoubtedly can occur, it would be hard to argue that it is the dominant procedure. Having disposed of what I believe are the two principle theories for the overthrow of democracy,[77] we are left without very much in the way of genuine theory.

Historically electoral systems have sometimes lasted very long periods of time. Venice was almost a thousands years old when it was finally destroyed by Napoleon (then a mere general).[78] Similarly, Bearn lasted a good five hundred years before once again the French Revolutionary troops overthrew it. Thus electoral systems can last for a long time. Some of the German city states lasted right up to the unification of Germany in 1870.[79]

Nevertheless, that has not been the normal history of electoral systems In general, they have fallen either because they failed to keep their arms up in peace time, or from internal causes. But the problem of developing any general theory of their fall has so far defeated me. There seem to be innumberable different distinct causes.[80] There is however, one thing that I think can be said fairly certainly they tend to be overthrown by the executive branch of the government rather than the legislative.

The reasons for this are I think, fairly simple and straight forward. In general, a clear majority of the legislature would normally lose from the removal of the electoral system, what ever it is, and the substitution of a dictatorial regime. The executive branch on the other hand, surely contains many people including whoever is head of the executive branch who would gain.

Note that the question of whether it is the strictly military part of the executive branch or other parts is relatively unimportant here. Traditionally, central governments have been very largely military machines. Thus, it is commoner for a military man like Napoleon to overthrow the government than a civilian like Dr. Francia. It does not seem likely however, that the predominance of military overthrows over civilian overthrows is any greater than the predominance of military men over civilians in the governments. Basically the executive branch is apt to be exalted by the movement to dictatorship regardless of whether it is a civilian or military man who heads it, and the legislative branch of the government reduced.

Why are in some cases, the executives able to overthrow the electoral government and in other cases not? I must confess, I have no clear answer, but it should be said that a great many electoral systems including those that have lasted a long period of time have had arrangements which kept the executive very weak. The Doge of Venice in the latter part of that republic's life was a mere decorative figure.[81] The actual executive work was carried out by a rotating committee called the council of ten, members of which rarely served more than one year successively.[82] The current Swiss republic has instead of a true president a council of seven.[83] The rapidly rotating executive leaders of most modern parlimentary governments also have the characteristic of probably not ever getting enough power to become dictators. Still, this is a statement of condition and nothing more. I have to admit this problem puzzles me and I would be delighted if any of the readers of this book provide a better explanation.

The reverse problem, is how do democracies replace dictatorship? Here there is for at least some cases a fairly straight forward explanation. South America, and I suspect that this will in time develop in Africa, have essentially temporary dictatorships. That is dictators who for one reason or another do not feel that they can remain dictator throughout the whole of their life and pass the throne on to their son. The reason, of course, may be that they fear their son would kill them if they made him their designated successor. They are also able to steal very large amounts of government money so that they can become independently wealthy.

Under these circumstances, retirement from office is desirable, but these dictators are aware of the fact that if they transfer the power to another individual dictator that dictator would have a very strong reason to have them killed since they would always be potential leaders of an opposition against him. On the other hand, if they transfer the power to a democracy, democratic leaders are likely to be grateful and in any event do not have such strong motives for killing their predecessor. No doubt the democracy will eventually become a dictatorship again, but by then, the dictator may be dead or will be elderly enough so that it is unlikely the successor dictator will feel it necessary to dispose of him.

Under these circumstances, establishing a democratic government has much to be said for it. A great many South American dictators have done so. They also of course, benefit from the fact that currently democracy is intellectually in very good odor and hence it looks as though they are behaving virtuously when they establish the democracy.

It is of course always possible that this kind of an arrangement will eventually lead to a permanent democratic government. So far in South America however, it has not done so, although the government of Venezuela has been democratic for a reasonable period of time now.[84] It is unfortunate in this regard that currently the far left, with its strongly anti-democratic traditions is dominant intellectually in much of the under developed world. Further, although the right in the United States, England, and Switzerland, is firmly democratic, it is not firmly democratic in places like South America or Africa. Thus a dictator can anticipate almost immediate support from at least one large body of intellectuals. Whether these are right-wing intellectuals, as they were in Brazil, or left-wing intellectuals as they are with the current government of Nicaragua, their influence is equally pernicious from the standpoint of democracy.[85]

This phenomenon is not something that I think we can regard as the basic reason why democracies are replaced by dictatorships. After all in Africa, and in South America, democracy never really got established. In those areas where electoral systems did become reasonably firmly established, a number of the Greek city states, Carthagenian city states, and for that matter Medieval city states, many of which were electoral,[86] and in Eastern Europe, the cause of the failure clearly was foreign conquest. Nevertheless, there are a number of cases in which electoral systems perished domestically. The sovereign roman people found a more sovereign Ceasar. A number of the Greek city states, and for that matter a number of the medieval city states, lost their electoral nature to a domestic dictator. Florence is of course the most prominent example.[87] I include the first and second French Republics in this category. They were established by a country which had only the feeblest electoral tradition and rather rapidly overthrown. At the time of the establishment of the Third Republic however, there was some electoral tradition and it developed to the point where as of now it seems likely that French democracy is about as secure as electoral institutions were in England in 1800. Petain was the result of a military defeat although the Germans did not directly impose him and in fact to a very considerable extent impeded the functioning of his government. DeGaulle was a rather unique phenomenon, and in any event except in the first couple of years, behaved as an exceptionally powerful democratic leader.[88]

Its obvious that democracies are indeed hard to overthrow if they're well established, simply because doing so requires quite a large number of people to take action following a leader and for at least some of them the prospects for the future will be less than if they remained an ordinary voting citizen. Simple inertia may also have meaning here.

Having said all of this however, we do still have the cases of Rome and Florence, and for that matter Syracuse, where democracy was completely removed.[89] There is also the overthrow of the Italian constitutional monarchy by Mussolini,[90] a very considerable time after the Italians had begun a fairly modern electoral government.[91] It is clear that it can be done, even if it isn't exactly easy to explain. Once again, I regret to say I have no theory explaining why it sometimes works and sometimes doesn't. The long run history of electoral institutions has not been one of success, but that may simply indicate that we have not waited long enough. The currently flourishing democracies may conceivably continue flourishing and gradually spread to take over the whole world.

I should however, not conceal from the reader my own feeling that despotism is in essence the equilibrium state of human society. This does not of course mean that I think it is a good thing. All buildings as Physicists know are in fact out of equalibrium and will eventually, given time enough,[92] fall down. I take it this is not an arguement for demolishing them. Similarly, the feeling that democracy is not the true equalibrium state, can be taken as an

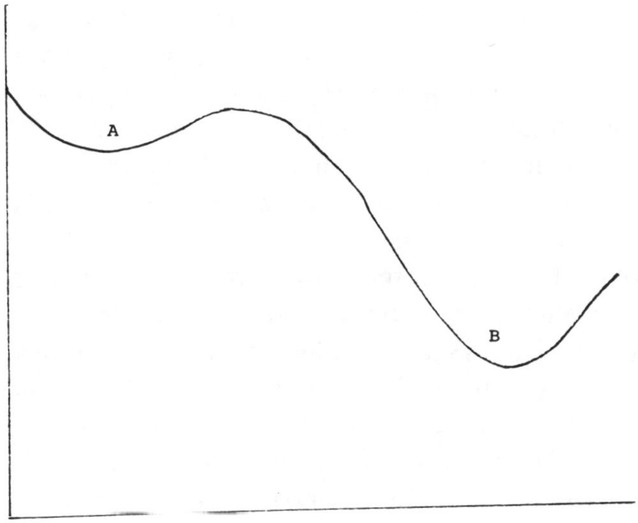

Figure 9.1

argument simply for guarding it more carefully in hopes that if we guard it carefully we can keep it or at least keep it a lot longer.

The situation is, I think, one in which electoral systems are in essence local equilibria. You can think of all possible governments as being arranged along the lines shown in figure 1. Electoral systems occupy a zone marked A and despotism is at B. Clearly, if we have a ball on this surface it would stay in A if it were there, but if it were sufficiently vigorously disturbed, it would go over the hill and down to B. Similarly, with really very vigorous disturbances, a ball which originated on B, might by accident go into A.[93]

This mechanical analogy is intended simply to indicate my view of the relationship between these two forms of government. Once again, it says nothing about their relative merits, only their relative stability. Of course if we were trying to have a really accurate analogy, we would have a hyper-surface in a multi-dimensional space, with some other possible forms of government, one of which certainly would be feudalism as local equilibria.

So far, this chapter has been even less satisfactory than the other chapters in this book. I regret this and hope that some of my readers can improve on it. What I've actually done is lay out the problems rather than my solution for them. Here however, I would like to turn to another intermediate form of government which at least arguably has been very successful. Montesque, in his *L'Esprit des Lois*, argued strongly for what he called constitutional monarchy, by which, roughly speaking, he meant England under George II.[94] By anybody's standard, this was indeed an extremely successful government. Not only did a country which was really not very big in terms of population compared to the other great powers of Europe become the dominant nation in Europe, but it also during this period laid the foundations for the industrial revolution, and had a higher per capita income for its population than almost anywhere else in Europe.[95] Montesque's admiration is therefore understandable, although whether he was right in believing that the cause was the form of government is not clear.[96]

Let us pause here and describe this government as it functioned in very rough terms. Firstly, we should say that the details are matters of great controversy. Montesque and Namier[97] for example, both thought that they knew as much about the government of England as possible, but their pictures are in many ways quite different. John Brewer,[98] is not so convinced that he himself knows how the constitution of England operated at that time, but he does in any event present a different picture than either of the two previous authorities.

The point of this is simply to indicate that at the time and for that matter now, the exact functioning of that government was a matter of considerable dispute. I am going to make what I think is a very general description, and which I think all of disputing parties would accept. It may be however, that this very general description is defective in that it misses certain vital details which one or more of the authories cited above included in their studies. Nevertheless, my description, as the reader will quickly discover, fits a number of reasonably successful modern governments. These modern governments are as the English government was in the 18th century, governments of underdeveloped countries. Thus it may be that this is a better form of government than those we normally find in underdeveloped areas.

What then is the situation? Firstly, there is at the top a man who is called king in England, dictator in the more modern examples, who has undeniably very great power. There is however, also a legislature. The exact split of power between the legislature and the dictator is not at all clear. Could, for example, George III simply appoint his own prime minister or could he not? I don't think anybody in 1776 was certain.

Secondly, if we look at the legislature itself, we find a number of rather odd characteristics. Firstly, the executive head, whether we call him a king or a dictator, clearly has a great deal of influence in determining who will hold seats in that legislature. To say he has a great deal of influence does not mean that he controls it. Characteristically, some members of the legislature will one way or another be directly appointed by him. Notably however, even these members of the legislature sometimes oppose him.

When I was in Korea recently, we drove by the legislature and as we went by my host, a professor of Economics, mentioned that one of his colleagues, had been appointed to the legislature. I responded by asking, 'Does he always vote with the President?' He apparently thought that I hadn't understood him and repeated that he was appointed to the legislature. I said, 'Yes, but does he always vote with the President?'[99] He responded by, 'I don't approve of people being appointed to the legislature by the President.' I said, 'I don't either, but does he vote with the President all the time?' He said, 'Not always.' This relationship would have been very familiar to George II or III.

Further, among those who are not put in their positions by by the dictator or King, a good many of them have gotten there by somewhat odd means. I previously mentioned, the ownership of seats in parliment, but seats were also sometimes bought. My favorite example was a well intentioned group of public spirited men, of a constituency in North England, who put their seats in Parliment up to auction. The money was to be used to repair roads.[100] Mostly however, it was less public spirited. Once again, this is characteristic of many of the countries that I will be discussing in a moment.

Lastly, it is not at all clear exactly why this institution exists, but it is clear that it is a restriction on the power of the man who otherwise would be an absolute ruler. Let me now turn to some modern examples. Mexico is a fairly clear cut example; as was Brazil.[101] South Korea, Taiwan, Singapore, and Thailand are also good examples.[102] Looking farther back, Rome from the time of Ceasar, until about the time of Severus, could be regarded as an example.[103] Further, almost all of the countries in Europe in the nineteenth century, were examples at one time or another.

If we look at the older examples, they all turned out to be transitional stages. Rome of course moved to a complete dictatorship and eventually hereditary monarchy. European countries generally speaking, moved to the modern type of constitutional monarchy where the king is a mere figure head or to outright republics. Russia, the country in which the movement to what I'm now calling constitutional democracy was the latest, occurring after 1905, went back to a monarchy which has many resemblances to that of Ivan the Terrible.[104]

Whether this indicates that the system is transitional, and hence that the modern examples that I gave would eventually be replaced either by democracies or by monarchies, is a question which I would not like to have to answer. Just at the moment, Brazil has become a democracy and Mexico may be moving in that direction. Developments in Thailand are sufficiently complicated so that it is not clear what is happening, but it could be argued that it is moving towards a democracy which would have a decorative king and hence would be the modern type of constitutional monarchy.[105]

The impressive feature of this list of countries however, is that all are examples of exceptionally successful countries. The modern set have all done very well economically, and certainly are pleasanter places for their citizens to live in than the average underdeveloped country. Rome seems to have gone up to its peak and then slid down again under the control of this form of government, but then it had it longer than any other country. England of course under George II was, as I mentioned above, almost fantastically successful as a country and the various governments of Europe in the nineteenth century had not only conquered most of the world in establishing their colonial empires, but also had a long period of rapid economic growth.

Does all of this indicate that this is a superior form of government? I regret to say, I cannot answer that question. The sample is too small. In addition, I cannot claim to know the history of all countries in detail, but for all I know there may be other examples of this form of government where things have gone very badly indeed. I can only say I know of none. It is also hard to predict the future. None of our historic examples lasted and the ones that I've picked out of the present world are in general quite young. The oldest, Mexico, is about 50 years old. This system had its attractions for Montesque, and for that matter for Locke, who argued for balanced governments.[106] Note, this was balanced between different forms of governments however, not anything more strenuous. He did not argue that it was for example, particularly likely to maximize the public interest.[107] In essence he thought that the two forms of government each had something to be said for it and the combination was desirable. Today, most of us would feel that the dictatorship-true monarchy, has little or nothing to say for it, and hence compromising democracy is not desirable. Nevertheless, this form of government does exist, and to repeat, as far as I can see, its had a rather good historical record.

This chapter has, I think, been rather more unsatisfactory even than the previous chapters. There do seem to be some general patterns, but I am unable to put my finger on any theory which explains them. I apologize for this, and hope that my readers, instead of simply repeating my own criticism of the chapter, will offer something to replace it.

NOTES

1. Israel is an exception to this rule since it is normally counted as a democracy in spite of the fact that west bank arabs are not permitted to vote for the Israeli government. Sometimes they are permitted to choose their own officials for local government organizations. See Dunnigan and Bay (19), on the limited political rights allowed West-Bank Arabs by the Israeli's; see also 'West Bank Arabs Have Rarely Felt so Cornered,' *The New York Times*, August 11, 1985, p. E5.

2. As Poowra (1957) points out: 'By the end of the eight century hereditary kings had almost ceased to count in Greece...and [were] replaced by written constitutions, which gave power to...oligarchies and democracies...the first of which...meant the rule of nobles.... A democracy, on the other hand, claimed that its government was in the hands of the whole free male adult population. This was a later growth than oligarchy and was always less common.' (p. 82). See also Forrest (1966), pp. 65-66.
A relatively small electoral class was also the case in Sparta's 'Democracy': 'In speaking of ''Democractic'' elements in the Spartan constitution, one must of course remember that the citizens as a whole were a ruling class fiercely tyranizing over the helots [Greek populations conquered by Sparta]. and allowing no power to the *Perioeci*' , free inhabitants of Laconia, (Sparta's capital) who had no political power. (Russell, 1945, p. 97.)

3. See for example, Kronenberger (1942), pp. 200-211; Spearman (1957), pp. 1-7, 52-59. Of course, as Muir (1924, p. 16) points out, 'All the Government proposals were carried by overwhelming majorities. And this was due not merely to the fact that corruption was employed on a wholesale scale - on a scale far more

lavish than Walpole even dreamed of - but still more to the fact that most of the country gentlement in the House of Commons were quite content that the King should control the Government, and had no quarrel with his policy...And there is no reason to suppose that in thus accepting the new regime the two Houses of Parliment ran counter to public feeling in the country at large. The King himself and the policy he pursued were by no means unpopular...If an election on quite democratic lines could have taken place at any time between 1770 and 1777, it is probable that the party which supported the King's policy would have obtained a majority quite as large as that which it enjoyed under the anomalies of the old representative system.'

4. Women could not vote. It wasn't until 1920 when the 19th Amendment was passed that they could, and of course in Great Britain universal suffrage began in 1918 when women over 30 were enfranchised. This was lowered to 21, a decade later. (See e.g. Grun, 1979, pp. 471ff.)

5. See for example, Fitzpatrick (1982), pp. 27,29. Of course, as Johnson (1983) points out (p. 64), 'Lenin astutely made the greatest possible use of the spurious legitimacy conferred upon his regime by the Soviets...[H]e carefully operated at two levels...on the surface was the level of constitutional arrangements and formal legality. That was for show,..the deep structures of a real power: Police, army, communications, arms..[On 12 November 1917] the elections proceeded with the Bolsheviks merely one of the participating groups. It was the first and last truly parlimentary election ever held in Russia.' Lenin formally dissolved the parliment on January 6, 1918. (See Johnson, 1983, pp. 71-72 for example.) Today of course, 'from the initial decision to hold elections on a particular day through the selection, nomination and registration of candidates, right through the count and post-election scrutiny of the ballots, the [communist] party is involved,...making ''authoritative suggestions''..., and leading the propaganda campaign, designed to get the voters to the polls and to refrain from voting against the one approved candidate in each constituency by crossing out the name....Nothing is left to chance or spontaneity...' (Hill and Frank 1983, pp. 110-111.) See also Hill (1973,1976); Scott (1969), esp. p. 97; Clarke (1967); Jacobs (1970, 1972); Gilison (1968), esp. p. 820; Friedgut (1979).

6. Harasymiur (1984) gives a discussion of Personnel and Recruitment policies with respect to membership in the Nomenklatura and Communist Party. See also, Armstrong (1961); Miller (1982); Hough (1980); Voslensky (1984); d'Encausse (1980), pp. 16ff, 70ff, 139-149, 320-322.

7. The expanding size of the communist party membership has been noted by many Sovietologists. Miller (1982) for example, suggest (p. 4) that this 'surprisingly large party presence in society', reaching more than 16 million in the early 1980s. Neuman (1956) in Blondel (1969); and Friedrich and brzezinski (1966), p. 49, for example, feel that the CPSU isn't 'really' a political party. Others (Merkl, 1970, pp. 271-272; Ball, 1977, p. 75; Blondel, 1973 pp. 82-83) believe it should be classified as a political party and analyzed as such. (The Soviets of course tend to side with the views of the latter.) Schapiro (1970, pp. 621, 625) and others look at the communist party simply as a 'monopoly' party; while others have concentrated on what they see as 'pluralistic tendencies' in Soviet politics, in recent years (see e.g. Miller, 1981, p. 604; Brown, 1983). C.F. d'Encausse (1980), pp.

207-209, on coalition stability in the CPSU; and *Ibid*, pp. 71-83, on the composition and growth of the Central Committee.

8. On Hitler's use of the Nazi party, see Bullock (1964), passim; See also Jarman (1961), pp. 79-94, 133-168. The Fascist party established on March 23, 1919 by Mussolini, as a means for gaining political control of Italy, is discussed in Johnson (1983), pp. 95-96, 97-103. Indeed, as Johnson notes (p. 100), in his use of the fascist party, Mussolini 'did not make any of Lenin's obvious mistakes. He did not create a secret police, or abolish parliment. The press remained free, opposition leaders at liberty. There were some murders, but fewer than before the coup. The Fascist Grand Council was made an organ of state and the Blackshirts were legalized, giving an air of menace to the April 1924 elections, which returned a large fascist majority. But Mussolini saw himself as a national rather than a party leader. He said he ruled by consent as well as force.'

9. The suggestions seem correct that to Franco, 'The army was the only truly national institution, ancient, classless, non-regional, apolitical, incorrupt, disinterested. If it was oppressed, it mutinied...; otherwise it served.' Franco 'Hated politics in any shape' and 'exploited the two insurrectionary movements, the Phalanage and the Carlists, amalgamating them under his leadership, but their role was subservient, indeed servile.' (Johnson 1983, p. 331. See also Ben-Ami, 1983, p. 396; and Wheatcroft, 1983, pp. 114-117 on Franco's Military Take-over.)

10. When it didn't sell all the citizens into slavery.

11. See Forrest (1966). He notes (p. 39) that the Athenian Empire 'is often described as a savage and selfish tyranny...But although Athenian enthusiasm may have led her occassionaly to impose or at least encourage democracy when it was not wholly necessary...to a considerable extent in fact,the ally remained autonomous...If Athenian rule was...harsh and unpopular..., it is curious how few of Athens' subjects' were anxious to exchange it for Spartan freedom; most of the allied contingents in Sicily preferred to face almost certain death beside the Athenians than to accept an offer of safety from the Syracusans; curious that when revolts occurred they were nearly always the work of dissident oligarchs while the people were often prepared actively to support the return of the Athenians; even more curious how many former members of the Empire were ready to join a new Athenian confederacy in the fourth century after less than thirty years' experience of Spartan freedom.' See also Eisenstadt (1963), p. 106.

12. On the Theban period in Greece (371-355 B.C.), see also Dupuy and Dupuy (1977) p. 43; Lander (1972), p. 77; Oman and Adam (1928), pp. 426-451ff.

13. And indeed also the Macedonians. See for example, Sinnigen and Boar (1977), pp. 59ff, 62ff, 97ff; Mommsen (1928), pp. 62-73. On the Macedonians, see Langer (1972), pp. 91-92.

14. Sinnigen and Boar (1977), pp. 133ff.

15. To a certain extent. though ruled by 'merchant Princes,' the Carthaginian state was nonetheless controlled in part by popular assemblies which were at liberty to 'freely discuss and oppose matters brought before th;em.' However, the assemblies' 'agenda' was determined by a council of elders who decided just what these 'matters' might be. Muller (1961), p. 104.

16. Sinnigen and Boar (1977), Chapter 8, 'Conqeust of the Mediteranean, First Phase: 264-201 B.C.', pp. 96-116; and Chapter 9, 'Conquest of the

Mediterranean, Second Phase: 200-167B.C.,' p. 117-127. See also Mommsen (1928), Part II, 'Conquest of the Mediterranean States, 264-133 B.C.,' pp. 89-168.

17. Gibbon (1914), Vol. I, pp. vff; Sinningen and Boar (1977), Chapter 23, 'The Public Administration Under the Autocracy,' pp. 431-450.

18. As Gershoy (1957, p. 93), for example, summarizes the process, 'In that part of Europe which lay closest to France, the guiding impulse [of the first republic (1792-1804)] had been in 1792-1793 to liberate the enslaved peoples...[C]ivilians and generals alike were imbued with the consciousness of their country as *La Grande Nation*, superior as well as victorious and entitled by the laws of nature to the natural frontiers that her armies had gained..people of the annexed and incorporated territory continued as before to pay for benefits received. The privileged aristocracy, both law and secular, had been dispossessed by 1799; the feudal and mandrinal regimes, totally uprootted. The sale of nationalized property was proceeding briskly. Careers were open, within the salutary limitations imposed by the occupying liberators, to the talents of the home population. To be sure, old grievances still rankled: omnipresent French civil and military officials, periodic requisitions of food and material, military service obligations, and sporadic religious persecution. But the people were free, practicing more or less popular sovereignty. Time, the great healer, was working, aided by his assistant, the pocketbook, to reconcile the old with the new.' See also *Ibid.*, pp. 57-58, 70-101; C.F. Blum, Cameron and Barnes (1970), pp. 480-491, 515, 604.

19. Of course, the industrial revolution these countries were experiencing at the time produced technological advances which contributed to the development of weapons, and as a result enhanced their military capacities. See McNeill (1982), Chapter 6, 'The Military Impact of the French Political and the British Industrial Revolutions, 1789-1850,' pp. 185-222; and Chapter 7, 'The Initial Industrialization of War, 1840-84,' pp. 223-261. See also Fieldhouse (1982), Part two, 'The Colonial Empires After 1815,' pp. 177-371.

20. These campaigns ae descirbed in Dupuy and Dupuy (1977), pp. 683-688.

21. In 1945. (See Langer, 1972, pp. 1344-1345.)

22. See for example, Johnson (1983), pp. 179-190ff; 719ff; Langer (1972), pp. 1344-1345 describes various constitutional changes in modern Japan's government.

23. See for example, Fieldhouse (1982) Chapter 2, 'The Spanish and Portuguese Empires in America,' pp. 11-33; Chapter 5, 'Myths and Realities of the American Empires,' pp. 84-99.

24. Bowra (1957), p. 77; see also Forrest (1966), p. 42.

25. Muller (1961), pp. 221-222; Langer (1972), p. 78; Oman and Adam (1928), pp. 471-520.

26. Langer (1972), Part III, SectionC, 'The Later Middle Ages,' pp. 287-391; Blum, Cameron, and Barnes (19), pp. 27, 31ff; Mango (1980), 46-59, 60, 220.

27. Until we decipher Indian script, we cannot be sure whether this was true there also.

28. See e.g., Silverberg (1963), passim; Langer (1972), pp. 27-34ff; Sayce (1928). The Sumerian government did have some aspects which can be interpreteted as electoral.

29. The short-term duration probelm of 'ready-made and superimposed'

western electoral regimes in this area of the world has been noted and examined in Lewis (1966), Chapter X, 'The Impact of West,' pp. 164-178.

30. As Johnson (1983), p. 703) observes, the chances for long-run political stabilityin Lebanon were of course quite poor from the beginning.

31. Sayce (1928), p. 125. Silberberg (1963) suggests (p. 127) that it is in fact 'wrong to refer to this land of the Phonecians as a "nation". Even using the name "Phonecia" to describe the area is somewhat inexact. There never was a Phonecian nation under one government. What existed was a group of independent cities, bound loosely together by ties of commerce and language and kinship.' See also *Ibid*, pp. 146-147. Sayce (1928), p. 124: 'The government of the several states was a monarchy tempered by an oligarchy of wealth. The king seems to have been but the first among a body of ruling merchants princes and powerful and wealthy chiefs. In time the monarchy disappeared altogether, its place being supplied by suffetes or "judges", whose term of office lasted sometimes for a year, sometimes for more, sometimes even for life.' He states (p,. 125) that though 'successor royalty was abolished for a time, and the Tyrians elected suffetes or judges..On Hiram of Tyre (969-936 B.C.), see also e.g. Langer (1972), pp. 47-48. In Carthage, 'There were also kings at first. But by 400 B.C. the hereditary monarchy had given way to a system involving two annually elected magistrates, a senate of 300 members appointed for life, and another assembly of 104 members whose role is unclear.' (Silverberg, 1963, p. 147) In fact, 'Carthage never founded a real empire. In Spain and Africa, the Carthaginian colonies seem to have been under direct political control ofthe mother city, but the other western Phonecian cities in the Mediterranean were only slightly affiliated with Carthage.'

32. As Blum, Cameron, and Barnes (1970) state (p. 9), 'Moloch demanded the best and dearest that the worshipper could grant him, and the parent was required to offer his eldest or only son as sacrifice, while the victim's cries were drowned by the noise of drums and flutes. When Agathokles defeated the Carthaginians, the noblest of the citizens offered in expiation three hundred of their children to Baal-Moloch... The priests scourged themselves or gashed their arms and breasts to win the favor of the god, and similar horrors wer perpetrated in the name of [the goddess] Ashtoreth. To here, too, boys and maidens were burned, and young men made themselves eunuchs in her honor.' (Sayce, 1928, pp. 127-128.)

33. See e.g. sayce (1928), pp. 117-136; Oman and Adam (1928), pp. 27ff, 18ff; See also Silverberg (1963), pp. 130ff.

34. I offer my opinion here with little false modesty because no one else knows much about the matter either. For an easily readable but nevertheless authoritative account of what little is known, see Sandars.

35. See for example, Forrest (1966), p. 45; Silverberg (1963), pp. 131,135-144-155.

36. The Greek Dark Age (1200 B.C., to approximately 800 B.C.) followed the 'First massive greek colonial movement' by the Dorians coming down from Asia Minor.' Cities were destroyed and trade was cut off. 'The Greeks became illiterate and were reduced to small local communities.' (Langer, 1972, pp. 60-61). See also Oman and Adam (1928), pp. 51ff.

37. In fact, it was Greeks setting up city states who first began noticing the place. See Bowra (1957), p. 20.

38. As Russell (1945) describes it(pp. 96-97), 'The constitution of Sparta was complicated. There were two kings, belonging to different families, and succeeding by heredity. One or other of the kings, commanded the army in time of war, but in time of peace their powers were limited. At communal feasts they got twice as much to eat as anyone else, and there was general mourning when one of them died.' Forrest (1966, p. 128) summarizes the double monarchy as 'a strange institution which the Spartains traced back to the twin sons of an early leader but is more probably to be explained by some earlier compromise and coalition of rival Dorian groups.'

39. Langer (1972), pp. 185, 258-259, 331-333, 341-342, describes the early political history of Novogorod, a city in Russia originally established by the Swedes (862 A.D.), later dominated by German traders as a commercial center (1150-1250 A.D.), and eventually conquered and made a territory of Russia by Ivan III (The Great) (1478 A.D.). In the 11th century, 'The assembly of freemen (*Vieche*) reached its fullest development' as a political system in Novogorod. (p. 259)

40. On Alexander Nevski (1236-1263 A.D.), Russian military leader, and 'Prince' (of Novogorod, and, of Vladimir after 1252), see for example Dupuy and Dupuy (1970), p. 378; Langer (1972), pp. 258-261, 340. See also Blum, Cameron, and Barnes, pp. 47-48. Nevski became, in effect, a 'vassal of the mongols' from 1240-1263, following their successful conquest in Russia.

41. I follow mainly Bury (1967) here.

42. More precisely, there were two distinct types of supreme rulers possible under the Germanic system, and tribes which had no monarch 'had an officer who was called the graf. The graf had functions and duties corresponding to these of the king', but with one noteworthy difference: 'The graf was elected by the assembly, and the assembly might elect anyone they liked. The king was likewise elected..., but in his case their choice was limited to a particular family, the royal family. In other words, the king was hereditary, and the grafship was not.' (*Ibid*, p. 13).

43. *Ibid.*, pp. 12, 13.

44. In fact, 'The presence of absence of a king might almost be described as a matter of convenience; it had almost no decisive constitutional importance. In every German state, whether there was a king or not, the assembly of the freemen was sovran...' (*Ibid.*, p. 12., See also pp. 14-15).

45. More commonly of course, it was subject to direct control from some superior. see e.g. Rank (1913), pp. 3ff, on the development of papal authority during this early period. On the movement toward centralization of the authority of the Roman church, see Sinnigen and Boar (1977), pp. 381, 480-485.

46. Sabine (1957, pp. 211-212) comments that 'in constitution making the Papacy led the way by the establishment in the second half of the eleventh century of an orderly process of election by the clergy, to replace the older informal kind of election which often made a Papal election the plaything of the petty Roman nobility or of imperial politics.'

47. Haskins (1957, p. 28) notes taht 'it was almost wholly as formulated in a few standard texts that the learning of the ancient world was transmitted to mediaeval times.' See also, *Ibid.*, pp. 66ff.

48. I believe that some of the Scandinavian countries, particularly Sweden, had a

development rather similar to that of England, but I must admit I don't know much about them.

49. Mackie (1957), pp. 562-567, describes relations between the monarchy and parliment during this time. In 1539, following the constitutional separation of Parlament into the two Houses, King Henry VIII nevertheless "packed" parliment judiciously before it met; he was ready with a programme, and he "managed" the debates...It is, however, uncertain how far the process of "packing" went....Parlament was not a "lion under the throne" which roared when the king pressed the hidden spring. It was, however, susceptible to "management" and Henry understood "management" very well.' (*Ibid.*, p. 437) See also, Fisher (1906), pp. 434-435.

50. On economic and political developments in England after William III see for example Heyney (1918), Chapter XVII, 'The Period of the Foundation of the British Empire, 1689-1763,' pp. 516-575: see also Muir (1927), pp. 701-702,710ff.

51. As MacDonald (1928, p. 211) writes, 'The acceptance of the constitution [of 1791] by the king [Louis XVI] was welcomed by contemporary France as the term of the revolution, rather than as an epoch in it...All that the men of 1789 had fought for was won; the grievances of the *Ancien Regime* were removed, and the constitution secured to France a modified form of that monarchial government to which the majority were sincerely attached. Men were tired of both the drudgery and of the excitement of politics, and desired to return to their civil occupations. Nothing was further form the heart of France than the deposition of Louis or the declaration of a *guerre a outrance* against Europe.' Of course, 'in spite of the wishes of the majority, both these misfortunes occurred.'

52. As one British scholar writes, 'The American war had profound results on the nascent democratic movement, because it roused strong opposition to the activities of George III and because so many people sympathized with the revolt of the colonies. "No taxation without representation" was certain of a cordial response on this side of the Atlantic. There was also a feeling that the defeat of the colonies would have encouraged the King in his suspected designs on the constitution...Englishmen no longer congratulated themselves on the superiority of their insitutions to those of other countires. The French Revolution was so spectacular that the similarly disturbing example of the United States is now forgotten, but it was very important.' particularly in its economic effects: 'Every year that democratic government existed in the United States it became a more damaging contrast to the Government of England. Many manufactureres had business contracts with the United States, as for example Cobden and the Radical manufactureres of Leicester...Everyone who was dissatisfied, the middle class, the working men, the dissenters, naturally asked why a system which worked in one country [The United States] would not work in another.' (Spearman, 1957, pp. 48, 68.)

53. See *Infra*, references in a previous note in this chapter.

54. But C.F. comments in *infra*, previous note in this chapter.

55. See Temperley (1925), pp. 69-73ff; Rigg (1925), pp. 423ff; see also, on the derangement of king George III, Griffin (1925), pp. 473-474. An added problem for Parliment at the time of the King's illness was that of discerning the political inclinations of the examining physicians. The doctors who were asked to report to

the Commons on the King's capacities tended 'to differ politically as well as professionally, thus adding to the difficulties of the situation.' (*Ibid.*, p. 473).

56. Cheyney (1918, p. 548) notes that 'this bad custom [of Parlimentary corruption] had been growing ever since the reign of Charles II, but it reached its height under Walpole. "All these men have their price," he once said to a friend, pointing to a group of members of the House of Commons.'

57. See Blum, Cameron and Barnes (1970), pp. 567-572.

58. Langer (1972) pp. 980-1120, summarizes political structures worldwide at this time. On Ethiopia in particular, see *ibid.*, pp. 872, 1078-1079; and see also Kapuscinski (1977), on the reign of Ethiopian Emperor Haile Selassie (1916-1974). It might be noted that Ethiopia in fact did not officially abolish slavery until 1924. Thailand's (Siam) political system during this period is discussed in Langer (1972) p. 906, 1104-1105; see also *The New York Times*, September 15, 1985, p. 2E, where 'Thailand's 15 to 20 Coup Attempts over the Last Half Century' are examined in light of current developments.

59. Dupuy and Dupuy (1977), 1048-1050; Langer (1972), pp. 1067-1069 (See also 1241-1245); see also 'The General's Still Run Latin "Democracies",' *The Washington Post*, Nov. 10, 1985, pp. D1,D4, on current developments.

60. Shortly after this time, of course, Argentina 'fell victim to both the twin evils which poison Latin America: Militarism and Politics.' As Johnson (1983, p. 616) continues, summarizing the problem in this region, 'in the nineteenth century the military *coup* had become a standard means to change government. This disastrous practice continued after the arrival of universal suffrage. In the years 1920-66, for instance, there were eighty successful military *coups* in eighteen Latin-American countries, Ecuador and Bolivia leading with nine each, Paraguay and Argentina following the seven each.'

61. So, for example, Langer (1972), pp. 1057-1066, 1239-1245. Moore (1967) suggests in passing that 'much of Latin America remains in the era of authoritarian semiparlimentary government.' (p. 438).

62. At the time this book was written there were only six dictatorships in the whole of Latin America. This was possibly a record, but at the time of the final revision it had risen to seven. Both numbers are low and perhaps portend a change.

63. In fact, a citizen's political eligibility for certain offices and function ws determined at least in part by the contribution he could make to the military needs of the state: 'Since the days of Solon (594 B.C.) Athenians had been divided into four census classes, the *Pentakosio medimnoi*, men whose estates could produce 500 measures of grain or there equilivant per annum; the *Hippeis* or cavalrymen, those who could afford to keep a horse and equip themselves for cavalry service; the *zeugitai* or hoplites, those fitted to arm themselves as infantrymen; and the thetes, those who could not. At first,...these classes had an important political significance in that membership carried with it qualification for certain offices of state. In the fifth century this was still officially the case, at least to the extent that *thetes* were barred by law from the highest purely civil office, the archonship and only *pentakosiomedomnoi* were trusted with the chief financial positions.' (Forrest 1966, p. 22. See also Langer, 1972, p. 65).

64. Sinnigen and Boar, 1977, p. 262. See also Luttwak, 1976, pp. 40ff.)

65. Montross (1944), pp. 417-439; Dupuy and Dupuy (1977), pp. 708-717;

Kreidberg and Henry (1955), pp. 1-22; Wheatcroft (1983), pp. 14-20.

66. Montross (1944), pp. 450-458; Dupuy and Dupuy (1977), pp. 678ff; McNeill (1982), pp. 137-8, 144-206; Wheatcroft (1983) pp. 21-29; Hart (1955), pp. 113ff; Dupuy (1980), pp. 154-158; Dunn-Pattison (1928), pp. 400-403.

67. 'The first great victory of Heavy Cavalry over Roman infantry came in the battle of Adrianople (A D. 378). Emperor Valens of the East Roman Empire had assembled a large army for a showdown with the Ostrogoths and Visigoths...The Roman losses were tremendous...perhaps as many as forty thousand men were killed...[T]he Roman cavalry...did not participate in the battle, succeeded in breaking out and escaping death.' (Dupuy, 1980, pp. 39-40. See also Montross, 1960, pp. 86-87, Dupuy and Dupuy, 1970, p. 157.)

68. See for example Eadie (1967); Sinnigen and Boar (1977), pp. 426ff; Dupuy (1980), pp. 36-41; Hart (1955), pp. 59-60.

69. Montross (1960), pp. 127-128 Discusses the replacement of cavalry with footsoldiers or 'foot-archers' in 10th century Byzantium.

70. See Montross (1960), pp. 168-172, for a discussion of the English Longbowmen, employed in England's army from the 12th through the 15th centuries. On the Swiss 'Halberdiers' or spearman of the 14th century, see *Ibid.*, pp. 172-175. Both types of men-at-arms, are also discussed in Dupuy (1980), pp. 81-89.

71. Dupuy and Dupuy (1977) pp. 43-44, gives a summary of Greece's fall to Maledonia (355-356 B.C.). As a result of King Phillip's reorganization of the Macedonian fighting force, 'The backbone of the army was its infantry.' (p. 44).

72. Dupuy and Dupuy (1977), p. 1341; Langer (1972), pp. 1251-1253; summarizes that 20th century history of these practices in Argentina. On similar events in Greece, see Macridis (1984); Dupuy and Dupuy (1970), pp. 1271-1272; *The New York Times*, November 21,1985, p. A7.

73. I am here using his definition of 'democracy' not mine. In his meaning of the word, the electorate was large, but not universal. Aristole's *Politics*, Book IV, in particular, discusses this problem. But see Sabine (1956), pp. 88-122 for a review and discussion of Aristotle's theory of tyranny and democracy; see also Jaszi and Lewis (1957), pp. 4-9 and passim.

74. See e.g. Sabine (1956), pp. 114-115.

75. Forrest (1966), pp. 82ff. Sinningen and Boar (1977, p. 76).

76. On Caesar's rise to power, see Mommsen (1928), pp. 374-376. He asserts (pp. 375-376) that, when Caesar became Emperor, 'no corps of guards - the true criterion of a military state - was even formed by him; even as general he dropped the bodyguard which had long been usual; and, though constantly beset by assassins in the capital, he contented himself with the usual escort of lictors.' He admits, however, that 'this noble ideal, of a kingship based only on the confidence of the people, could be but an illusion; amid the deep disorganization of the nation it was impossible for the eighth king of rome to reign merely by virture of law and justice. Just as little could the army which had placed him on the throne be really absorbed again into the state...Thousands of swords still flew at Caesar's signal from their scabbards, but they no longer returned to their scabbards at his signal. Caesar's creation could not but be a military monarchy; he had overthrown the *regime* of the aristocrats and bankers only to put in its place a military *regime*.' Of

interest is Caesar's introduction of the use of mercenaries in his cavalry, a policy innovation to which 'He was driven by the untrustworthiness of the subject cavalry' (Mommsen, 1928, p. 374).

On Lenin's acquisition of control, see Wolf (1969), pp. 82-99; Treviranus (1944), pp. 75-140; Fitzpatrick (1982), passim; Johnson (1983), pp. 52ff, 66-86, 384; d'Encausse (1980), pp. 109-110. As Johnson (1983) points out, 'In the initial stages of his takeover, Lenin depended entirely on the armed bands Trotsky had organized through the Petrograd Soviet. They were composed partly of politically motivated young thugs, the "men in black leather jerkins", partly of deserters, often Cossacks'. (p. 65) Though on December 7, 1917, the military committee overseeing this political police force was disbanded, one section was retained, to become the 'cheka' ('All Russian Extraordinary Commission') and was 'charged with combating "counter-revolution and sabotage". The decree which created the Cheka was not made public until more than ten years later (*Pravda*, 18 December 1927), so that Lenin's security force was from the beginnin and remained for the rest of his life a secret police in the true sense, in that its very existence was not officially acknowledged.' (pp. 67-68).

Stalin of course, also employed secret policy; with his political behavior becoming (from the average citizen's viewpoint) 'characterized by the total absence of rules...[and] for this reason unpredictable. One example provides evidence. In the late forties, when the future purge was in a preparation, the police, as a first step, carried out massive arrests on the periphery of the Soviet state, in the regions where prisoners who had completed their terms were confined. These former prisoners, trying to understand the logic governing their arrests, finally discovered that it was simply alphabetical; because of the first letter of his name, an individual might escape from the purge or experience [it] again'. (d'Encausse, 1980, pp. 41-42; see also Antonov-Ovseyenko, 1981, passim.)

77. There is of course the very old one under which demagogues who are for some obscure reason very powerful, succeed in overthrowing it. There is an equally ancient one under which people who are simply wicked (usually soldiers) overthrow it, but in neither case is there any explanation as to why they can do it.

78. Pirenne (1937), pp. 198-200; Vernon (1925), pp. 605-607; Langer (1972), 238-240, 322-323, 496-497, 634-635, 700; see also Braudel (1979), pp. 466-467, 489-490; Blum, Cameron and Barnes (1970), p. 102.

79. Langer (1972), pp. 715-742.

80. Such as changes in coalition formations, and in the organizational costs of forming such groups for political gain. see my article, 'The Roots of Order' (1981), where I discuss this and other factors affecting the structure and stability of governments.

81. On the origins and development of the post of Venetian Doge see for example, Langer (1972), pp. 238-240, 322-323.

82. The Council of Ten, invented in 1335 A.D., followed from a series of electoral institutions which began in 687 with the election of the first Venetian Doge. In 1032, a coalition of aristocrats attempted to establish a hereditary doge, but they were defeated, and a council and senate were created instead. later, the appointment of the doge became the council's responsibility (1171). A popular uprising (1300) was the result of moves to restrict membership on the council 'in

favor of a narrow, hereditary, commercial oligarchy' (Langer, 1972, p. 240). A more serious revolt, Tiepolo's rebellion (1310) finally prompted the formation of an 'emergency committee on public safety,' the council of ten, in 1335. 'The Venetian government thus consisted of: the great council (i.e., the patrician caste); the senate (a deliberative and legislative body dealing with foreign affairs, peace, war, finances, trade); the council of ten, (a secret, rapidly acting body concerned with morals, conspiracy, european affairs, finance [and] the war department, which could override the senate); the *collegio* or cabinet (the administrative branch); the doge and his council, which, sitting witht he ten, made the council of seventeen.' (*Ibid.*, p. 240; see also pp. 238-239).

83. The origins of Swiss political institutions are discussed in Oechsli (1928), passim; see also Langer (1972), pp. 714-715, 1192; Blum, Cameron, and Barnes (1970), pp. 738-740; Johnson (1983), pp. 605-607. Current structures no doubt evolved from the introduction of 'concordant democracy', under which all major political parties were given representation in the executive body (the Federal Council). The system was first established in the late 1800's following a series of reforms requiring voter decision-making in direct elections to create new legislation.

84. Wheatcroft (1983), p. 159; see also Langer 91972), pp. 1258-1259.

85. General discussions of this problem are found in Revel (1984); Gasset (1957), Chapter 8, 'Why the MAsses Intervene,' pp. 68-77; Hayek (1979); Popper (1950), Chapter 23, 'The Sociology of Knowledge,' esp. pp. 402-403; d'Ecausse (1980), pp. 16-17; Mises (1963), Chapter IX, 'The Role of Ideas,' Esp. pp. 178ff; Weaver (1960), esp. pp. 90-98.

86. Mango (1980), pp. 46-59, 60, 220; Blum, cameron, and Barnes (1970), pp. 20-23; Langer (1972) pp. 155-286.

87. Pireene (1937), p. 204; Blum, Cameron, and Barnes (1970), p. 39; See also Braudel (1979), pp. 488-490.

88. See Bourgeois (1928a); Bourgeois (1928b); Bourgeois (1928c); see also Langer (1972), pp. 627-640, 679-683, 686-693, 1180-1181; Blum, Cameron, and Barnes (1970), pp. 480-485, 616-621, 722-279, 979-980, 1040-1042; Johnson (1983), pp. 587-598; Fieldhouse (1982), pp. 322-324.

89. Syracus instituted democratic reforms in 413-410 B.C., but these were quite short-lived; in 405, Dionysius I, after winning election as one of ten generals, appointed himself dictator. His son, Dionysius II, followed him and ruled tyrannically until 345, when the Syracusans requested the political services of two foreign rulers; Hicetas, tyrant of Leontini; and later Timoleon of Corinth. See for example, Oman and Adam (1928), Chapter XXXVII, 'The Greeks of the West, 413-338 B.C.,' pp. 407-418.

90. See Blum, Cameron, and Barnes (1970), pp. 930-934.

91. See for example Langer 91972), pp. 700-711, 998-1000, for a summary of the development of the electoral system of modern Italy.

92. Which in many cases may be more than one million years.

93. The similar analogy, (and a figure similar in nature to my figure 1) has been suggested by Carneiro (1982, p. 111-112); 'Elasticity in the Capacity of a body to undergo deformation and, when the deforming forces are withdrawn, to regain its original shape...a force of a certain magnitude is applied to the free end of a metal rod

and then withdrawn, the rod will spring back into place. If the force is increased so that it pushes the rod beyond its elastic limits, the rod will take a permanent set. So it is with human societies. Every social system has a margin of elasticity. It can be subjected to certain forces - wars, floods, famines, riots, plagues, strikes, inflation, unemployment - and as long as the magnitude of these forces is not excessive, the system will essentially return to its original conditions once the impinging forces abate. If it is not pressed beyond this margin, the society will be able to reestablish its old equilibrium...But if the society is subjected to forces that exceed this margin of elasticity, its existing institutions will not be able to cope with these forces. Under heavy stress, the society will be permanently deformed, that is, it will be forced to change its structure.'

94. E.g., Spearman (1957), pp. 1-7.

95. See Buer (1926); Cole and Deane (1965); George (1926); Ashton (1962); see also Mantoux (1962); Ashton (1963).

96. I myself, have argued that at least one aspect of this government was one of the major reasons for the development of modern economic systems. See, 'Why Did the Industrial Revolution Occur in England?', unpublished monograph. Public Choice Center, George Mason.

97. See Namier (1965).

98. See Brewer (1976).

99. Apparently he was under the impression that I didn't know that South Korea was basically a dictatorship.

100. Relations between Mexico's legislative Chambers of Senators and Deputies and its president are discussed in Hellman (1983), pp. 126-128ff; Johnson (1984), Chapter 5, 'The Practice of Estoteric Democracy,' pp. 116-159. See also Deland (1981), pp. 329-395, for example on conflicts between Brazil's president and its congress.

101. Summaries of these countries' current political institutions is given in Paxton (1985), pp. 395 (Taiwan), 766 (South Korea), 1055-1056, (Singapore), 1170-1171 (Thailand).

102. Mommsen (1928), pp. 29-55.
This was also true of the Spartan system. In addition to two kings, the government was controlled by 'the Council of Elders, a body consisting of thirty men (including the kings)...chosen for life by the whole body of citizens, but only from aristocratic families. The Council tried criminal cases, and prepared matters which were to come before the Assembly. This body (the Assembly) consisted of all the citizens; it could not initiate anyting, but could vote yes or no to any proposal brought before it...branch of government, peculiar to Sparta. This was the five ephors. These were chosen out of the whole body of the citizens, by a method which Aristotle says was "too childish," and which Bury says was virtually by lot. They were a "democratic" element in the constitution, apparently intended to balance the kings...When either king went on a warlike expedition, two ephors accompanied him to watch over his behavior. The ephors were the supreme civil court, but over the kings they had criminal jurisdiction.' (Russell, 1945, p. 97). The Spartan constitution was, according to myth, due to a god nameed Lycurgus, meaning 'Wolf-Repeller.' (*Ibid.*, p. 97) The Spartan Assembly (or 'Apella') is discussed also in Oman and Adam (1928), p. 64.

Similar (but weaker) institutional constraints were also present in ancient Athens: 'The political game was played in and around an aristocratic Council which, with the king, if one existed, was the sole organ of government. Mass assemblies might be held occasionally to show approval or disapproval of vital decisions which could lead to disaster without mass suppport (A declaration of war for example)...' Forrest (1966), pp. 54-55; see also Oman and Adam, (1928), pp. 62-63ff.

103. On political events prior to the revolution in 1917, see for example Werstein (1967); Fitzpatrick (1984), pp. 26-33. See also Johnson (1983), p. 59; d'Encausse (1980), pp. 8-10; Wheatcroft (1983), pp. 78-95.

104. See 'Thailand's Military Suffers Some Self-Inflicted Wounds,' *The New York Times*, September 15,1985,p. 2E.

105. Though Locke of course believed that certain 'just' and non-arbitrary procedural rules should be followed by any majority-rule government, he nonetheless felt that 'the majority, having...upon men's first uniting into society, the whole power of the community naturally in them, may employ all that power in...a perfect democracy; or else *may put the power of making laws into the hands of a few select men,...an oligarchy; or else into the hands of one man;...a monarchy*; or and if to him and his heirs; it is an hereditary monarchy; if to him only for life,...an elective monarchy. And so accordingly of these *the community may make compounded and mixed forms of government, as they think good.' Locke goes on to stress that 'by commonwealth, I must be understood all along to mean, not a democracy or any form of government, but any independent community...'* Locke, (1947ed.) pp. 186-187, emphasis added. See also Sabine (1956), pp. 534ff.

106. Through of course the replacement of such a 'balance' of political institutions by a structure desired by a single faction is not necessarily preferable, especially if it is accomplished through revolution. I discuss this problem in *The Social Dilemma* (1974).

ENVOI

It is my hope that by now the reader knows more about autocracy than he did when he started the book. It is also my hope that he has new questions about autocracy, and that these questions are better formulated than the questions with which he started. To return to a theme which was mentioned in the preface and reitterated several times. My intent was to improve our knowledge of autocracy, but I certainly would not claim that I have solved all the problems. I hope that at least some of my readers will proceed to either develop my ideas, attempt their refutation, or develop an alternative general approach. Autocracy is, by all odds, the commonest form of government both in history and in the present day world. It may not be a good form of government, but we should do our best to understand it. The book has been a step in that direction, but many more steps are necessary.

APPENDIX

Appendix

The propositions below are not strictly speaking, testable hypotheses. They are proposals for empirical research suggested by a new approach and detailed reasoning of this book. Nevertheless, the research would not only improve our knowledge of what is the commonest form of government today, but also in this case, offer evidence as to whether the general approach in this book, and the detailed reasonsing is correct. Once again, I hope that this book is the beginning of research in autocratic government, it does not purport to be the last word.

CHAPTER I: INTRODUCTION

1. Most dictators (who are overthrown are overthrown by higher officials of their own regime rather than by popular uprisings. (Line 692)

2. Change of dictator by coup, normally makes relatively modest changes in policy. (Line 712)

3. Genuine popular uprisings are rare. (Line 750)

4. Dictators do not have strong attachments to most specific policies. This can be tested by looking at those dictators who have been involved for long periods of time and observing how often they have stuck to the policies they start with when it is politically unwise to do so. (Line 850)

CHAPTER II: COUPS AND THEIR PREVENTION

1. Dictators and other autocrats are fundamentally insecure. This has not really been tested, but it would be very useful to develop a table showing frequency with which different dictators hold power. For hereditary monarchs, a similar table showing how long specific dynasties have held power would be helpful. ((Line 20)

2. It should be possible through careful study, to get some qualitative idea of the average intelligence of a random sample of hereditary rulers and of dictators. Kings should be, if this book is correct, less intelligent than dictators who have risen to power on their own. (Line 90)

3. People and organizations who save dictators from removal tend to be given material rewards, but reductions in power as a result. (Line 717)

There have been fairly few testable hypotheses proposed in connection with this chapter. The reason is not that I think in the eye of God there might not be such hypotheses, but that the data on what goes on in the immediate circle around a dictator are exceptionally bad. Everyone is strongly motivated to keep his own acts secret, and most of them are reasonably successful.

CHAPTER III: WAR

1. Military success by an army is likely to lead the heads of the army to attempt to overthrow the existing ruler. (Line 185)

2. There is a positive correlation between the strength of military force any country maintains, and the probability that the dictators would be overthrown by it. (Line 182)

3. There is a negative correlation between the strength the military forces maintain by any dictator and the probability that he will be overthrown by foreigners. (Line 182)

4. Armies that rotate officers and units are less likely to overthrow the government than armies that do not. (Line 691)

5. Armies and Navy's with committees as their supreme command are less likely to overthrow dictators. (Line 792)

CHAPTER IV: 'POPULAR' RISINGS

1. It is a thesis of this chapter, that what appears to be a popular uprising isnormally a split within the governemnt, with possibly the more popular of the two groups winning. Genuine popular risings are rare this is readily testable by counting. (Line 720).

2. The number of people actually involved in the overthrow of a government is normally quite small. Certainly much less than the majority of the population and probably much less than two or three percent. (Line 770)

3. Secret conspiricies among anyone except high officials of the government have rarely been successful in overthrowing a government. (Line 780)

4. Governments in which the level of corruption is high are far more likely to use torture as a method of detecting subversion than a relatively honest government. (Line 800)

CHAPTER V: LEGITIMACY AND ETHICS

1. Foreign armies of occupation are rarely driven out by popular uprisings.

CHAPTER VI: THE USES OF DICTATORSHIP

1. Most dictators who succeed in retiring are very well off, but not immensely wealthy.

2. The lack of firm policy preferences on the part of dictators can most readily be tested by observing the policy of those dictators

who have remained in office for long periods of time. If they had strong personal preferences for policy, then the policies would tend to remain stable through out the period. (Line 400)

3. The average change of dictator leads to relatively modest changes in policy. Most are no larger than those which occur when republican replaces democrat in the presidency.

CHAPTER VII: BECOMING A DICTATOR

1. The normal coup is carried out against the previous dictator by someone who has already achieved fairly high position. (Line 300).

2. Less commonly, a coup will be carried out by someone who rose to high rank in the government and then for one reason or another, left the country and organized opposition from outside.

3. Most dictators do not have a formal successor appointed while they are in office. (Line 450)

4. Carefully worked out plots among high officials to overthrow the dictator are rare. (Line 585)

5. Juntas normally condense to control by one man. (Line 810)

CHAPTER VIII: THE PROBLEM OF SUCCESSION

1. Dictators who are not overthrown have a strong tendency to remain in power until they die rather than retiring. This is true even if they're seriously ill. (Line 20)

2. When a dictator does have a formal successor appointed, he is very likely to remove the successor because he suspects him. The test here would be whether formal successors to dictators tend to remain in office (when there is one) for only short periods. (Line 70)

3. Hereditary monarchies tend to be domestically more peaceful than other forms of autocracy. Note this is only true when the rules of inheritance specify some individual person.

4. Counting the number of political murders by a son or other successor of a king is extremely difficult because of the facilities which such a man has to conceal his crime. Careful historical research should however, produce reasonably good figures here, and my hypothesis that this would turn out to be a very common cause of death, probably the commonest, could thus be tested.

5. My prediction that current dictatorships will eventually become hereditary is theoretically testable, but unfortunately requires waiting at least one hundred years.

6. Coups which overthrow democratic governments tend to originate in the executive rather than the legislative or judicial branches. (Line 1320)

7. Military forces are more likely to overthrow democracy by a coup than other members of the executive branch, but this preponderance is no greater than the personel preponderance that the military characteristically has over other parts of the executive branch. (Line 1330)

8. Limited autocracies tend to be considerably above average efficiency. (Line 1650)

CHAPTER IX: DEMOCRACY AND DESPOTISM

1. Whether democracy is really associated with the military predominance of drafted infantry is easily testable by statistical regression analysis.

2. The aristotelean theory of the rise and fall of democracies, tyrannies, and oligarchies could be fairly easily tested by simply counting the number of cases in which such changes went in the right direction. The problem would be making certain that the various governments met Aristotle's rather vague definition of these three forms.

Bibliography

Abraham, Henry J.,*The Judiciary: The Supreme Court in the Governmental Process*, (5th Edition) (Boston: Allyn and Bacon, Inc., 1980).

Allen, Richard C., *Korea's Syngman Rhee* (Rutland, VT: Charles E. Tuttle Company, Publihsers, 1960.)

Antonov-Ovseyenko, Anton, *The Time of Stalin: Portriat of a Tyranny*, (New York: Harper & Row, Publishers, Inc., 1981).

Ardrey, Robert, *The Hunting Hypothesis*, New York, NY: Atheneum, 1976.

Armstrong, Edward, 'The Burbon Governments in France and Spain,' in Ward, A.W., Prothero, G.W., and Leathes, Stanley, *The Cambridge Modern History, Volume VI: The Eighteenth Century*, (New York, The MacMillan Company, 1925), pp. 120-144.

Armstrong, John A., *The Politics of Totalitarianism: The Communist Party of the Soviet Union from 1934 to the Present* (New York: Random House, 1961).

Ashley, Maurice, *The Greatness of Oliver Cromwell*, (New York: Collier Books, 1966).

Ashton, T.S., *The Industrial Revolution*, 1760-1830 (Cambridge: Cambridge University Press, 1962).

–, 'The Treatment of Capitalism by Historians,' in Hayek, F.A. (ed.), *Capitalism and the Historians*, (Chicago: Phoenix Books [The University of Chicago Press], 1963), pp. 36-61.

Aubyn, Giles St., *The Year of Three Kings: 1483*, (New York: Atheneum, 1983)

Axelrod, Robert, *The Evolution of Cooperation*, (New York: Basic Books, Inc., 1981).

Baer, Gabriel, 'Social Change in Egypt: 1800-1914,' in Holt, D.M. (e.d.) *Political and Social Change in Modern Egypt: Historical Studies from the Ottoman conquest to the United Arab Republic* (London: Oxford University Press, 1968), pp. 135-161.

Bakhash, Shaul, *The Reign ofthe Ayatollahs: Iran and the Islamic Revolution*, New York: Basic Books, 1984.

Ball, Alan R., *Modern Politics and Government*, (2nd ed.) (London: Macmillan, 1977).

Bargeois, Emile, 'The French Republic', in Ward, A.W., Prothero, G.W., and Leathes, Stanley, *The Cambridge Modern History: Volume XI*, (New York: Macmillan, 1928); pp. 96-141.

Barnett, Correlli, *The Desert Generals*, New York: Ballantine Books, 1960.

Batchelder, Robert C., *The Irreversible Decision, 1939-1950*, New York, NY: Macmillan, 1961

Bemis, Samuel F., *The Diplomacy of the American Revolution*, Bloomington, IN: Indiana University Press, 1957.

Ben-Ami, Shlomo, *Fascism from Above: The Dictatorship of Primo de Rivera in Spain, 1923-1930* (Oxford: Clarendon Press, 1983).

Berdyaev, Nicolas, *The Origin of Russian Communism*, (London: Geoffrey Bles, 1948).

Bingham, Woodbridge, *The Founding of the T'ang Dynasty: The Fall of Sui and Rise of T'ang, A Preliminary Survey* (New York: Octagon Books, 1970).

Bjorklund, Oddvar, Haakon Holmboe, Anders Rohr, and Berit Lie, *Historical Atlas of the World*, (new edition), New York, NY: Barnes and Noble, Inc., 1980.

Blennerhassett, Lady, 'The Doctrinaires,' in Wart, A.W., Prothero, G.W., and Leathes, S. (eds.), *The Cambridge Modern History: Vol. X, The Restoration*, New York: The Macmillan Company, 1907, pp. 40-70.

Blondel, Jean, *An Introduction to Comparative Government* (London: Weidenfeld & Nicolson, 1969).

5 Blum, Jerome, Cameron, Rondo, and Barnes, Thomas G., *The European World, A History* (2nd Edition) (Boston: Little, Brown and Company, 1970).

Bornet, Vaughn Davis, *The Presidency of Lyndon B. Johnson* (Lawrence, Kansas: University Press of Kansas, 1983).

Bourgeois, Emile, 'The Orleans Monarchy,' in Wark, A.W., Prothero, G.W., and Leathes, S. (eds.), *The Cambridge Modern History: Vol. X, The Restoration*, New York: The Macmillan Company, 1907, pp. 475-516.

–, 'The Fall of Constitutionalism in France (1840-1848),' in Ward, A.W., Prothero, G.W., and Leathes, Stanley (eds), *The Cambridge ModernHistory, Vol. XI: The Growth of Nationalities* (New York: Macmillan Co., 1928a), Chapter II, pp.22-42.

–, 'The French Republic (1848-1852),' in Ward, A.W., Prothero, G.W., and Leathes, Stanley (eds), *The Cambridge ModernHistory, Vol. XI: The Growth of Nationalities* (New York: Macmillan Co., 1928b), Chapter V, pp. 96-141.

–, 'The Third French Republic,' in Ward, A.W., Prothero, G.W., and Leathes, Stanley (eds), *The Cambridge ModernHistory, Vol. XII: The Latest Age* (New York: Macmillan Co., 1928c), Chapter V, pp. 91-133.

Bowra, C.M., *The Greek Experience*, (New York: New AmericanLibrary, Inc., 1957).

Brams, Steven J., & William Riker, 'Models of Coalition Formation in Voting Bodies', *Mathematical Applications in Political Science*, Vol 6. University Press of Virginia; Charlottesville, VA, 1972.

Braudel, Fernand, *The Wheels of Commerce, Vol. II*, in *Civilization and Capitalism, 15th - 18th Century* (New York: Harper & Row Publishers, 1982).

Brewer, John, *Party Ideology and Popular Politics at the Accession of George III*, (Cambridge: Cambridge UniversityPress, 1976).

Brown, Archie, 'Leadership Succession and Policy Innovation,' in Brown, Archie and Kaser, Michael, editor, *Soviet Policy for the 1980's* (Bloomington, IN:

Indiana University Press, 1982), pp. 223-253.

Bruce, Anthony, *The Purchase System in the British Army, 1660-1871*, London: Royal Historical Society, 1980.

Buer, M.C., *Health, Wealth and Population in the Early Days of the Industrial Revolution*, (London: G. Routledge & Sons, 1926).

Bullock, Alan, *Hitler: A Study in Tyranny* (revised edition) (New York: Harper and Row Publishers, 1964).

Bunce, V., *Do New Leaders make a Difference?: Executive Succession and Public Policy Under Capitalism and Socialism* (Princeton, NJ: Princeton University Press, 1981).

Burg, Steven L., *Conflict and Cohesion in Socialist Yugoslavia: Political Decision Making Since 1966* (Princeton, NJ: Princeton University Press, 1983).

Burgess, John W., *The Middle Period, 1817-1858*, in the *American History* series (New York: Charles Scribner's Sons, 1897).

Burn, A.R., *The Pelican History of Greece*, (Great Britain: Penguin Books, 1984).

Bury, J.B., *The Invasion of Europe by the Barbarians* (New York: W.W.Norton & Co, 1967).

Callahan, Raymond, *The East India Company and Army Reform, 1783-1798*, Cambridge, MA: Harvard University Press, 1972.

.ti -5 Camp, Roderic A., *Mexico's Leaders*, (Tucson, AZ: The University of Arizona Press, 1980).

Cantor, Norman, F., *The English: A History of Politics and Society to 1760*, (New York: Simon and Schuster, 1970).

Carneiro, Robert L., 'Successive Reequilibrations as the Mechanism of Cultural Evolution,' in Schieve, William C., and Allen, Peter M. (eds.), *Self-Organization and Dissipative Structures: Applications the Physical and Social Sciences* (Austin: University of Texas Press, 1982), pp. 110-115.

Caro, Robert A., *The Years of Lyndon Johnson: The Path to Power*, (New York, NY: Alfred A. Knopf, Inc., 1982).

Carr, Raymond, 'Spain and Portugal, 1793-1840,' in Crawley, C. W. (ed.), *The New Cambridge Modern History: Vol. IX*, Cambridge: at the University Press, 1965, pp. 439-461.

Carrere D'Encausse, Helene, *Confiscated Power*, New York, NY: Harper and Row, 1980.

Carter, April, *Democratic Reform in Yugoslavia: The Changing Role of the Party*, (Princeton, NJ: Princeton University Press, 1982).

Chadwick, Henry, *The Early Church*, (New York, NY: Penguin Books, 1976).

Chang, David W., *Zhou Enlai and Deng Xiaoping in the Chinese Leadership Succession Crisis*, Lanham, MD: University Press of America, Inc., 1984).

Chase, Gilbert, *America's Music* (New York, NY: McGraw-Hill Book Co., Inc., 1955).

Cheyney, Edward P., *A Short HIstory of England*, (Revised Edition) Boston: Ginn and Company, 1918).

Chorley, Katherine C., *Armies and the Art of Revolution* (London: 1943).

Clarke, Alan, *Barbarossa: The Russian German Conflict, 1941-1945*, New York: New American Library 1966.

Clarke, Roger A., 'The Composition of the Supreme Soviet, 1958-66,' *Soviet*

Studies, Vol. XI (1967): p. 53-65.

Clausewitz, Carl von, *On War* (Baltimore, MD: Penguin Books, 1968).

Cole, W.A., and Deane, Phyllis, 'The Growth of National Incomes,' in Habakkuk, H.J. and Postan, M, *The Cambridge Economic History of Europe, Volume VI: The Industrial Revolutions and After: Incomes, Population, and Technological Change (Part I)*, (Cambridge: Cambridge University Press, 1965), Chapter I, pp. 1-55.

Cornford, Francis M., 'Introduction', to *The Republic of Plato*, New York, NY: Oxford University Press, 1945.

Corning, Peter A., *The Synergism Hypothesis: A Theory of Progressive Evolution* (New York: McGraw Hill Book Co., 1983).

Cottrell, Leonard, *The Warrior Pharaohs* (New York, NY: G. P. Putnam's Sons, 1969).

Crassweller, Robert D., *Trujillo: The Life and Times of a Caribbean Dictator* (New York, NY: Macmillan Company, 1966).

Crofts, Alfred and Buchanan, Percy, *A History of the Far East*, New York, NY: Longsman Green and Co., 1958.

Crozier, Bernard, *DeGaulle*, New York, Charles Scribner's Sons, 1973.

Dahl, Robert A., *Polyarchy Participation and Opposition*, (New Haven, CT: Yale University Press, 1971).

Daland, Robert T., *Exploring Brazilian Bureaucracy: Performance and Pathology*, (Washington D.C.: University Press of America, 1981).

Davies, Norman, *Heart of Elrode A Short History of Poland*, Oxford: Clarendon Press, 1984.

DeJouvenel, Bertrand, *On Power: Its Nature and the History of its Growth*, (Boston: Beacon Press, 1962).

Dermejian, R. Hrair, *Egypt Under Nasir* (Albany, NY: State University of New York Press, 1971).

Diederich, Bernard, and Burt, Al, *Papa Doc: The Truth About Haiti Today* (New York, NY: Avon Books, 1969).

Dmytryshyn, Basil, *U.S.S.R.: A Concise History*, New York, NY: Charles Scribner's Sons, 1984.

Domes, Jurgen, *The Government and Politics of the People's Liberation Army*, Boulder, CO: Westview Press, 1985.

Downey, Fairfax, *The Grande Turke: Suleyman the Magnificant, Sultan of the Ottomans* (New York, NY: Minton, Balch, and Co., 1929).

Downs, Anthony, *An Economic Theory of Democracy* (New York: Harper and Row, 1957).

Dunn-Pattison, R.P., 'The General War,' in Ward, A.W., Prothero, G.W. and Leathes, Stanley, *The Cambridge Modern History Series Volume VIII, the French Revolution* (New York: MacMillan Co., 1925 Chapger XIV, pp. 398-446.

Dunnigan, James, and Bay, Stephen, *A Quick and Dirty Guide to War: Briefings on Present and Potential Wars*, New York: William Marrow and Company, 1985.

Dupuy, R. Ernest, and Dupuy, Trevor, N., *The Encyclopedia of Military History, from 3500 B.C to the Present*, (revised edition) New York, NY: Harper and Row Publishers, 1977.

Dupuy, T.N., *THe Evolution of Weapons and Warfare* (New York: Bobbsw-Merrill Co., Inc., 1980).

Dziewanowski, M.K., *Poland in the 20th Century*, New York, NY: Columbia University Press, 1977.

Eadie, John W., 'The Development of Roman Mailed Cavalry,' *Journal of Roman Studies* 57 (1967): pp. 161-173.

Eisenstadt, S.N., *The Political Systems of Empires* (New York: The Free Press, 1963).

d'Encausse, Helene Carrere, *Confisciated Power: How Soviet Russia Really Works* (New York: Harper & Row, Publisehrs, Inc., 1980).

Evans, Bergen, *Dictionary of Quotations*, New York, NY: Delacarte Press, 1968.

Evans, Rowland, Jr., and Novak, Robert, D., *Nixon in the White House: The Frustration of Power*, New York, NY: Random House, 1971.

Fainsod, Merle, *Smolensk Under Soviet Rule*, Cambridge, MA: Harvard University Press, 1958.

Farago, Ladislas, *The Last Days of Patton*, New York: Berkley Books, 1982.

Fiechter, Georges-Andre, *Brazil Since 1964: Modernization Under a Military Regime, A Study of Interactions of Politics and Economics in a Contemporary Military Regime* New York, NY: John Wiley and Sons, 1975.

Fieldhouse, D.K., *The Colonial Empires A Comparative Survey from the Eighteenth Century* (2nd Edition) (London: The Macmillan Press Ltd., 1982).

Fisher, H.A.L., *The History of England from the Accession of Henry VII to the Death of Henry VIII (1485-1547)*, New York, NY: Kravs Reprint Co., 1969.

Fisher, H.A.L., *The History of England from the Accession of Henry VII to the Death of Henry VIII (1485-1547)*, in Hunt, William and Poole, Reginald L. (eds.) *The Political History of England (in Twelve Volumes)*, New York: Longsmans, Green and Co., 1906, Vol. V. Reprint Co., 1969.

FitzGibbon, Constantine, *20July*, New York: Berkley Publishing Co., 1956.

Fitzpatrick, Sheila, *The Russian Revolution, 1917-1932*, New York, NY: Oxford University Press, 1984.

Forrest, W.G., *The Emergence of Greek Democracy*, 800-400 B.C., (New York: World University Library, 1979).

Fortescue, G.K., 'The Directory,' in Ward, A.W., Prothero, G.W., and Leathes, Stanley (eds.), *The Cambridge Modern History, Vol. VIII: The French Revolution* (New York: Macmillan Co., 1928), Chapter XVI, pp. 487-520.

Friedgust, Theodore H., *Political Participation in the U.S.S.R.* (Princeton: Princeton University Press, 1979).

Friedrich, Carl J., and Brzezinski, Zbigniew K., *Totalitarian Dictatorship and Autocracy* (2nd Edition) (New York: Praeger, 1966).

Friedrich, Carl J., *An Introduction to Political Theory*, (New York, NY: Harper & Row, publishers, 1967).

Fugate, Bryan I., *Operation Barbarossa*, Novato, CA: Presidio Press, 1984.

Gasset, Jose Ortega y., *The Revolt of the Masses* (New York: W.W. Norton & Co., Inc. 1957).

Gelman, Harry, *The Brezhnev Politburo and the Decline of Detente*, Ithaca, NY: Cornell University Press, 1984.

George, M. Dorthy, *London Life in the Eighteenth Century* (New York: A.A.

Knopf, 1926).

Gershoy, Leo, *The Era of the French Revolution, 1989-1799: TenYears That Shook the World*, (Princeton, N.J.: D. Van Nostrand Co., Inc., 1957).

Gibbon, Edward, *The History of the Decline and Fall of the Roman Empire, in Seven Volumes*, London: Methuen and Company, 1914.

Giliberg, T., 'Political and Social Deveopments in Rumania,' *Current History* (November 1984), 83, pp. 375-94.

Gilison, Jerome M., 'Soviet Elections as a Measure of Dissent: The Missing One Percent,' *American Political Science Review*, Vol. LXII (1968): pp. 814-826.

Gipson, Larence Henry, *The British Empire Before the American Revolution, Vol. V, Zones of International Friction: The Great Lakes Frontier, Canada, The West Indies, India, 1748-1754*, New York, NY: Alfred A. Knopf, 1942.

Gittings, John, *The Role of the Chinese Army*, London: Oxford University Press, 1967.

Glubb, John Bagot, *The Empire of the Arabs*, (Inglewood Cliffs, NJ: Prentice-Hall, 1965).

Goldhamer, Herbert, *Reality and Belief in Military Affairs*, Rand Report, R-2448-NA, Santa Monica, CA: Rand Corporation, 1979.

Grampp, William, *Economic Liberalism: Volume 1*, Chicago: University of Chicago Press, 1960.

Green, V.H.H., *The Hanoverians 1714-1815*, London, England: Edward Arnold, 1965.

Griffeth, Samuel B., *The Battle for Guadal Canal*, New York: Bantam Books, 1980.

Griffin, Martin J., 'Great Britian (1756-93) The Years of Peace and the Rise of the Younger Pitt (1782-1793),' in Ward, A.W, Prothero, G. W., and Leathes, Stanley (eds.), *The Cambridge Modern History, Vol. VI: The Eighteenth Century* (New York: Macmillan Co., 1925), Chapter XIII, pp. 475-478.

Grum, Bernard, *The Timetables of History A Horizontal Linkage of People and Events*, New York, NY: Simon & Schuster, Inc., 1979.

Gulick, E.V., 'The Final Coalition and the Congress of Vienna, 1813-1815,' in Crawley, C. W. (ed.), *The New Cambridge Modern History: Vol. IX.* (Cambridge: at the University Press, 1965); pp. 639-667.

Gungwu, Wang, *The Structure of Power in Noreth China During the Five Dynasties*, Stanford, CA: Stanford University Press, 1963.

Haberstam, David, *The Making of a Quagmire*, New York: Random House, 1965.

Hamill, Hugh M., Jr.,(eds) *Dictatorship in Spanish America* (New York, NY: Alfred A. Knopf, 1965).

Han Woo-Keun, *The History of Korea*, (Translated by Kyung-Shik Lee), Honolulu, HI: East-West Center Press, 1970.

Harasymiw, Bohdan, *Political Elite Recruitment in the Soviet Union*, New York, NY: St. Martin's Press, 1984.

Haring, clarence H., *Empire in Brazil: A New World Experiement with Monarchy*, Cambridge, MA: Harvard University Press, 1958.

Hare, Paul, and Kirby, Maurice, *An Intorduction to British Economic Policy*, London, England: Wheatsheaf Books, 1984.

Harris, William H., and Levey, Judith S., (Editors), *The New Columbia*

Encyclopedia, New York, NY: Columbia University Press, 1975.
Harris, J.R., *The Legacy of Egypt* (2nd edition), Oxford: Clarendon Press, 1971.
Harrison, G. B., *Shakespear: The Complete Works*, New York, NY: Harcourt, Brace, 1952.
Hart, B.H. Liddell, *Strategy* (New York: Frederick A. Praeger, 1955).
Hayek, F.A., *The Counter-Revolution of Science: Studies on the Abuse of Reason*, (Indianapolis Liberty Press, 1979).
Haskins, Charles Homor, *The Rise of Universities* (Ithaca, NY: Cornell University Press, 1957).
Hellman, J.A., *Mexico in Crisis* (2nd Edition), New York, NY: Holmes and Meier Publishers, 1983.
Henderson, Gregory, *Korea: The Politics of the Vortex*, Cambridge, MA: Harvard University Press, 1968.
Henderson, Nicholas, *Prince Eugen of Savoy*, New York, NY: Frederick A. Praeger Publishers, 1964.
Hibbert, Christopher, *The Days of the French Revolution*, New York, NY: William Marrow and Company, 1980.
Hill, Ronald J., 'Patterns of Deputy Selection to Local Soviets,' *Soviet Studies*, Vol. XXV (1973): pp. 196-212.
Hill, Ronald J., 'The CPSU in a Soviet Election Campaign,' *Soviet Studies*, Vol. XXVIII (1976): pp. 590-598.
Hill, Ronald J., and Frank, Peter, *The Soviet Communist Party* (2nd Edition), Boston, MA: George Allen and Unwin, 1983.
Himmelfarb, Gertrude, *Lord Acton* (Chicago, IL: University of Chicago Press, 1968).
Hirschman, Albert O. 'On Democracy in Latin America,' *The New York Review*, Vol., XXXIII, No. 6, April 1986.
Hirst, David, and Beeson, Irene, *Sadat*, London, Faber and Faber, 1981.
Holborn, Hajo, *A History of Modern Germany: 1840-1945*, Princeton, NJ: Princeton University Press, 1982.
Hostetler, John A., *Amish Society* (Revised Edition), Baltimore, MD: The Johns Hopkins Press, 1968.
Hough, Jerry F., *Soviet Leadership in Treansition*, Washington, D.C.: The Brookings Institution, 1980.
Hough, J.F., and Fainsod, M., *How the Soviet Union is Governed* (Cambridge, Mass: Harvard University Press, 1979).
Hoveyda, Fereydain, *The FAll of the Shah*, New York, NY: Wyndham Books, 1980.
Hume, David, Esq., *Essays, Literary, Moral, and Political*. Ward, Lock & Co., Warwick House; London, England, p. 23.
Ingram, J. K., 'Marx Karl', in Higgs, Henry, ed. *Palgrave's Dictionary of Political Economy: Volume 2* (London: Macmillan 1925); pp. 704-706.
Jacobs, Everett M., 'Soviet Local Elections: What They Are, and What They Are Not,' *Soviet Studies*, Vol. XXII (1970): pp. 61-76.
Jacobs, Everett M., 'The Composition of Local soviety, 1959-1969,' *Government and Opposition*, Vol. 7 (1972): pp. 503-519.
Jarman, T. L., *The Rise and Fall of Nazi Germany*, New York, NY: Signet Books, 1961.

Jaszi, Oscar, and Lewis, John D., *Against the Tyrant: the Tradition and Theory of Tyrannicide*, Glencoe, IL: The Free Press, 1957.

Jennings, George H., *An Anecdotal History of the British Parliament*, New York, NY: D. Appleton and Co., 1883.

Johnson, Chalmers, *Revolutionary Change* (Stanford, Ca: Stanford University Press, 1966).

Johnson, John J. *The Military and Society in Latin America*, (Stanford, CA: Stanford University Press, 1974).

Johnson, Kenneth F., *Mexican Democracy: A Critical View* (3rd Edition), New York, NY: Praeger Publishers, 1984.

Johnson, Paul, *Modern Times: The World from the Twenties to the Eighties*, New York: Harper and Row, 1983.

Jouvenel, Bertrand de, *On Power: Its Nature and the History of its Growth*, Boston, MA: Beacon Press, 1962.

Kapuscinksi, Ryszard, *The Emperor: Downfall of an Autocrat* (New York: Harcourt Brace Jovanovich, 1977).

Kay, Hugh, *Salazar and Modern Portugal*, New York, NY: Hawthorn Books, Inc., 1970.

Karnaw, Stanley, *Mao and China*, New York: Viking Press, 1972.

Keegan, John, *Six Armies in Normandy*, New York, NY: Viking Press, 1982.

Kelidar, A.R., 'Government and Ideology,' in Sinai, Anne, and Pollack, Allen (eds.), *The Syrian Arab Republic: A Handbook*, New York, NY: American Academic Association for Peace in the Middle East, pp. 45-58.

Kessler, Lawrence D., *K'ang-hsi and the Consolidation of Ch'ing Rule, 1661-1684*, Chicago, IL: The University of Chicago Press, 1976.

Kinross, Lord, *The Ottoman Centuries*, New York: Morrow Quill, 1977.

Knollenberg, Bernhard, *The Origin of the American Revolution 1759-1766*, New York: The Free Press, 1961.

Kreidberg, Marvin A., and Henry, Merton G., *The History of Military Mobilization in the United States Army, 1775-1945* (Washington D.C.: Department of the Army, 1955).

Kronenberger, Louis, *Kings and Desperate Men: Life in Eighteenth-Century England*, New York, NY: Vintage Books (Random House), 1942.

Kung, Hans, *Does God Exist?: An Answer for Today* New York, NY: Doubleday, 1980.

Kushler, Dorothy, *The British Redcoat, 1775-1783* [text accompanying chart] Washington D.C.: National Park Service, 1976.

Laband, D. N., 'Is There a Relationship Between Economic Conditions and Political Structure'. *Public Choice Journal*, Vol. 42, No. 1, 1984, p. 25-38.

LaCourture, Jean, *Nasser, A. Biography*, New York, NYU: Alfred A. Knopf, 1974.

Langer, William, L., *An Encyclopedia of World History*, (5th revised edition) Boston, MA: Houghton Mifflin, 1968, and 1972.

Langer, William, L., *An Encyclopedia of World History*, Boston, MA: Houghton Mifflin, 1972.

Larson, Arthur, *Eisenhower, the President Nobody Knew*,New York, NY: Scribner's Sons, 1968.

Lewis, Bernard, *The Arabs in History*, New York, Harper Torchbooks (Harper and Row Publishers), 1966.

Lewis, Naphtali, and Reinghold, Meyer (eds.), *Roman Civilization, Sourcebook I: The Republic* (New York: Harper Torchbooks [Harper & Row] publishers), 1966.

Lewitter, L. R., 'The Partitions of Poland,' in Goodwin, A. (ed.), *The New Cambridge History: Vol. VIII*, Cambridge: at the University Press, 1965; pp. 333-359.

Lloyd, Christopher, 'Armed Forces and the Art of War,' in Goodwin, A. (ed.), *The New Cambridge History: Vol. VIII*, Cambridge: at the University Press, 1965; pp. 174-190.

Locke, John, *Two Treatiese of Government*, edited by Cook, Thomas I. (New York: Hafner Publishgin Co., Inc., 1947).

Loewenstein, *Political Reconstruction*, (New York, NY: Macmillan Co., 1946).

Lunt, William E., *Papal Revenlles in the Middle Ages, Vols. I and II* (New York: Octagon Books, 1965).

Luttwak, Edward, N., *The Grand Strategy of the Roman Empire*, Baltimore, MD: The Johns Hopkins University Press, 1976.

Lynskey, Elizabeth M., *The Government of the Catholic Church*, New York, NY: P. J. Kennedy and Sons, 1952.

Machiavelli, Niccolo, *The Prince*. The Oxford University Press, 'World's Classics' translation by Luigi Ricci, revised by E.R.P. Vincent. New York & Scarborough, Ontario, Canada, p. 96 & 117.

Macdonald, J.R.M., 'The Thermidorian Reaction and the End of the Convention', in Ward, A.W., Prothero, G.W., and Leathes, Stanley, *The Cambridge Modern History: Volume XIII*, (New York: Macmillan, 1928); pp. 372-397.

MacDonald, J.R. Moreton, 'The Legislative Assembly,' in Ward, A.W., Prothero, G.W., and Leathes, Stanley (eds.), *The Cambridge Modern History, Vol. VII: The French Revolution* (New York: Macmillan Co., 1928), Chapter VIII, pp. 211-244.

Mackie, J. D., *The Early Tudors, 1485-1558*, in Clark, G. N. (ed.), *The Oxford History of England (Oxford: The Clarendon Press, 1957.*

MacMullen, Ramsay, Soldier and Civilian in the Later Roman Empire, Cambridge, MA: Harvard University Press, 1963.

Macridis, Roy C., *Greek Politics at a Crossroads: What Kind of Socialism?* (Stanford, California: Hoover Institution Press, 1984).

Mahan, Alfred T., *The Influence of Sea Power upon History 1660-1783*, New York: Sagamore Press, 1957.

Main, Jackson T., *The Soverign States, 1775-1783*, New York, NY: New Viewpoints, 1973.

Mair, Lucy, *African Kingdoms*, Oxford: Oxford University Press, 1977.

Mango, Cyril, *Byzantium: The Empire of New Rome*, New York, NY: Charles Scribner's Sons, 1980.

Mantoux, Paul, *The Industrial Revolution in the Eighteenth Century* (New York: Harper & Row Publishers, Inc., 1962).

Marr, Phebe, *The Modern History of Iraq*, Boulder, CO: Westview Press, 1985.

Martin, John Bartlow, *Overtaken by Events: The Dominican Crisis from the Fall of Trujillo to the Civil War*, Garoen City, NY: Doubleday and Company, Inc., 1966.

McNeill, William H., *The Pursuit of Power: Technology, Armed Force, and Society Since A.D. 1000* (Chicago: The University of Chicago Press, 1982).

Merkl, Peter H., *Modern Comparative Politics* (New York: Holt, Rinehart & Winston, 1970).

Miller, John H., 'The Communist Party: Trends and Problems,' in Brown, Archie, and kKaser, Michael (eds.) *Soviet Policy for the 1980sw* (Bloomington, Indiana: University Press, 1982), pp. 1-34.

Miller, Norman N., *Kenya: The Quest for Prosperity*, Boulder, CO: Westview Press, 1984.

Mills, Richard M., 'The Soviet Leadership Problem,' *World Politics*, Vol. XXXIII, No. 4 (1981), pp. 590-613.

Mises, Ludwig von. *Human Action: A Treatise on Economics* (Chicago: Contemporary Books, Inc., 1963).

Mommsen, Theddor, *Rome, from Earliest Times to 44 B.C.*, in Lodge, Henry Cabot (ed.), *The History of Nations*, New York, NY: P.F. Collier and Son, Co., 1928, Volume II.

Montague, F.C., 'Louis XVI,' in Wart, A.W., Prothero, G.W., and Leathes, S. (eds.), *The Cambridge Modern History: Vol. VIII, The French Revolution*, New York: The Macmillan Company, 1928, pp. 79-118.

–, 'The National Assembly and the Spread of Anarchy,' in Ward, A.W., Prothero, G.W., and Leathes, S. (eds.), *The Cambridge Modern History: Vol. VIII, The French Revolution*, New York: The Macmillan Company, 1928, pp. 145-275.

–, 'The Elections of the States General,' in Ward, A.W., Prothero, G.W., and Leathes, S. (eds.), *The Cambridge Modern History: Vol. VIII, The French Revolution*, New York: The Macmillan Company, 1928, pp. 119-144.

Montross, Lynn, *War Through the Ages* (Revised 3rd ed.) (New York: Harper & Row, Publishers, 1960).

Moore, Barrington, Jr., *Social Origins of Dictatorship and Democracy*, Boston, MA: Beacon Press, 1966.

Morton, W. Scott, *China, Its History and Culture*, New York, NY: Liddencott and Crowell, 1980.

Mosher, Steven, *BrokenGround: The Rural Chinese*, New York, NY: The Free Press, 1983.

Muir, Ramsay, *A Short History of the British Commonwealth: Vol. II: The Modern Commonwealth (1763 to 1919)*, Yonkers-on-the-Hudson, New York: World Book Company, 1924.

Muller, Herbert J., *Freedom in the Ancient World* (New York: Harper & Brothers, 1961).

Mustafa, Abdel Rahim, 'The Breakdown of the Monopoly System in Egypt after 1840,' in Holt, P.M., (ed.), *Political and Social Change in Modern Egypt: Historical Studies from the Ottoman Conquest to the United Arab Republic*, London: Oxford University Press, 1968.

Nagy, Charles J., *Political Parties and System Flexibility* (Washington, D.C.,

University Press of America, 1981).

Namier, Sir Lewis, *England in the Age of the American Revolution*, London, England: Macmillan, 1963.

– , *The Structure of Politics at the Accession of George III*, London, England, Macmillan, 1965 (2nd edition).

Needler, Martin, *Mexican Politics: The Containment of Conflict*, Stanford, CA: HooverInstitution Press, 1982.

Nelson, Harold D., (editor) *Poland: A Country Study*, Washington, D.C.: American University Area Handbook Series, U.S. Government Printing Office, 1983.

Newhall, Richard A., *Muster and Review: A Problem of English Military Administration, 1420-1440*, Cambridge, MA: Harvard University Press, 1940.

North, Douglas C.,and Thomas, Robert Paul, *The Rise of the Western World: A New Economic History*, (London: Cambridge University Press, 1973).

North, Douglas C., *Structure and Change in Economic History*, (New York: Norton and Co., 1981.).

Nutting, Anthony, *Nasser*, New York, NY: E. P.Dutton and Company, Inc., 1972.

Nyrop, R. F. (ed.), *Syria: A Country Study (Area Handbook for Syria)*, American University Area Handbook Series (Washington, D.C.: American University, 1979.

– , (ed.), *Iraq: A Country Study (Area Handbook for Iraq)*, American University Area Handbook Series (Washington, D.C.: American University, 1979.

– , (ed.), *Panama: A Country Study (Area Handbook for Panama)*, American University Area Handbook Series (Washington, D.C.: American University, 1980.

O'Dea, Thomas F., *The Mormans*, Chicago, IL: The University of Chicago Press, 1957.

Oechsli, W., 'The Achievement of Swiss Federal Unity,' in Ward, A.W., Prothero, G.W., and Leathes, Stanley (eds.), *The Cambridge Modern History, Volume XI: The Growth of Nationalities* (New York: Macmillan Co., 1928), Chapger VIII, pp. 234-261.

Oliveira Marques, A. H. de, *History of Portugal, Volume II: From Empire to Corporate State*, New York, NY: Columbia University Press, 1972.

Oman, C.W., 'The Undred Days, 1815,' in Ward, A.W., Protero, G.W., and Leathes, Stanley, (eds.), *The Cambridge ModernHistory, Vol. IX: Napoleon* (New York: Macmillan Co., 1907), Chapter XX, pp. 616-645.

Oman, C.W.,C, and Adam, G. Mercer, *Greece*, In Lodge, Henry Cabot (ed), *The History of Nations* series (New York: P.F. Colleir & Son Co., Publishers 1928), Vol. II.

Onate, Andres D., 'Hva Kuo-Feng andthe Arrest of theGang of Four', *China Quarterly*, 75 (September 1987); pp. 540-566.

O'Neill, Richard, *Suicide Squads*, New York, NY: Ballantine Books, 1981.

Parry, V. J., et. al., *A History of the Ottoman Empire to 1730*, London: Cambridge University Press, 1976.

Paxton, John, *The Statesman's Yearbook: 1983-1984*, New York, NY: St. Martin's Press, 1983.

–, *The Statesman's Yearbook: 1985-1986*, New York, NY: St. Martin's Press, 1985.

Penkovskiy, Oley, *The Penkovskiy Papers*, New York, NY: Doubleday, 1965.

Perrin, Bernadotte (transl.), *Plutarch's Lives*, Cambridge, MA: Harvard University Press, 1968.

Pirenne, Henri, *Eocnomic and Social History of Medieval Europe*, (New York: Harcourt Brace Jovanovich, 1937).

Polanyi, Karl, Arensberg, Conrad M., and pearson, Harry W. (eds.), *Trade and Market in Early Empires*, (Chicago: Henry Regnery Co., 1957).

Polo, Marco, *The Travels of Marco Polo*, New York, NY: Grosset and Dunlap, 1931.

Popper, Karl R., *The Open Society and Its Enemies* (Princeton: Princeton University Press, 1950).

Potholm, Christian P., *The Theory and Practice ofAfrican Politics*, Englewood Cliffs, NJ: Prentice Hall, 1979.

Prifti, Peter, R., *Socialist Albania since 1944: Domestic and Foreign Developments*, Cambridge, MA: MIT Press, 1978.

Ranke, Leopold von, *The History of the Popes During the Last Four Centuries, Volumes I-III*, London: G. Bell and Sons, Ltd., 1913.

Rather, Dan and Gates, Gary Paul, *The Palace Guard*, New York, NY: Harper and Row Publishers, 1974.

Revel, Jean-Francois, *How Democracies Perish* (New York, NY: Doublday & Co., Inc., 1984).

Ridgeway, Mathew, *The Korean War*, Garden City, NY: Doubleday and Co., 1967.

Rigby, T. H., *Communist Party Membership in the U.S.S.R., 1917-1967*, Princeton, NJ: Princeton University Press, 1968.

Rigg, J. M., 'Great Gritian (1956-93): The King's Friends,' in Ward, A.W., Prothero, G.W., and Leathes, Stanley (eds.), *The Cambridge Modern History, Vol. VI: The Eighteenth Century*, (New York, NY: The Macmillan Co.., 1925), Chapter XIII, pp. 423-456.

Rodzinski, Witold, *The Walled Kingdom: A History of China from Antiquity to the Present*, New York, NY: The Free Press, Macmillan, 1984.

Roett, Riordan, *Brazil: Politics in a Patrimonial Society*, New York, NY: Praeger Publishers, 1978.

Rose, J. Holland, 'Bonaparte and the Conquest of Italy,' in Ward, A.W., Prothero, G.W., and Leathes, Stanley (eds.,) *The Cambridge Modern History, Vol. VIII: The French Revolution* (New York, NY: Macmillan Co., 1928), Chapter XVIII, pp. 553-593.

Rosser, Richard F., *An Introduction to Soviet Foreign Policy*, Englewood Cliffs, NJ: Prentice-Hall, 1969.

Russell, Bertrand, *A History of Western Philosophy*, New York, NY: Simon and Schuster, 1945.

Sabine, George H., *A History of Political Theory* (New York, NY: Henry Holt and Co., 1956).

Sanders, N.K., *The Sea Peoples: Warriors of the Ancient Mediterranean*, (Revised Edition), (London: Thames and Hudson Ltd., 1985).

Sartori, Giovanni, *Parties and Pary Systems A Framework for Analysis* (Cambridge: Cambridge University Press, 1976).
Sayce, Archibald Henry, *Ancient Empires of the East*, in Lodge, Henry Cabot (ed.), *The History of Nations series (New York, NY: P. F. Collier & Sons, Co., 1928), Vol. I.*
Sayyid-Marsot, Afaf Lutfi Al, Egypt in the Reign of Muhammad Ali, Cambridge, MA: Cambridge University Press, 1984.
Schapiro, Leonard, *The Communist Party of the Soviet Union* (2nd Edition) (London: Methuen, 1970).
Schelling, Thomas C., *The Strategy of Conflict*. Harvard University Press; Cambridge, Mass., 1960.
Schwartz, Charles, *Gershwin: His Life and Music*, New York, NY: Da Capo Press, Inc., 1979.
Scott, Derek J.R., *Russian Political Institutions* (4th Edition) (London: Allen & Unwin, 1969).
Scott, Robert E., *Mexican Government in Transition* (Revised Edition), Urbana, IL: University of Illinois Press, 1964.
Sculc, Tad *Twightlight of the Tyrants*, (New York, NY: Holt,Reinhart, & Winston, 1959).
Seward, Desmond, *The Hundred Years War: The English in France, 1337-1453*, New York, NY: Atheneum, 1978.
Sheridan, James E., *Chinese Warlord, the Career of Feng Yu-Hsiang*, Stanford, CA: Stanford University Press, 1966.
–, *China in Disintegration: The Republican Iraq in Chinese History, 1912-1949*, New York, NY: The Free Press, Macmillan, 1975.
Silverberg, Robert, *Empires in the Dust: Ancient Civilizations Brought to Light* (New York, NY: Chilton Books, 1963).
Sinnigen, William G., and Boak, Arthur E., *A History of Rome to A.D. 565*, (6th Edition), New York, NY: Macmillan Publishing Co., Inc., 1977.
Slobodan, Stankovic, *The End of the Tito Era*, Stanford, CA: Hoover Institution Press, 1981.
Smith, Dennis Mack, *Mussolini*, New York, NY: Alfred A. Knopf, 1982.
Smith, Peter, *Labyringhts of Power: Political Recruitment in Twentieth Century Mexico*, Princeton, NJ: Princeton University Press, 1979.
Smith, Richard J., *China's Cultural Heritage: The Chi'ing Dynasty, 1644-1912* (Boulder, CO: Westview Press, 1983).
Soustelle, Jacques, *Daily Life of the Aztecs on the Eve of the Spanish Conquest*, Stanford, CA: Stanford University Press, 1970.
Spearman, Diana, *Democracy in England* (New York, NY: The Macmillan Co., 1957).
Spence, Jonathan D., *Emporer of China: Self-Portrait of K'ang-His*, New York, NY: Alfred A. Knopf, Inc., 1974.
Springborg, Robert, *Family, Power, and Politics in Egypt*, Philadelphia, PA: University of Pennsylvania Press, 1982.
Starr,Chester G., *The Roman Empire, 27 B.C- A.D. 476*, New York, NY: Oxford University Press, 1982.
St. Aubyn, Giles, *The Year of the Three Kings: 1483*, New York, NY: Atheneoni,

1983.

Tapsell, R. F., *Monarchs, Rulers, Dynasties and Kingdoms of the World*, New York: Facts on File, 1982.

Temperley, H.W.V., 'The Age of Walpole and the Pelhams,' in Ward, A.W., Prothero, G.W., and Leathes, Stanley (eds.) *The Cambridge Modern History, Vol. VI: The Eighteenth Century* (New York, NY: Macmillan Co., 1925), Chapter II, pp. 40-89.

Theodoracopulos, Taki, *The Greek Upheaval*, New Rochelle,NY: Caratzas Brothers, 1978.

Thomas, Hugh, *Cuba, or thePursuit of Freedom*, London: MacMillan, 1971.

Tolkien, J.R.R., *The Silmarillion*, Boston, MA: Houghton Mifflin, 1977.

Tolstoy, Nikolai, *Stalin's Secret War*, New York: Holt, Rinehart and Winston, 1981.

Treviranus, G.R., *Revolutions in Russia* (New York,NY: Harper & Brothers, Publishers, 1944).

Trevelyan, G.M., *History of England, Volume II: The Tudors and Stuart Era*, Garden City, NY: Doubleday, 1953.

Trythall, John, *Franco: A Biography*, London: Macmillan Press, 1970.

Tullock, Gordon, *The Politics of Bureaucracy* Washington D.C.: Public Affairs Press, 1965).

–, *The Organization of Inquiry* (Durham, NC: Duke University Press, 1966).

–, *The Social Dilemma: The Economics of War and Revolution*, Blacksburg, VA: University Publications, 1974.

–, 'The Roots of Order,' in Tullock, Gordon (ed.), *Toward a Science of Politics* (Blacksburg, VA: Public Choice Center, 1981), pp. 121-130.

–, 'Why Did the Industrial Revolution Occur in England?', unpublished monograph (Fairfax, VA: Public Choice Center, George Mason University, 1985).

Turner, Paul, *Selected Lives from the Lives of the Nobel Grecians and Romans, Volumes I and II*, Carbondale, IL: Southern Illinois University Press, 1968.

Vernon, H.M., 'Italy and the Papacy,' in Ward, A.W., Prothero, G.W., and Leathes, Stanley (eds) *The Cambridge Modern History, Volume VI: The Eighteenth Century* (New York,NY: Macmillan Co., 1925), Chapter XVI, pp. 586-610.

Von Hayen, Victor W., *Realm of the Incas*, New York: Mentor Books, 1957.

Voslensky, Michael, *Nomenklatura: The Soviet Ruling Class, An Insider's Report*,(Translated by Eric Mosbacher) Garden City, NY: Doubleday and Co., 1984.

Vreeland, Nena, Et. Al., *Area Handbook for South Korea*, (2nd Edition), American University Area Series, Washington, D.C.: American University, 1975.

Wakeman, Fredric, Jr., *The Fall of Imperial China*, New York, NY: The Free Press, Macmillan, 1975.

Ward, A.W., Prothero, G.W., and Leathes, Stanley, *The Cambridge Modern History: Volume IX: Genealogical Tables and Lists*, (New York: Macmillan, 1907).

Ward, A.W., Prothero, G.W., and Leathes, Stanley, *The Cambridge Modern*

History: Volume XIII: Genealogical Tables and Lists, (New York: Macmillan, 1911).

Ward, A.W., Prothéro, G.W., and Leathes, Stanley, *The Cambridge Modern History: Volume XI: The Growth of Nationalittes*, (New York: Macmillan, 1928).

Weaver, Richard M., 'Concealed Rhetoric in Scientistic Sociology,' in Schoeck, Helmut, and Wiggins, James W. (eds.), *Scientism and Values*, (New York, NY: D. Van Nostrand Co., Inc., 1960), pp. 83-99.

Weigley, Russell F., *Eisenhower's Lieutenants*, Bloomington, IN: Indiana University Press, 1981.

Weil, T.E., et.al., *Area Handbook for Paraguay*, Washington D.C.: U.S. Government Printing Office, 1972.

Weinstock, Stefan, *Divus Julius*, Oxford: Oxford University Press, 1971.

Werstein, Irving, *Ten Days in November: The Russian Revolution* (Philadelphia: Macrae Smith Co., 1967).

Werth, Alexander, *Russia Under Kruschev*, New York: Hill and Wang, 1961.

Wheatcroft, Andrew, *The World Atlas of Revolutions*, New York, NY: Simon and Schuster, 1983.

Whittlesey, Derwent, *The Earth and the State: A Study of Political Geography* (New York,NY: Henry Holt and Co., 1944).

Wilson, Edward O., *Sociobiology*, Cambridge, MA: Harvard University Press, 1975.

Wilson, H.W., 'The War of 1812-1815,' in Ward, A.W., Prothero, G.W., and Leathes, Stanley (eds), *The Cambridge Modern History, Vol. VII: The United States* (New York, NY: Macmillan Co., 1907), Chapter X, pp. 335-348.

Wittfogel, Karl, *Oriental Despotism: A Comparative Study of Total Power*, (New York: Vintage, 1981)

Wolf, Eric R., *Peasant Wars of the Twentieth Century* (New York, NY: Harper Torchbooks (Harper & Row, Publishers), 1969).

Wright, Arthur, F., and Twitchett, Denis (eds.) *Perspectives on the T'ang* New Haven, CT: Yale University Press, 1973

Young, G.F., *The Medici*, New York, NY: Modern Library, 1930.

Young, Peter, and Lawford, J.P., *History of the British Army*, New York: G. P. Putnam's Sons, 1970.